The
Courageous Mosaic
Awakening Society, Systems, and Souls

To Sandi,
Thank you so much,
for all your guidance!

Love
Ross

3/23/14

Other Books by
Ralph H. Kilmann
(as author, co-author, co-editor)

The Management of Organization Design
Social Systems Design
Methodological Approaches to Social Science
Producing Useful Knowledge for Organizations
Corporate Tragedies
Beyond the Quick Fix
Gaining Control of the Corporate Culture
Corporate Transformation
Escaping the Quick Fix Trap
Managing Beyond the Quick Fix
Making Organizations Competitive
Workbook for Implementing the Tracks
Logistics Manual for Implementing the Tracks
Managing Ego Energy
Quantum Organizations

The
Courageous Mosaic
Awakening Society, Systems, and Souls

Ralph H. Kilmann

 SM NEWPORT COAST, CALIFORNIA

Published and Distributed by Kilmann Diagnostics
1 Suprema Drive, Newport Coast, CA 92657
www.kilmanndiagnostics.com
info@kilmanndiagnostics.com
949-497-8766

Cover, layout, typography, and illustrations by Ralph H. Kilmann.

05 04 03 02 01   10 9 8 7 6 5 4 3 2 1
Printed in the United States of America

Publication Data
Kilmann, Ralph H.
     The Courageous Mosaic: Awakening Society, Systems,
     and Souls / Ralph H. Kilmann.
          p. cm.
     Includes illustrations and bibliographical references.
     ISBN 978-0-9895713-0-2
     1. Consciousness. 2. Mind/body/spirit modalities.
     3. Spiritual autobiography. 4. Bringing Consciousness
     into organizations. I. Title.

FIRST EDITION
First Printing 2013

Pieces of My Mosaic

Preface   vii

1. When Time Began   3
2. One Awakening Was Not Enough   7
3. The Quashed Rebellion   13
4. Mistreating Buttons   17
5. My First Round of Therapy   21
6. Resolution with Dad, But Not Mom   25
7. The Moveable Eye Chart   31
8. The Full Circle of My Work Life   35
9. Getting to Know My Dad   43
10. Transitioning with My Dad   53
11. Additional Rounds of Therapy   63
12. Damaged Boundaries, Damaged Lives   67
13. Expanding My Consciousness   75
14. Revisiting When Time Began   101
15. Resolution with Mom   115
16. Varieties of Resolution   129
17. My Accidental Death   153
18. My Energetic Awakening   161
19. Energy, Healing, and Soul   181
20. Society, Systems, and Souls   203
21. Transitioning with My Mom   225

Epilogue   243
Bibliography   247
About the Author   251

To Rosie, my beloved twin sister

You were with me all the time
and always will be

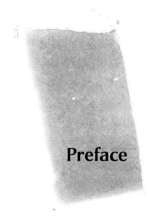

Preface

Even before I sat down to write *The Courageous Mosaic*, I had already touched many people's lives in various ways—as a professor, author, consultant, friend, lover, and father. But as I began seeing my life on paper, I soon realized I'd been born for a special purpose. And that purpose is *to invite people to accelerate their awakenings* by (1) seeing how they've been recreating unconscious patterns in their mind; (2) choosing to break the unproductive patterns that have become stuck in their body; and (3) transcending those self-defeating patterns so they can live with love, joy, peace, and compassion. By painstakingly sharing how I expanded my own mind/body/spirit consciousness— evolving from a traumatized child to an awakened adult—I hope I can inspire others to take that same journey to wholeness and then bring that expanded consciousness into all their organizations.

The *Mosaic* in the title refers to the separate pieces of one's life that can be sorted into useful patterns with concepts and theories of human behavior. The *Courageous* portion of the title represents the ceaseless, fearless, dedicated, and everlasting investigation of one's existence, which can be shown as three superhighways for pursuing an examined life: mind consciousness, body consciousness, and spirit consciousness.

From reading my stories and theories, you'll see why all three aspects of consciousness—*mind, body, and spirit*—must be included in the pursuit of self-discovery. Indeed, any modality for expanding self-knowledge must be explored in a holistic, integrated manner—since the development of each highway of consciousness is so highly interrelated with the other two. Thus, an integrated mind/body/spirit modality involves looking into your mind, breaking into your body, and transcending your ego—so you can live your soul's purpose.

Perhaps you have spent years clarifying your mind by reading personal growth and self-help books (and participating in one type of psychotherapy or another), but are wondering why you are still recreating the same patterns and attracting the same people. Maybe you've already developed a strong, flexible, and "tension-free" body through a number of modalities (including physical exercise, yoga, massage, and chiropractic care), yet you are still distracted by your old traumas, troubled with your personal relationships, and unhappy with your work life. Or maybe you've read many books about Spirit and attend religious services or participate in spiritual retreats (and practice one or more forms of prayer or meditation), but you're still unable to experience bliss at other times.

The Courageous Mosaic resolves the typical paradoxes that stem from specialized (singular) efforts at living an examined life. As such, I illuminate these integral principles and practices: Without already having a fairly conscious mind and a secure ego, you won't choose to work through the accumulated tension and painful memories in your body. And without maintaining an energetically flowing and feeling body, you won't have an easy time directly experiencing the Divine. Yet I am convinced that a magnificent life is available to all people who diligently examine all three aspects of human consciousness. Said differently, my book illustrates how participating in a series of mind/body/spirit modalities can transform childhood traumas into unique opportunities for resolving your primal relationships, which enables you to awaken to *your* destiny—not someone else's.

The Courageous Mosaic also reveals how the systems in society play a major role in the evolution of consciousness. This book thus investigates how our organizations and institutions (public schools, religious organizations, health-care organizations, governments, and workplaces) can be—must be—designed for conscious living. If this mission can be achieved, many more citizens—not just a privileged few—will be able to radiate a higher level of human consciousness. One thing is clear: *It's only by expanding consciousness in people—and their organizations—that humankind can wake up and stop war, violence, hatred, poverty, hunger, disease, hopelessness, and the destruction of Mother Earth herself.*

Regarding the numerous mind/body/spirit modalities utilized in this book, a few people's names have been changed to honor their personal and professional privacy. Moreover, my account of all these modalities is strictly from my own unique experience. Other people will naturally be affected differently, based on *their* unique traumas and challenges. Since my account of these various modalities covers my journey through the summer of 2006, these modalities—just as people—have grown and evolved, year after year. Experiencing them in the present, therefore, would be another reason why their impact could be different from my experience years earlier. For example, in the case of Network Spinal Analysis (NSA) and Somato Respiratory Integration (SRI), both developed by Dr. Donald Epstein, additional modalities have evolved: Epstein's Reorganizational Healing (ROH) and the emerging Epstein's Energetic Discipline (EED). The reader is urged to "search the Internet" for the most current version of all the mind/body/spirit modalities mentioned in *The Courageous Mosaic*.

The
Courageous Mosaic
Awakening Society, Systems, and Souls

The unexamined life is not worth living.

Socrates, in *Plato, Dialogues, Apology*
Greek philosopher in Athens (469 BCE TO 399 BCE)

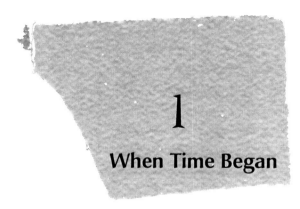

1
When Time Began

The first vivid memory I have of being awake in this lifetime took place in 1950, at age three. In a New York City hospital, I woke up blindfolded—bandaged across both eyes. And each of my arms had been placed in a heavy cardboard sleeve. The result: I wasn't able to bend my arms at the elbow, so I couldn't use either hand to touch other parts of my body. But I did feel the metal bars on the sides of the bed with my knees, feet, and arms. I was imprisoned. I was also nauseous, dizzy, and dazed: I felt like I had to throw up.

The first thoughts I recall having in my lifetime were a string of questions: Why were my eyes bandaged? Why was I imprisoned and nauseous? Why did I hear children screaming in the background?

Keep in mind that I'm using the language of an adult here, not the actual words of a three-year-old child. While I don't remember the kind of language I would have used for my inner dialogue way back then (to make sense of my experience), I do recall exactly what I did upon awakening: I started crying: no screaming—but a steady stream of tears.

I next heard a woman's voice (a nurse?), which gifted me with the first spoken words that I ever remember hearing in my lifetime: "If you cry, you'll lose your eyes."

While I don't recall much after those words were spoken, all I can imagine is that I must've tried hard not to cry so I wouldn't lose my vision, perhaps losing my eyes entirely. And I must've wondered what I could possibly have done—in the measly three years of my life—to be treated in this manner. What mistakes had I made? More important, why was I viewed as "bad," in need of punishment?

When I was much older, I learned the reason why my both eyes were blindfolded: If only my bad eye had been bandaged, my good eye would have moved around to see what was going on. These kind of wanderings would've caused my repaired eye to move around as well. Excess movement would've hindered the healing process, since the surgery was done on the eye muscles to reposition my lazy right eyeball. Also as an adult, I learned that my arms, and thus my hands, were incapacitated with stiff sleeves to prevent my removing the big bandage across my eyes (which a three-year-old child would be prone to do). I also learned that my nausea was the side effect of the ether that had been used for a general anesthesia. And who were all those screaming kids? We were all in ward, recovering from surgery.

I also learned years later that, in those days (around 1950), the guiding philosophy in the medical community was not to tell young children much of anything about what they might experience before, during, and after surgery. The belief was that the less children knew, the better. Consequently, I was left to my own imagination to figure out why, what, how, and who...and when this bizarre torture might be inflicted on me again. And I could imagine a lot.

What made matters even worse? In that hospital, around 1950, visiting hours were just one hour per day for parents as well as for other relatives. So I only saw—or rather experienced—my mom for one hour a day during that frightening ordeal. The rest of the time—twenty-three hours a day—I was completely alone. I'd wait for my mom to appear; and it seemed like I was waiting forever. Where was she? When would she arrive? How much longer? I was perpetually waiting for my mother—while hoping the *other* woman (the nurse) would never be near me again…ever.

During that hospital experience, I "saw" my dad for short visits every day, because he was an eye surgeon—an ophthalmologist—on staff in the same hospital. While he didn't perform the eye surgery (he had a colleague do that for him), I later learned that my dad was in the operating room "to make sure everything would be all right."

Decades later, I saw the 1952 documentary by James Robertson: *A Two Year Old Goes to Hospital.* This thirty-minute film dramatically captured the trauma of a young child who, like me, hardly saw her mother or father throughout a stay in a hospital. Even though Laura's minor surgery (an umbilical hernia repair) didn't require her to be blindfolded or tied down, she still experienced major trauma from having been abruptly separated from her mom and dad—during all that confusion, anxiety, and fleeting strangers (nurses and doctors). Robertson's dramatic film is credited for having revolutionized the in-patient care of young children—by allowing parents not only to visit their child daylong, but also to sleep in their child's hospital room overnight. But my 1950 ordeal occurred two years before that documentary was produced, and many more years before hospitals began eradicating their trauma-inducing policies.

How long was I in the hospital? My best guess is five to seven days. But it felt like a lifetime. I had absolutely no concept of time in those days. I only knew my time had begun. Later, I'd learn that the rest of my life would be affected—fueled—by this awakening.

2

One Awakening Was Not Enough

When I was seven years old, my parents planned a family vacation to Europe, a major part of which would involve another eye surgery. My lazy eyeball had moved off course again, gravitating to the near corner of the eye socket. As historical evidence, I still have numerous photos of myself at five and six years of age. In each case, the image captures me looking away, with my head pointing somewhere else, even though I had fixed my gaze straight on the camera.

This time around, I knew, in advance, I was going to have eye surgery, but the details were again not discussed—even though I was several years older than before. I must have been deemed a seasoned veteran, who didn't need any question-and-answer discussion. I was simply informed that the surgery would be performed in a clinic in St. Gallon, Switzerland, because some doctor there had developed a new technique called "tucking the muscle," which would make this operation more successful than before.

My only wish was that this new technique would enable me to see better out of my right eye. It had become obvious to me that my right eye had weak vision, while my left eye was in better shape. But because of my condition, I couldn't see in 3-D: My brain wasn't able to put the complementary perspectives of my two eyes together so I would have true three-dimensional vision. I was led to believe that this second surgery would surely correct the lazy eye—stimulating its vision and enabling me to see depth.

Did you ever see one of those classic movies that involve eye surgery? At some point after the recovery period, the bandages are slowly taken off the patient's eyes and head. There's this anticipation (drum roll) to see if the patient has restored vision. Sometimes the focus of the camera is blurred at first to represent the patient's eyes adjusting to the light and the surroundings. Then, in most cases (or at least in the films I choose to remember), the focus gets sharp and the patient realizes he can see.

This powerful scenario became my most cherished fantasy. This hoped-for outcome was what gave me the courage to have positive expectations about the upcoming surgery in Switzerland.

For this second eye surgery, I can neither recall waking up nor experiencing my confinement. I don't recall if I was tied down again (with those solid arm sleeves) and if I was nauseous. All I remember is being very alone in a private hospital room with a large window next to my bed that gave me a view of the valleys and mountains in St. Gallon. This indicates that only one eye was bandaged after the surgery. Or perhaps I can only remember what life was like after the doctor took the bandage off my good eye. I don't remember.

But my loneliness was extreme, and that I can remember well. I didn't see my parents very often, and I didn't see my only sibling, my brother, Peter, who is eighteen months older. I was told that my father was in the operating room, but I don't recall him visiting me any more often than my mom. Neither do I recollect the hospital's visitation policies. But it was vacation time, so I suppose the family, except for me, was out enjoying Switzerland, while I was all alone— once again—in my hospital room.

When it was time to take my bandages off, I was hoping I'd see better with my right eye and I'd see depth as well. Neither happened. I saw everything the same as before—except that my iris and pupil were now in the center of my very blood-shot eye.

Back in the United States, when I was thirteen, my tonsils were removed, which replayed another round of stressful surgery for me. I didn't need to get rid of them due to frequent colds or tonsillitis. It was my older brother, a year before, who presumably had to have his tonsils taken out for good reasons. This year, it was simply my turn to have a tonsillectomy. I guess you might call this: preventive surgery. But just like a rose is a rose, surgery is surgery, regardless of what you call it or how it's done—at least to me.

When I was sixteen, my mother told me it was time again for surgery. This next round took place in between my sophomore and junior years in high school, when kids want to do many other things during their summer break. By this time, however, I believed I had no control over my own body: It wasn't mine. Even though I never complained about my right eye to anyone else, how it looked or how well I could see, my mother decided that this is what I needed.

I have no recollections about that surgery. It took place in the early part of the summer, so I'd be fully healed by the time school began in September. In fact, my mom told me that by doing it this way, "Nobody will ever know you had to have surgery." I wondered why we began keeping this a family secret. Is eye surgery shameful? Why shouldn't I tell anyone?

In retrospect, it's remarkable that I can remember vivid details about my first eye surgery at age three, but I don't recall much of my surgery in Switzerland (at seven years of age). I remember even less about my tonsillectomy (at age thirteen), and cannot recall much of anything about my third eye surgery (at sixteen). You'd predict my memory of more recent events would be sharper, not fuzzier, than earlier events. Was I choosing to forget each successive surgery? Was I learning to disconnect from my experiences—and my body?

My fourth eye surgery took place when I was twenty-three years old. There are several startling things about this operation that were different from the others. By the time I was twenty-three, you'd have thought I'd have a mind of my own: I was living away from home. I was already in graduate school. I'd been married for a year. And yet, I still hadn't claimed ownership of my body or realized I had a right to make decisions about my eyes separate from my parents.

I don't remember what I did or what went wrong, but my mom simply informed me, once again, that it was time for surgery. Since I'd be getting my bachelor's degree and master's degree in May and wouldn't be starting a doctoral program at another university until September, June was the perfect time for the surgery: My eye would have plenty of time to heal so, by the time September came around, no one would have to know I'd undergone surgery in the summer. The big family secret would continue.

It never occurred to me that I could announce to my mother, the decision maker, or to my father, the ophthalmologist, that I did not want to have more eye surgery. Nor did it enter my mind that I could get a second opinion from another ophthalmologist, or from another mother. Nor did I realize that I could explore *other avenues* for correcting what could be a serious problem. And so on. So like a sheep going to its slaughter, I passively accepted my fate and silently agreed to the surgery.

While my father never said much of anything before the prior surgeries, he did have more to say about my fourth eye operation: "This surgery is going to hurt." Keep in mind that this comment was coming from a man who could never acknowledged pain, had never teared in my presence, nor had spoken of any kind of discomfort or inconvenience. He was a very traditional, German man who kept all his feelings—and experiences—to himself. So for him to say that my upcoming eye surgery was going to hurt would surely turn out to be a gross understatement.

My dad was absolutely right. For my fourth eye surgery, I only received a local anesthesia, not the general anesthesia I had always been given before. The reason? My dad said that by using only local anesthesia, the muscles in my right eye would stay in the same elastic state that occurs for daily use. As such, repositioning the eye muscles during surgery could be done much more accurately than would be the case under general anesthesia.

The powerful by-product of this game plan, however, was that I'd be fully awake during the operation. Indeed, *I can still vividly see the surgical knife coming straight into my right eye.* And, just as I'd been explicitly forewarned, the procedure was extremely—immensely—painful. My dad and a nurse had to hold down my legs as I screamed out loud—again and again—every time anything was done to those tiny, very sensitive muscles surrounding my right eyeball.

In the past, I'd always been told that my father would be there in the operating room during my eye surgery (as an "observer," not as the surgeon). But this time, I could see him live for myself. On the one hand, seeing him there was reassuring. (I can still see him in his surgical clothing and mask.) On the other hand...I developed mixed feelings about actually seeing him there, especially when he had to hold my legs down every time I screamed in pain.

Given my unique history, a fundamental lesson I learned from this fourth eye surgery was loudly said by me in the recovery room: "Nobody is ever going to do this to me again!" I was thus done with eye surgery—unless *I* decided that this is what I wanted to do.

Finally, after two decades of recurring trauma and victimhood, I reclaimed my body. I was never again going to turn my physicality over to mom, dad, or anyone else. This particular awakening was at least as profound as my first awakening at age three. Apparently for me, one awakening was not enough.

3

The Quashed Rebellion

I was afraid to challenge or confront my parents. For one thing, they had the power over me (or so it seemed at the time) to decide when I'd have my next eye surgery. I never knew their magical formula— what I must have done that prompted those surgery decisions—so I always had to be a good boy and behave myself at all times. It was in my own best interests, therefore, not to annoy them in any manner whatsoever. But there was this one time when I actually stood up to my mom that I'll never forget.

It was 1956. I was ten years old. It was a warm day after school and I was having a good time playing in the empty dirt lot adjacent to my parent's home on Long Island. It must've been about 5:00 PM. My mom came out the back door of the house, along the path to the lot, and told me it was time to go inside.

I can't think of why I picked this particular moment to take a stand, but it all started by my saying: "No, I'm not ready to go inside right now." I'm sure she was surprised by my noncompliance to such a simple request, so naturally she repeated it: "Right now, I want you to come inside the house!" But again I failed to obey and probably responded along these lines: "I'm not going inside. Leave me alone!" This deadlock continued for another minute as she and I gradually walked closer to each other, ensuring that each of us would hear what the other was saying.

When it became obvious to me that neither of us was going to budge, I put it all on the line, looked straight into her eyes (as best I could at the time), and told her: "Go fuck yourself!"

She was so shocked by my graphic instruction that not a word came out of her mouth. She simply turned around and walked back into the house. My best guess is that I felt pretty good about standing my ground for the first time in my life. But had I thought through the possible consequences of this rebellion before or after the event? No. I just continued playing on the lot until I was good and ready to go back into the house. I passed my mom in the kitchen on the way up to my room, but no words or glances were exchanged.

Everything proceeded pretty much as normal for a school day. Dinner was ready about 7:00 in the evening—since we always waited for my dad to return from his practice in Manhattan. There we were, my mom, dad, brother, and I, finishing our dinner. Everything had gone very well: My mom hadn't said one word about what I'd yelled to her a few hours earlier.

Just before dinner was officially over, my dear brother decided to start a new conversation: "Does anyone want to know what Ralph said to Mom this afternoon?" I was shocked! I couldn't believe that my brother was about to betray me. Then I remembered he had not even been there when the mega-incident took place, so my mother must have told him a bit later. Meanwhile, there was zero response from my dad, who was busy gobbling up his dessert. And my mom didn't respond to my brother's question either. So my brother tried to be heard once again: "Doesn't anyone want to know what Ralph said to Mom this afternoon?" To this my dad finally replied: "Okay, what did he say?" With this invitation, my dear, sweet, twelve-year-old brother said it out loud: "Ralph told Mom to go fuck herself."

In less than a microsecond, my dad turned bright red, stood up, and smacked me hard across the face, which knocked me off my chair and down to the kitchen floor. At the top of his lungs, he shouted at me to go to my room. As I lifted myself off the floor, he hit me again. He followed me down the hallway, up the stairs, and into my room, hitting me as many times and as hard as he could. Once in my room, he ordered me to take off my clothes and get to bed. As I pulled off my clothes (I slept in my underwear), he hurled me on the couch. A moment later, he picked me up off the couch and hurled me across the room so I landed on top of my bed. All during this time, he hit me every chance he could get. A few minutes later, I was lying in bed, crying hysterically and uncontrollably, when he stormed out of my bedroom and slammed the door behind him.

I cried and whimpered for an hour. But I wasn't ready to fall asleep. So I walked slowly out of my room into the upstairs hallway, softly crying, still clutching my tiny security pillow against the side of my face. As I walked by my dad's study, I noticed he was reading at his desk. I gingerly entered the room and walked over there, while keeping a safe distance between us. As he slowly turned toward me, before he had a chance to speak, I asked him in a childish, sheepish voice: "Dad, what does that word mean?"

It was now my father who looked shocked and bewildered: It had never occurred to him that I might've said that word to my mom, which an adult (or even an adolescent) would know is "vulgar," but an innocent ten-year-old child would not. I kept up this pretence as he squirmed around in his chair, while he tried to decide whether to tell me what it meant or to apologize for his violent outburst. But he just stammered away for a short while, before he promised he would explain that word to me one day.

As anticipated, he never did explain to me what the word "fuck" meant or what it meant to tell your own mother to go fuck herself. He wasn't inclined to explain much of anything in those days. Now the truth is this: Although I *didn't* know the details, I did know that "fuck" was not a nice thing to say to your mother, or anyone else for that matter, but I wasn't going to let him know that. He had hurt me badly on that day, physically and emotionally, by hitting me so hard, again and again.

My first attempt at a rebellion had been quashed. I learned it wasn't a good idea to take a strong stand against my mother, even if I succeeded in derailing her for a couple of hours.

4
Mistreating Buttons

In September 1959, a month before I turned thirteen, my parents decided that my brother and I were old enough to care for a dog. My parents found a family that had to get rid of a nine-month-old, black cocker spaniel, named Bender's Boy Buttons. Their teenager's allergic reaction to his dog had become too severe to manage.

Soon after Buttons arrived in our home, I bought a few books on how to train a dog to do tricks. The first thing I decided to teach Buttons was to "shake hands." One book showed the five easy steps for teaching your dog to extend his right paw on command.

After I rehearsed the instructions in my mind, I helped Buttons sit in the proper position. I then raised my right hand and said "paw" (per the manual). But before I had a chance to pick up his right paw and shake it, Buttons raised his right leg and gave me his paw! I was overcome with wonder: "Buttons is brilliant!"

Then I realized that the Bender family must've taught him this trick during his nine-month stay with them. My next inspiration was to realize that Buttons might know many tricks besides handing me his paw. So I started vocalizing all the basic commands, one at a time, while I waited for his response: "Sit. Heel. Stay. Roll over. Beg. Jump. Hop." But nothing happened. After a while, I concluded that Buttons had only learned the one paw trick. During the next several months,

Buttons and I took the time to learn and practice many new tricks—and we became the best of friends.

As with most dogs, every now and then Buttons misbehaved by jumping on the kitchen table to steal freshly prepared gourmet food (or leaving occasional gifts for our amusement). So how did I teach Buttons that he needed to break these canine habits?

I don't remember how it began, what I was thinking, or if I was thinking at all. But when Buttons made a mistake, I proceeded to tie him up, blindfold him, and put him in a small closet. I did this again and again as the primary way to teach him self-control—and also to punish him for being bad.

Neither my parents nor my older brother were involved in this training method. *Only me.* I cannot recall if anyone else was present when I disciplined Buttons this way. Maybe I only punished Buttons when nobody else was around. But I do know that this unique form of punishment wasn't mentioned in any of the books I read on how to train and care for your family pet.

Well, it should be clear by now where, when, and how I learned my teaching style with Buttons: In my disciplinary approach, *I was doing to Buttons exactly what had been done to me.* I tied him up so he couldn't move any of his "arms." He couldn't see through either eye because I bandaged both of them with a rag or T-shirt. Even though he couldn't see, I still found it necessary to put him into a very small closet—so the walls of the closet imprisoned him (serving the same purpose as the metal bars that had surrounded my small hospital bed). And I kept him there alone for a significant length of time. He didn't know when I'd return or when he'd be freed.

Did inflicting this cruel punishment on Buttons make me feel better as a person? Of course not. Did I expect it to? Absolutely not. Was I expecting anything at all? I don't think so. The best I can say is that I was blindly recreating the pattern that was lodged in my numb body and my unconscious mind—a repeating pain that I hadn't yet been able to feel, let alone resolve.

When I finally was able to examine this "acting out" during my first round of therapy (fifteen years later), I could truly empathize with all the other acting out that goes on in our world—all the way from individuals to nations. It became clear to me that unless we're prepared to revisit our past, we're doomed to recreate our patterns with others, including pets.

In October 1967, when my brother, Peter, and I were both away at college (he in California and I in Pittsburgh) my parents decided they were going to downsize from the four-bedroom home on Long Island to a two-bedroom apartment in Manhattan. In anticipation of that relocation, they sent Buttons to Peter. My brother had rented an apartment that allowed dogs.

In the summer of 1968, I traveled to California to visit Buttons. He was almost ten years old by then and had aged quite a bit. But he did remember me! After I hugged, kissed, and petted him a while, I sat him back down on the ground and said: "Paw." Sure enough, he still remembered his first trick. We had several hours of fun together, just as we used to have years before.

It was hard leaving Buttons in California. I knew I'd never see him again. And even though it was still several years before I'd start psychotherapy, I realized I hadn't always been kind to my beloved dog. Before I said good-bye to him, I knelt down where he was calmly sitting and told him I was sorry I'd been so tough on him. He was a very good dog and didn't deserve to be mistreated. But I would soon learn that I was talking to myself as much as I was apologizing to my childhood friend.

5

My First Round of Therapy

I distinctly recall the exploratory meeting I had in early 1975 with the first therapist in my life, Dr. Stanley A. Chasin, a psychoanalyst. Between taking frequent puffs on his Freudian cigar, he asked me why I was interested in therapy at this time in my life. I told him my marriage had been falling apart for quite some time and I wanted to understand why.

Then Dr. Chasin asked me about my family history, questions that were rather easy to address, except for the one that caught me completely off guard: "Did you have any surgery in your childhood?" I quickly answered no. But then I thought about it for a few seconds before I modified that immediate response: "Well, I did have a *little* eye surgery, but that was nothing much." Dr. Chasin just nodded, as if to say: "We'll see about that."

When I started seeing Dr. Chasin for one fifty-minute session every week, I was twenty-eight years old. I portrayed my childhood to my analyst as having been ideal, the only distraction being some minor eye surgery (which, for sure, I only mentioned because of his background question). But in my state of mind, strange as it might seem, I really believed that my early years had been virtually perfect: I was happy; I was loved; I had been well cared for; I'd lived in a nice home, next to a large lot, where we could play baseball and ride our bikes. I went to Camp Laurel almost every summer and learned to swim, scuba dive, water ski, hike, climb cliffs, play tennis, and create mosaics. I'd received virtually every toy I ever wanted.

Keep in mind: Everything I wrote about in the first two pieces of my mosaic—especially my statements about the fear, pain, and brutality of those four eye surgeries—was still very much buried in my mind and body. It was only through several rounds of therapy (and other mind/body/spirit modalities) that I discovered the truth of my thoughts, feelings, and inner being. Mine was a long journey to awakening, but essential if I was to know myself, speak my truth, and deeply connect with other human beings.

At first, as I began talking with Dr. Chasin about my childhood, I had a difficult time remembering what actually took place in my family of origin—versus the many homegrown publicity statements about everything being so happy, wonderful, and perfect. It was so important to my mom, and therefore to me, for her to be the perfect mother (no matter what really transpired at home). Early on, I had convinced myself that she didn't and couldn't do anything wrong.

Think about it this way: If my mom *wasn't* perfect, whom was I entrusting to take care of very dependent me? Who was ensuring I'd be kept safe in this cold, cruel world? It seems I *had* to be sold on her perfection if I was to have any sense of security during my turbulent childhood. But these survival-based beliefs gradually disappeared as I began grappling with my feelings, relieved of the fear that I'd again, without warning, be driven to a hospital for more surgery.

Indeed, at some point in the therapy process, I even wished I'd been physically beaten throughout my childhood so I'd have known, without a doubt, that something was terribly wrong. The illusion of a perfect family significantly delayed my self-discovery and ability to move forward.

That I was successfully peeling away the many hidden layers of self-deception was initially demonstrated through my dreams, while asleep. At first, I'd have dreams about my looking at some beautiful country scene through binoculars. But then these binoculars would accidentally fall out of my hands and the lenses would shatter on the ground before my eyes. In my dream, I would scramble to pick up all the shattered pieces of glass and frantically try to repair the broken lenses—so I could see the beauty around me.

Later in therapy, a second set of recurring dreams would find me walking across a hilly expanse of large rocks and slippery stones, making it tough to walk without stumbling or falling. I was carrying a round, transparent bucket that had an open, *oval* top, which was filled to the brim with a weird off-white liquid. If I lost my balance, the liquid would easily spill out. For some unknown reason, I had to avoid this at all costs. Although it wasn't explained in the dream, I had to travel across that challenging terrain and make it to the other side. If only I could keep walking ever so slowly and carefully, I'd be sure not to lose a single drop of that precious fluid while reaching my final destination.

Naturally, in the first set of dreams, I am safely feeling out the fear of losing my eyes and not being able to repair them. While in the second set, I'm addressing the anxiety of letting any loss of liquid— the tears from my crying—ruin my eyes (recall the nurse's comment to me in the recovery room). In these latter dreams, it also seemed I felt solely responsible for taking care of my eyes—even under the most difficult and challenging circumstances. And I had to reach the other side of the destinations in my life, all on my own. I could only count on me. I certainly couldn't count on Mom, Dad, or Peter!

Eventually, my dreams allowed me to experience deep cuts on my wrists and arms that had to be bandaged for them to heal. I also dreamt about cuts on my face, around my cheeks and directly above my eyebrows, which needed medical attention in a first-aide station or a doctor's office. Gradually, my dreams took me closer and closer to my eyes.

When I was finally ready to see the stark truth of my childhood experiences, I had a dream about an actual eye surgery in a hospital, including the surgeons with green gowns and masks, their surgical instruments, and several nurses. I was so thrilled to finally get to the point where it was safe enough for me to relive and witness some of the scariest moments in my life. I woke up early one morning and declared: "Fantastic! I dreamt about eye surgery again!"

Several times, Dr. Chasin would ask me what it felt like when I first awoke from my earliest surgery, blindfolded and tied down in a hospital bed. I'd say: "I am sure I must have been scared." Then he would rephrase his question: "What did you actually *feel?*" And I'd respond along these lines: "Any child awakening in such a horrible situation would be confused and frightened."

In just a few years, I had made a lot of progress in uncovering the truth of my surgeries: They did take place, they were painful, and they weren't handled well. Nevertheless, I still had a long way to go in recovering the buried feelings inside my body, so I could become a whole—awakened—human being.

6

Resolution with Dad, But Not Mom

It was September 1976 and I was almost thirty years old. My father was seventy-seven and my mother was sixty-nine. I was a year and a half into my first round of psychotherapy. Armed with some initial self-knowledge about my childhood, I felt that now was the time to confront my parents about my surgical traumas.

Why do it at this time in my life? Once I discovered—or rather recalled—what my childhood was really like, I felt I was living a lie. I'd have phone conversations every week with my parents as well as regular visits during the major holidays. But increasingly, I realized I was only pretending with them that my childhood years had been perfect and that they were the perfect parents. At some point during the therapy process, I concluded that to be truly authentic, healthy, and growthful, I either had to stop relating with my parents or begin talking to them about my childhood experiences. I chose the latter, so my parents and I would have a chance to resolve our differences and finally be *real* with each other. I felt I had nothing much to lose by telling them my truth: Any consequence from such an unexpected confrontation couldn't be as bad as the surgeries themselves.

I made a deliberate choice to have separate conversations with each parent in their apartment in Manhattan, starting with my dad. I wanted to find out directly from him (without any interference from my mom) why I had to have all those surgeries (the medical reasons) and who made the decision about each surgery (why my mother was the go-between when he was the licensed ophthalmologist). I also wanted to know why he didn't ask me *my* opinion about my eyes and whether I wanted surgery at all, since it was *my* body and *my* life that were at stake.

I still remember exactly how we were sitting at the dining room table. I can vividly see the sun making its distinctive shadows on my father's face, revealing the many lifelines that had been carved out of his own traumas.

After I outlined the agenda for our meeting, I began by asking my dad to just listen, without saying anything, so I could share my childhood experiences. This meeting turned out to be his finest hour as a father. Rather than having to manage my deep-seated fear about challenging my cold dad and the distant ophthalmologist, only pure love and complete understanding were before me.

In about forty-five minutes, I described what I had learned in therapy and what I could now remember about each of those four eye surgeries. I revealed what it was like to live in constant fear from three years old until I was twenty-three, when I finally decided that no one was ever going to do that to me again.

Once I finished my uninterrupted account of my experiences and feelings, I asked my dad if there was anything he wanted to ask me. He didn't. I then invited him to tell me his reactions.

My dad was tearing before he began. This might have been the first time I ever saw tears develop in his eyes. He paused, and with a posture and tone of authentic, heartfelt emotion that only a loving, dedicated parent could possibly convey, he affirmed: "If I knew then what I know now, I would have done everything differently."

That was it. That was all he said. And yet, in the particular way he said those few words, all I could feel was this huge gap: not a gap in understanding, but a gap in *expectations*. The huge gap was in the difference between the big effort I thought it would take for him to "get it" versus the divine ease with which he resolved our thirty-year history. What he said was all it took: nothing more, nothing less. It was truly that easy. From that moment on, for the rest of his life, we became best friends, who together developed a deep understanding of one another that words alone can't possibly express.

For the next hour, he answered virtually every question I asked. I learned many of the medical facts of the surgery that I never knew before. Some of these, as I noted before, had to do with the hospital's very restrictive visiting hours. Furthermore, eye surgeons didn't know much about child psychology, so they didn't know what could have been done to ease a young child's fear and anxiety about surgery.

Then in the most forthright manner, my dad acknowledged to me, for the first time in his life, the true objective of each of my eye surgeries: trying to get my eyes physically straight so they could work together, which was supposed to improve the sight in my right eye as well as enable me to see in three dimensions. That was the prevailing medical, ophthalmologic wisdom at the time. My dad then confessed that only for my very first operation, when I was three years old, was there any real hope of restoring the quality and depth of my vision. For all the subsequent surgeries, he knew, *ahead of time*, that it was already too late, age-wise, to fix any aspect of my vision. *For my last three eye surgeries, therefore, the sole objective was to straighten my right eyeball to improve my appearance.*

On one hand, maybe the oddest irony of my eye traumas stems from the radically different assumptions that ophthalmologists and optometrists make about how to improve the sight of a lazy eye and restore the stereovision of two crossed-eyes. *Ophthalmologists believe in strabismus surgery*, the assumption that adjusting the length of the tiny muscles around the weak eye (so the eyeball stays in the middle of its socket when looking straight ahead) will get both eyes working together. But it takes *several* surgeries to perfectly align the eyes, which still doesn't give the brain the basic know-how to process the visual information from each eye—even when the operation is performed on an infant. As I learned the hard way, strabismus surgery is mostly cosmetic surgery—since enhancing the appearance of an eye doesn't improve its vision.

On the other hand, *optometrists use vision therapy*, based on the assumption that utilizing special lenses, prisms, filters, and exercises (non-surgical treatments) will teach the brain how to assemble the visual information coming from both eyes. In sharp contrast to eye surgery, vision therapy directly improves eyesight—which enhances the appearance of both eyes. How? Each eyeball is gradually drawn to perfect alignment in its socket—because that's where the brain can make the most effective use of visual information. Even though vision therapy was developed in the late nineteenth century, I didn't learn about it until several decades after my surgeries. *Paradoxically, if instead of being an ophthalmologist my dad had been an optometrist, I wouldn't have experienced those repetitive eye surgeries and vision therapy might have greatly improved my eyesight and stereovision.*

Back to my story: There was only one time when I saw my dad noticeably squirm while he was trying to answer my questions about my eye surgeries (which thus revealed the ignored opportunities in his own personal development): Who decided when it was time for me to have eye surgery: the ophthalmologist or the mother?

By then, I knew that my dad had grown up with great fear of his own abusive mother. And he always seemed to have a difficult time asserting himself with his wife (my mother), who is a domineering woman. I did not need, for my own benefit and understanding, for my dad to investigate what only could be addressed during his own therapy, if he ever chose to follow such a path. So I decided to leave this line of questioning alone for the time being: I now knew who'd made those decisions about the last three surgeries and who'd made it seem that they were being done to improve my sight, which now could only be viewed as a deceptive ploy, whether deliberate or not, to ensure my ongoing compliance with repeated cosmetic surgeries on my right eye.

Next, I had a one-on-one meeting with my mom. But she was not up to the task: She couldn't even sit still while I tried to describe my childhood experiences with the surgeries. She kept interrupting me to correct my feelings, so they were consistent with her image of the perfect mother. Regardless of what I shared with her, she would talk over me by saying, "That's not how it was. You're crazy. I don't know what that therapist has put into your head. You're obviously ill. How could you possibly think we could do anything that wasn't best for you? I'm your mother. How could I possibly hurt you?"

That day, I couldn't break through my mom's sturdy walls. She was Perfect Mother, once again, and she seemed ready to die if that was what it would take to maintain her self-image. Facts, feelings, and someone else's perceptions and experiences were all irrelevant to the discussion; all that really mattered was to keep her world the way she needed it to be.

But I got to see my mother in action—in a way I was never able to see her before. How could I, as a young child, have reached her? How could I have put up much of a fight—a real rebellion—with her strength and determination to be right at all costs? There was hardly any point in continuing the discussion. It was clear: There would be no resolution with my mom on this day—or perhaps ever.

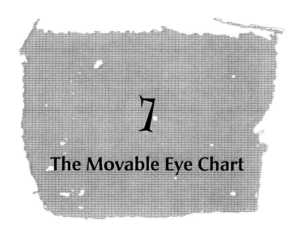

7
The Movable Eye Chart

When I was six years old, the eye chart was introduced into my life. Even though I needed to know each letter in the alphabet so I could learn how to read and write, perhaps the most pragmatic use of these basic elements of a literate society was to test how well I could *see*—with each eye separately and with both eyes together.

For me, there was always a particular kind of anxiety associated with how well I could see the eye chart and thus call out each letter. In my youth, success at correctly identifying these letters was one of the key determinants (besides my mother's mysterious formula), as to whether I'd need more surgery.

Toward the end of seventh grade, all students in my junior high school were given a tour of the industrial arts shops: woodworking, arts and crafts, pottery, electicity, and graphic arts. After the tour, each student was asked to choose which of these shops he wanted to take in eighth grade.

The graphic arts shop caught my eye—literally and figuratively. The movable type mesmerized me into a new world of seeing, being, and becoming.

On the tour, we were briefly shown the separate pieces of metal type that make up the entire alphabet, including numbers, symbols, and spaces. I didn't know it then, but I surely know now, why these pieces of type, sorted into their different compartments in a wooden type case, would so dramatically catch my attention: *When I looked at a type case filled with metal type, I was looking at an eye chart*—but not one that was twenty feet away, out of reach, and out of sight. When I picked up a little piece of type out of a type case and held it in front of me, I felt complete, I felt secure, and I felt safe. In the graphic arts shop, I'd discovered a movable eye chart that I could experience in three-dimensions—using all my senses—up close and personal.

Once our tour group of seventh-grade students had a chance to play with some movable type, we next experienced a printing press. *This single event of seeing how movable type meets the printing press set in motion the next forty years of my work life.* Can you even imagine what it was like for me to see the creation of an eye chart from beginning to end? Not only could I pick up a piece of movable type from a type case and hold it straight in front of my eyes, but I could learn how to prepare the metal type, as independent letters or meaningful words, for printing on any sheet of paper.

As it turned out, I was able to study graphic arts in the first half of the eighth grade. For Christmas, I received a surprise present from my parents: a small cylinder printing press and movable *rubber* type. It was a start! I spent the entire Christmas holiday—and many other weeknights and weekends—printing away with my press: business cards, letterheads, announcements, and party invitations.

For my ninth-grade surprise Christmas gift, I received a small Kelsey hand letterpress (with a three-by-five-inch steel chase) and my first font of movable *metal* type. Now I was in business! During that year, with the money I made from my quality printing business (and from allowance), I bought at least ten more fonts of movable type and additional supplies and accessories to enhance my graphic arts experience.

During the next months, I discovered that the two best colleges for printing processes and graphic arts management were Rochester Institute of Technology in Rochester, New York (which focused on the production process for the graphic arts industry) and Carnegie Institute of Technology (Carnegie Tech) in Pittsburgh, Pennsylvania (which focused on the management science aspects). Since I figured I'd prefer to study the big picture and ultimately manage a printing business, I decided that in my senior year in high school, still three years away, I would apply to only one college: Carnegie Tech.

My grades during my past three years in junior high averaged about 75 out of 100—mediocre at best. In the fall of 1961, I began my sophomore year in Jamaica High School. From this moment on, grades really mattered for getting into a selective college. Knowing that, my dad, on his own initiative, proposed a challenge I couldn't refuse: If I achieved an average grade of 90 or better for the fall term in tenth grade, he'd buy me a Kelsey letterpress with a six-by-ten-inch steel chase for printing a large area of type.

For my tenth-grade Christmas present, my mom gave me a type case cabinet that held ten type cases, which also had a sturdy top to support my printing press. She had bought this cabinet used, in bad repair, and had secretly spent many long hours fixing it, sanding it, staining it, and then varnishing it—so not only was it functional for use, but it also was so beautiful. I can't recall receiving another gift from my mom that embodied more of her time, effort, and love than this cherished cabinet—except, perhaps, when she gave me life.

In January 1962, it was time to face my final grades for the fall term in tenth grade. After I quickly and anxiously opened the official envelope in my homeroom class, I realized I'd achieved an average grade of 91, which also put me on the honor roll: "Yes! I did it!" And my dad made good on his promise: In March 1962, my brand-new printing press arrived by truck from the Kelsey factory.

Being placed on my high school's honor roll certainly boosted my confidence about being able to perform well in school. Because I'd already decided to apply to only one university, I knew I had to maintain, if not improve, my grades. And that is exactly what I did: I became a serious student in high school for the next two years.

In the fall of my senior year in high school, I followed my three-year plan by applying for admission to Carnegie Tech. My parents repeatedly encouraged me, even begged me, to apply to one or more backup schools, just in case I got turned down by my dream college. But I ignored all their pleas.

January 23, 1964, was one of the happiest days of my life. On that day I was accepted into Carnegie Institute of Technology. I had overcome the potentially defeating fate of my early eye surgeries by transforming my wounds into gifts.

8

The Full Circle of My Work Life

It was a dream come true every time I strolled across the Carnegie Tech campus in the fall of 1964. I spent the next few years majoring in graphic arts management—just as I had planned. But eventually my emphasis in college shifted from graphic arts to a deeper interest in managing organizations.

During two summers in high school, I had worked in a printing factory, so I could gain skill and experience operating much larger Heidelberg presses than a six-by-ten-inch Kelsey press. During two summers in college, however, rather than gaining more of the same printing experience, I decided to work for my uncle, Morris, who was the owner and president of a manufacturing company. My uncle had me work in each area of his business—accounting, marketing, sales, finance, production, and human resources. He also had me follow him around during the course of his workday. Spending those two summers with my uncle seeded my subsequent interest in studying and improving organizations.

In my junior year at Carnegie, because I had excellent grades, I was accepted into graduate school for a master's degree in science in the same university. So instead of entering my senior year of college in the fall of 1967, I began my first year in Carnegie's Graduate School of Industrial Administration (GSIA). This highly selective honor was designated the *3/2 Program:* three years in the undergraduate school and then two years in the graduate school, with the awarding of two degrees, B.S. and M.S., after the fifth year of study.

In early 1969, even though I was initially planning to graduate that June with both university degrees and then enter the job market to begin my business career, the war in Vietnam was still raging. And there was increasing talk in the media about escalating the war and drafting more men. Throughout 1969, however, it was still possible to get a college or graduate school deferment from your local draft board, if you were making satisfactory progress toward completing your degree. Technically, I hadn't finished my undergraduate work, since I'd entered graduate school in the beginning of what would've been my senior year in Carnegie. Thus, I was still eligible for a draft deferment if I could remain in graduate school.

Basically, I was facing two career choices as the spring of 1969 approached: whether I should (1) enter the workforce with my two degrees in hand, take my chances with the draft board, and thereby proceed with my business career or (2) postpone my entry into the job market for another year or so, by taking more graduate courses and, of course, making satisfactory progress toward completing my two degrees—which might keep me out of the war.

I shared these two career choices with my favorite professor, Dr. Kenneth D. Mackenzie. During the past several years, he'd been my instructor in several undergraduate and graduate courses. Early on, I had developed a great deal of respect for him—because of his good nature, dry wit, and brilliant mind. You might say he was my mentor, more so than any other professor.

As soon as I shared with Dr. Mackenzie my dilemma of either getting a job in the spring or one year later, he told me straight out: "You don't want to do either. You want to get your Ph.D., so you can do research at a university." I meekly responded with one question: "I do?" Dr. Mackenzie said, "Yes."

This short dialogue changed the entire course of my graduate studies—and my career. Perhaps I was still used to following orders regarding what I should and shouldn't do. In this case, however, the advice seemed obviously to my benefit. I don't know how he did it, but Dr. Mackenzie knew my special gifts and cared enough about me to speak his truth in no uncertain terms. More than forty years later, I can only conclude that he was absolutely correct.

As a result of Dr. Mackenzie's unquestionable belief in me, I applied to and was accepted for admission into the Ph.D. program in Carnegie's GSIA in the fall of 1969—majoring in organizations. (Note: I didn't have to be awarded my B.S. or M.S. degree, which was entirely acceptable to the graduate admission's committee, since all my coursework and teachers were in the same school. But if I had enrolled in another university's doctoral program, I would first have to receive both my degrees before leaving the newly named Carnegie Mellon University [CMU]—which would've made me immediately eligible for the draft. Result: My decision to purse a Ph.D. degree at CMU seemed the perfect solution for staying out of Vietnam.)

On December 1, 1969, a dramatic change in draft procedures shocked all college students: A birthday lottery was held to guide all local draft boards in selecting men for military service—whereby a *random process* would replace college deferments.

The general expectation was that if the random process placed your birthday in the bottom 100 of the list (birthdays between days 267 and 366), it was very unlikely you'd be drafted. If your birthday fell in the middle of the list (between 101 and 266), you might get picked if the war continued to escalate. But if your birthday randomly appeared in the top 100, it was highly probable you'd be drafted.

December 1, 1969, wasn't one of my luckier days: My birthday of October 5 was Number 24 on the list. Consequently, it was rather certain that I'd be drafted. Indeed, a few months later, I was notified by my draft board in New York to report to the Federal Building in downtown Pittsburgh to complete my aptitude and physical tests—so the Selective Service System could classify me for the draft.

Without having to think about it, I already knew I wasn't going to rebel and move to Canada to avoid the draft, as many thousands of students did in that era. I decided, instead, I'd do my best to find a way to beat the draft. If I couldn't succeed at outwitting the system, I was prepared to join the U.S. Army. As a result, my battle cry was, "If they can get me, they deserve me!"

Early one morning, I arrived at the Federal Building. As I began taking the various aptitude tests, I immediately realized it'd be really ridiculous for me to purposely fail these tests, while I was currently enrolled in a doctoral program. But a little later that morning, it was time for the physical exam and it included an *eye test*—replete with an *eye chart.* Now my battle with the draft board was on very familiar territory: I had the home-court advantage.

In those days, there wasn't an optical instrument for assessing a person's vision by directly examining his eyes or by analyzing the properties of his eyeglass lenses. Instead, the vision assessment was entirely based on a person first seeing and then correctly naming—out loud—the sequence of letters on the eye chart, row by row. On that particular day in the Federal Building, for some *strange* reason, my right eye wasn't seeing very well, so I couldn't correctly identify *any* letters on the chart. Because the Army's physicians didn't believe I couldn't see anything with my right eye, they briskly escorted me outside the building to have my eyes examined by two independent optometrists in downtown Pittsburgh.

Both of these optometry practices placed that all-too-familiar eye chart at my service. In both offices, I consistently voiced almost blind vision with my right eye. Regardless of my apparent difficulty in seeing that day, what seemed to convince the optometrists of the veracity of my responses was that my lazy eyeball was sporadically orbiting around its "normal" focal position in the eye. Even better, noticeable scar tissue, from those past eye surgeries, was present on either side of my right eyeball.

When the authorities received the results from these additional tests, I was officially given an I-Y classification: "Registrant qualified for military service only in time of war or national emergency." Now, what was the practical meaning of this policy? Since the U.S. never officially declared war on North Vietnam nor treated the escalation of police action in the Vietnamese conflict as a national emergency, *I wasn't going to Vietnam any time soon.*

Years later, during my first round of therapy, when I first came to accept the emotional traumas I'd experienced because of my eyes, *I had to realize that my eyes might've saved my life.* After being assigned Number 24 on the birthday lottery, if I hadn't been blessed with my orbiting, surgically scarred right eye, I would've been dumped into a nasty battlefield in a life-threatening jungle in South Vietnam. Sure, I might have made it out alive, but there was also a decent chance I would have been seriously injured—or killed. Eventually, I would be extremely grateful that I'd been born with a lazy eye. What a joy—the silver lining on all those dismal days in my earlier life.

In June 1970, safe from the draft board and the war in Vietnam, I received my two degrees from CMU. At the end of that same month, I experienced the last of those four eye surgeries, when I exclaimed: "Nobody is ever going to do this to me again!"

In October 1970, I entered the Ph.D. program at the University of California, Los Angeles (UCLA), majoring in social systems. Ever since my parents took my brother and me on an extended vacation to the West Coast in 1959 (when I was twelve years old), I wanted to return there. And UCLA was considered to have one of the best Ph.D. programs for my area of study. This was my golden opportunity to build a new life—having reclaimed my personal power.

I thrived at UCLA: For the first time in my life, I was exposed to self-discovery and self-understanding—through direct experience in sensitivity training groups (called T-groups) and by reading research studies on organizational change. Because I was so energized by these topics, I was motivated to complete the doctoral program quickly, so I could begin my heart's work: teaching, researching, and consulting on transforming social systems.

After fourteen months at UCLA, I'd completed all my required coursework and examinations, except for my dissertation, which I completed in a short time after arriving in Pittsburgh, Pennsylvania, in December 1971. For the next thirty years, my work thrived at the University of Pittsburgh's Katz School of Business.

During the 1970s, I wrote the drafts of my articles and books on an IBM Selectric typewriter, which utilized removable, pivoting, metal typeballs with different proportional fonts. I could switch fonts on the fly, which brought me back to my early printing days, when I set movable metal type.

In the early 1980s, I bought my first IBM personal computer with two 320K floppy-disk drives. Now I could type my articles and books on screen and print them on a dot-matrix printer or with my IBM Selectric typewriter, making use of a special converter box that connected my computer directly to the typewriter. The computer-to-typewriter connection was rather slow, but it provided me with the look—and feel—of letterpress printing.

In the late 1980s, desktop publishing was born. At the start of this new era, I felt compelled to switch from the IBM-based PC world to an Apple Macintosh. With a new Apple LaserWriter printer, I could enjoy an enhanced printing experience. It was a thrill for me to draft my articles and books on a bright color screen, hit the print button, and then quickly see my words printed on high-quality paper with precise laser technology.

In the early 1990s, with my Apple computer and a laser printer, I completed a book on transforming organizations. Besides writing the words, I designed the layout, chose the fonts, and delivered the files to my publisher, who then printed the book with an offset press.

The dedication page, which included an illustration, identified the inspiration behind all my published creations: "To my mother, Lilli Kilmann, who took me from eye charts to type cases."

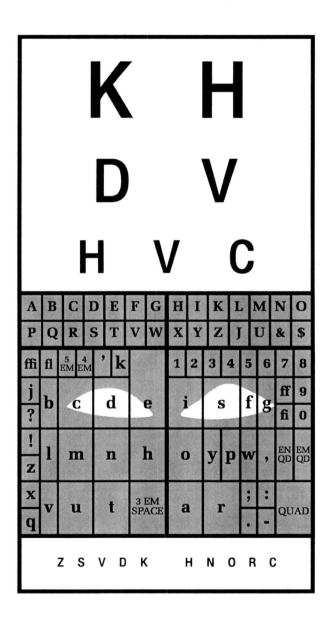

In retrospect, the full cycle of my work life—from my early eye surgeries to my timely exposure to moveable type, to my majoring in graphic arts management, to my writing articles and books, and to my creating the desktop-publishing files for printing my words—has always been about seeing, being, and becoming my true self on my own terms.

9

Getting to Know My Dad

Once I experienced the resolution with my dad in September 1976, he and I became best friends. A few weeks later, I invited him to visit me in Pittsburgh (without my mom present), so I could get to know him—adult to adult. Although my dad and I had always been able to connect by playing cards or chess, these activities were undertaken to *do* something together—rather than to *learn* about one another. And since my mom always spoke over my dad and, therefore, dominated the discussion (whether in person or during a three-way phone call), this time, I wanted to interact with my dad, one on one.

At first, my mom had a hard time accepting that I didn't want her to join my dad on his travel to Pittsburgh—especially since this arrangement had never before been attempted in our family. But I insisted, my father concurred, even if passively, and my mother had no choice but to concede.

My dad visited me in Pittsburgh for a four-day weekend. That's the most concentrated time I'd ever spent with him. We talked non-stop. I learned, directly from him (rather than hearing it piecemeal from my mom), his struggles as a child and what he'd experienced growing up in Germany—including the life-altering circumstances that led him and my mom to escape their homeland and then move to the United States.

My father was born on February 3, 1899, in the small village of Trachenberg, Germany. He grew up in a family with ten children. His mom and dad were extremely poor—and thoroughly disheartened. My dad's father, my grandfather, had been born with only one good eye (sound familiar?) and then lost his remaining eyesight when an arrow accidentally pierced his good eye. Being completely blind, he couldn't get a job, nor could his wife find suitable employment. They were so poor, in fact, that the family would regularly go into the fields and eat weeds just to stay alive.

When my dad was sixteen, he decided to run away from home, so his family would have one less mouth to feed. He lied about his age, saying he was eighteen, so he could join the Imperial German Navy in 1915, during World War I. While onboard a naval ship for the next four years, a highly educated and sophisticated Greek sailor recognized the genius in my dad and proceeded to teach him Greek, Latin, literature, and science.

Even though my father never completed high school (because he'd left home at sixteen), after he had completed his tour of duty in 1919, he spent one year in a special program for ex-service men. There he was able to pass all the examinations—not only for completing high school, but also for completing his college requirements. Then my dad applied to the University of Heidelberg Medical School, was accepted, and graduated first in his class in 1924.

In terms of choosing a specialization for his residency, my dad considered psychiatry and ophthalmology. He decided to become an ophthalmologist because his father had lost both eyes. My dad said he wanted to learn more about eyes, since they'd touched his life in many ways. Indeed, while he was pursuing his residency, he began doing research on eye diseases and published a number of articles in medical journals, working with several prominent eye researchers in Germany. His dream was to become a full professor in a top medical school, so he could have the support to do leading-edge research on the diagnosis and treatment of eye diseases.

While I'd heard pieces of these family stories before from my mom, it wasn't until I heard the whole story from my dad that the ancestral roots of my life began to illuminate me. Prior to his visit, I believed that my desire to become a professor had been exclusively shaped by my mentor, Professor Mackenzie, while I was a graduate student at CMU—not because of my dad's unfulfilled dreams. And previous to his visit, I'd seen my dad as an ophthalmologist—not as an aspiring research professor.

My dad next described his early years with my mom: In 1926, when he was twenty-seven and my mom was nineteen, their initial contact took place near the small town of Mutterstadt, Germany. My dad was doing some office work in his local medical practice on the second floor of a building, when he just happened to gaze out the window. He noticed a beautiful girl walking down the street. In that moment, he decided he was going to marry her. He then proceeded to find out who she was and took the next steps. They were married on September 5, 1929—he Christian, she Jewish.

In January 1933, Hitler was appointed chancellor, the head of the German government. Only two months later, the Enabling Act, *Ermächtigungsgesetz*, gave Hitler dictatorial powers to enact new laws without the voice of Germany's parliament. The presumed purpose of giving Hitler such sweeping powers was to provide autocratic—emergency—leadership to remedy supposed communist threats that had recently been publicized about the inexplicable Reichstag fire.

Using the Jews as a scapegoat to rally the Aryan population into a revitalized Germany, Hitler and the Nazi Party then proceeded to strip the Jews of their rights and property and, ultimately, their lives. In August 1934, German President Paul von Hindenburg died, and Hitler quickly combined the separate powers of the chancellor and the president into one all-powerful office, thus becoming *The Führer*. Thereafter, he required every public official in the government and every soldier in the military to swear a loyalty oath, not to Germany, as would have been customary, but to Adolf Hitler himself.

As a stream of new laws were enacted to annihilate the Jews and their culture (for the avowed purpose of cleansing and purifying the Aryan race), my parents had to divorce or else my father would have been thrown in jail: According to a new law, a German man was not allowed to be married to a Jewish woman. Nevertheless, my parents still rented an apartment and met in secret. But it was a dangerous situation: Besides his well-being, my father was risking his position as head doctor of the eye department and the eye dispensary of the state hospital of the Federal Police in Berlin. (Note: Previously, my mom had told me that most German men who'd married a Jewish woman before Hitler came to power quickly left their wives when the new laws came into being—and then pledged allegiance to the Führer and their fatherland: "Deutschland über alles." My mother virtually worshiped my dad for his steadfast loyalty to his principles [and to her], although she often felt sad and guilty that her religion had "caused" their hardships.)

At one time between 1933 and 1934, during that tumultuous, ominous period in Germany history, my father decided to read Adolf Hitler's book: *Mein Kampf*. My dad wanted to determine what Hitler was really thinking, and what he was likely to do. It became evident to my dad that Hitler was planning to purify the Aryan race not only throughout Germany, but also throughout Europe and Russia—so Germany would have enough "living space": *Lebensraum*. Soon after reading Hitler's book, my dad recognized that he and my mom had to get off the continents of Europe and Asia. While many Jews *and* Germans were still living the illusion that the unthinkable political developments they saw occurring just couldn't continue (thus many people chose to sit back and wait it out), my dad was one of a small group of German citizens who'd seen the handwriting on the wall— *Mein Kampf*—and knew that he and my mom had to leave Germany no matter what.

By 1935, my parents had devised a secret plan to immigrate to the United States, which, by necessity, required a lot of deceit and trickery. (Note: Neither my dad nor my mom ever shared with me the painstaking details of their courageous escape from Germany. My intuition tells me that my mom, at a minimum, suffered some sort of horrible ordeal. Perhaps some devastating violation, which took place during their daring escape, wounded her so deeply that she had to shut off a noble part of herself to survive. But it was a subject that she'd never discuss, and therefore could never heal. I'm only guessing here, but I have no other way of explaining the very troubled nature of my childhood and adult experiences with her— and the way she talked about Hitler and the Nazis. Occasionally, I wondered if her incessant need to be the Perfect Wife—and Perfect Mother—partially stemmed from her guilt over her Jewish religion and her traumatic ordeal in escaping Germany.)

My father said it took them six months to get out of Germany. My parents arrived in New York City in March 1936 with hardly any possessions—except the sheer will to start a new life in America.

Dad was able to learn English quickly, benefiting from the Latin he had acquired from his mentor during his stint with the Imperial German Navy. As a result, it didn't take much time for him to pass the medical exams in New York State and set up his practice in New York City.

During the next seven years, he performed many eye surgeries every week in Lenox Hill Hospital in Manhattan. Yet it became more and more difficult to proceed with "business as usual" after the U.S. entered the war against Germany in 1941. As Germany escalated its assaults in Europe and Russia, my dad couldn't look the other way— it wasn't his nature. Consequently, in 1943, at the age of forty-four, my father closed his office and then enlisted in the U.S. Army, so he could help his new country beat Germany. Amazing! During World War I, my dad had fought *for* Germany and then, almost thirty years later during World War II, he fought *against* Germany. To this day, I'm so proud of him for truly living his core beliefs—again and again— and not just talking about them.

Naturally, at his age, the Army wasn't going to put my dad on the front lines. Instead, after surviving boot camp in Indiana, he was given the rank of captain and became the head of the eye department at Walter Reed General Hospital in Washington, D.C. My father was stationed there for two years. In March 1945, my brother was born in the same hospital. And just weeks later, in early May, the war against Germany came to a successful end. While the Army offered my dad a promotion to major, he declined. My parents had other plans: They moved back to New York to re-establish their civilian life and raise a new family.

Eighteen months later, I was born in Manhattan. When I was six months old, my parents decided it would be better to raise their two children in a relaxed suburban environment, while still having convenient access to the city. So in March 1947, the family moved to Jamaica, Long Island, only fifty minutes by subway train to my dad's office and Lenox Hill Hospital.

My mom used to say: "Not until you've lived through a world war, do you have any idea of what it can do to you." My parents, of course, had lived through *two* world wars. But it wasn't until I was getting to know my dad during his visit to see me in Pittsburgh that I experienced a deeper sense of what she really meant—the immense geographical, emotional, cultural, and linguistic challenges that my parents had to overcome so my brother and I could be born in a free country. My parents left everything behind in Germany—including relatives and friends who would later die in concentration camps— to make that courageous move to America. Based on my dad's many stories, *I developed a deep respect for the powerful forces that had shaped his life, which subsequently shaped my life.*

After my father's visit to Pittsburgh, we regularly talked on the phone about two or three times a week. If my mom was home and got on the phone in a three-way conversation (which, as mentioned, she tended to dominate), I'd eventually say: "Mom, I want to talk to dad now, so could you please get off the phone?" My mom did not like this very much, but I still asserted myself. But other times, my dad would choose to call me when she was out shopping or visiting with friends. In those cases, I'd get a call from my dad around 10:00 or so in the morning, not for any particular purpose, but just so we could talk. Many times, he would begin his conversation by saying: "I miss you." This warm, loving expression from my delightful dad was a huge shift from the distant relationship I'd experienced while growing up with a cold ophthalmologist. Our phone conversations were now relaxed and smooth: It was as if we had known each other throughout our entire lives (and perhaps in other lifetimes as well), even though it was only very recently that we'd broken through our parent-child barriers and had resolved our relationship to the core of our being.

In April 1978, I was attending a local conference in midtown Manhattan, where I'd be presenting my new research on designing and improving organizations. I invited my best friend—my dad—to attend. This would be the first time he'd see me deliver a research presentation in front of an academic audience (or *any* audience for that matter).

I met my dad in the hotel lobby early, so I could get him a good seat in the assigned conference room. Just a few people were there when we first entered the ballroom, including the chairman of the session, Professor Mackenzie, my mentor at CMU. I introduced them and soon left the two of them talking, while I arranged the materials for my presentation.

When the audience was settled in their seats at the appointed time, Dr. Mackenzie began by introducing me as well as the subject of my presentation. He then proceeded to tell the audience that he'd met my dad about fifteen minutes ago. Dr. Mackenzie then publicly shared their private conversation. He had asked my dad why he was attending my presentation. Apparently, my dad had answered: "I sent my son to the college of his dreams with all expenses paid. I'm here to find out if I made a good investment!" The audience roared with laughter, and I'm sure I was beaming from ear to ear . With this warm audience reception, I described my latest research on organizational design and transformation.

The presentation and question-and-answer session went very well. When it was over, I looked for Dad to see if he still wanted to stay for lunch. When I found him and reminded him of our tentative lunch plans, he just mumbled that I should go out to lunch with my friends. I wasn't sure what he meant, but I thanked him for having attended my presentation. I then hugged him good-bye, since I was taking a flight back to Pittsburgh in the evening.

A few days later, I called my parents from Pittsburgh. My dad was out doing some errands, so I decided to ask my mom: "Did Dad say anything to you about my presentation? He didn't stay for lunch and didn't say much when we said good-bye."

My mom then recounted that my dad had taken a taxi back to their apartment. The very moment he returned, she asked him how it all went. My father could barely talk. He started choking up as he tried to explain his experience at the presentation, but my mom had difficulty understanding him. While crying, my dad kept saying: "How did he do that? I never saw anything like it! I don't understand. Who did he get that from? He didn't get it from me."

My dad was obviously moved to see his child in command of his profession. But I must wonder if, through me, my father finally came to terms with the unfortunate demolition of his research plans, which were shattered simply because Hitler had taken command of the German scene and then dictated which individuals—and which marriages—were pure and which ones were not. Now, maybe for the first time in his life, my dad could fully honor that pivotal journey he'd taken from Germany to America more than forty years earlier: While he couldn't live his silent dream of conducting eye research as a professor in Germany, his son would live the essence of that dream for him right here in America, because his son's eye traumas brought him from printing to writing to research.

And so, after all was said and done, my dad's life-long dream was ironically realized: From that unique academic vortex in a New York hotel, my father and I discovered that my eye-inspired future resolved his arrow-piercing past.

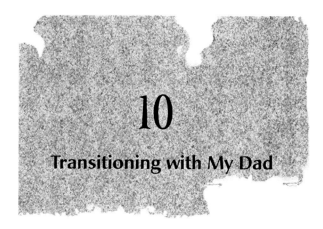

10

Transitioning with My Dad

In 1974, at age seventy-five, my dad decided to stop performing eye surgeries: He felt his concentration and stamina weren't what they used to be. Nevertheless, he continued treating patients in his office for another two years, but then he felt it was time to retire altogether. So he sold his practice in 1976 and officially concluded his career.

When I visited him a few months after his retirement, he told me he had something important to share. He took me into his study in my parents' apartment, closed the door, and asked me to sit down. I wasn't sure what this was all about, but I feared it had something to do with either his or my mom's health. Well, the meeting was about my dad: "They found a cancer in me," were the precise words I recall hearing. It was prostate cancer and he was going to receive radiation treatments and maybe surgery. He told me not to worry: Everything would be fine.

During the next few years, even though my dad proceeded with radiation treatments, followed by surgery, his health only got worse. Yet I still had nice times with him, between his trips to the hospital.

For the Christmas holiday in 1979, I traveled from Pittsburgh to New York to visit my parents. I picked up my daughter, Cathy, who was seven years old at the time, and brought her with me to visit my family. (Cathy lived with her mother on Long Island.)

On December 30, my dad was brushing his teeth. He became extremely dizzy and collapsed. My mother called out to me in a panic and I rushed into their bathroom. She and I were able to get my dad onto their bed, but he was extremely pale and couldn't move. I called for an ambulance to take him to Lenox Hill Hospital.

Before the ambulance arrived, I asked Cathy to go into the guest bedroom and stay there with the door closed, until I came back for her. I told her that Opa suddenly became very ill and I didn't think it was a good idea for her to see him in that condition. I knew Cathy was a bit scared of what was occurring. But at her young age, I didn't want her to have an unnecessarily traumatic experience—above and beyond what I'd already described to her. Basically, I didn't want my daughter to see her pale and unconscious grandfather being hauled away on a stretcher. I wanted her to remember Opa as he had always been. I knew that my dad wouldn't be returning to the apartment— and that Cathy wouldn't be seeing her grandfather again.

After the doctors in Lenox Hill Hospital had a chance to run a few tests, they determined my father's cancer had spread to his lungs and lymph glands. This wasn't that surprising to the doctors, because they knew my father had smoked cigarettes for at least fifty years— between one and two packs a day. The prognosis from the tests wasn't good: My dad was not expected to live more than a few weeks, since his lungs were frequently filling with liquid, making it very difficult for him to breathe.

During the next weeks, I traveled from Pittsburgh to New York every Thursday morning (the day after I finished teaching my MBA class on Wednesday evening) and then I flew back to Pittsburgh on Sunday (so I was prepared to teach my doctoral seminar on Monday afternoon). I kept this schedule week after week, just so I could spend quality time with my dad.

There was a life-clinging-to-a-death-freeing transition that took place during those successive weekends that I shared with my father in January 1980.

In the beginning, I was wishing and hoping he wouldn't die: I wasn't ready. I just couldn't bear the thought of living the rest of my life without him. He was my best friend. We had developed our deep connection only three years before.

Every Thursday afternoon, my dad would radiate as soon as I entered his hospital room for my weekly pilgrimage. I'd spend a lot of time with him, even if he fell asleep. Each day, after seeing him in the morning and in the early afternoon, I would next go out for a run in the park. I'd then take a shower and change clothes, so I could spend several more hours with him in the evening. At times, it was rather strange *me seeing him* in a hospital bed instead of *he seeing me* while I was recovering from eye surgery. And it was unusual having such long visiting hours in the same hospital that used to have such a restrictive, one-hour-per-day visitation, when I was only three years old. But I put these ironies aside, as I focused on being fully present with my dad, since I needed him to be fully present with me.

Toward the end of January, however, the transition with my dad shifted to a different kind of wishing and hoping: I didn't want my dad to suffer anymore. He wasn't going to get better, so what was the point of him staying alive just for the sake of my mom, my brother, and me. Near the end of January, on a very sunny day, I let him go. While I never said anything to him out loud, I knew my best friend could read every one of my thoughts: "Everything's great, Dad. I'm happy. I'm successful. I can take care of myself. I'll miss you, but I'm ready to take my next steps on my own. Now it's time for you to take care of yourself and be at peace. It's time for you to go."

I've often heard that dying people stay alive just long enough to reach some important milestone in their lives, such as a birthday or an anniversary. Perhaps the timing was perfect: I was able to let go of my dad and his birthday was just a few days away.

My last weekend with my dad started on Thursday, January 31, 1980, and ended on Sunday, February 3—his eighty-first birthday. Prior to that weekend, my mom told me on the phone that he was no longer moving much: He couldn't switch from lying on one side to the other—and there was no way he could gather the strength to sit up in his hospital bed. My mom was trying to prepare me for his weakened and worsening condition.

Yet, when I walked into my dad's hospital room on that final Thursday, he instantly began beaming—as soon as he saw me. And then, in his last act of will power, with a little help from his closest friend, he sat up and dangled his legs off the side of the bed. He did this incredible feat so I could look straight in his eyes and give him a huge hug and a warm kiss. My mother was absolutely amazed, as she saw this scene unfold, but I wasn't. I'd learned about my dad's monumental determination from those stories he'd told me during his visit to Pittsburgh, just a few years before: My dad could always do exactly what he wanted to do—or felt he had to do—to achieve some virtuous purpose.

On that Sunday afternoon, my mom and I celebrated my dad's birthday. That evening, I sat next to my dad on the hospital bed and told him how much I loved him. We then sat in a long silence, as we looked at each other boy to boy and man to man. We'd been through so much together—all the way from that first barbaric eye surgery, when I awakened blindfolded, tied up, imprisoned, and nauseated with zero forewarning (at age three); to my quashed rebellion, when he severely beat me, because I finally took a stand and told my mom to go fuck herself (when I was ten); to his very generous grade-point-average proposal and my subsequent academic success, resulting in him buying me my fantasy printing press (when I was fifteen); to my fourth brutal eye surgery, when he had to hold down my legs while I screamed in pain (when I was twenty-three); to my total resolution with him in New York and his follow-up visit with me in Pittsburgh, when I discovered the ancestral roots of my eye operations and my career decisions (at age thirty); to my presentation at a management conference, with him beaming in the audience, presumably there to assess the results of his college investment in me and, yet, through me, to resolve his own dream of becoming a professor in Germany (at age thirty-two); and, most recently, to my holding a sacred space for him, weekend after weekend, during the ultimate transition on his deathbed (when I was thirty-three).

My delightful dad and I re-experienced the entire history of our unconditional love in complete silence, and we left it at that. Deeply inspired silence can express more love—and cover more ground—than any kind of eloquent words and phrases. Just before I left for the airport for my return trip to Pittsburgh, I kissed him good-bye.

At 7:20 AM on Tuesday, February 5, 1980, my mom called to let me know that my dad had fallen into a deep coma during the night. He wasn't expected to live much longer. I quickly said: "I'll be there as soon as I can. Good-bye."

Twenty minutes later, I was on route to the Pittsburgh airport. I'd already called the airlines and made a reservation for an 8:30 AM flight to LaGuardia in New York. Although there was morning rush traffic in Pittsburgh, I treated every stop light as a stop sign, while I instantly became an adept race-car driver. As a result, I made it to the airport in record time, ran to the front of the line of the US Airways' counter to purchase my ticket for the flight (quickly explaining that my dad was dying), and then I raced to the gate. I made the flight to LaGuardia with only five minutes to spare.

After the jet parked at the gate in New York, I bolted out of the airport to the curbside taxi line. Not much of a surprise, it was a very long line—and stacked with many impatient New Yorkers. But I still went directly to the front of the line and said I had to get to Lenox Hill Hospital before my dad died. I didn't ask for their help; I just let them know why I had jumped ahead of them on the line and how much I truly appreciated their help in this life-and-death situation. Well, they got out of my way and let me grab the next cab.

I told the driver about the desperate situation facing us, and so I asked him to show me what a New York taxi can do when it really mattered. He quickly took my challenge to heart (he also had a great relationship with his own dad) and proceeded to speed through the busy parkways and crowded streets in a fashion worthy of the speed-demon reputation of New York cabbies.

As soon as I arrived at the hospital, I sprinted to the elevators. I was almost there. Moments later, I walked into my father's hospital room at 11:00 AM. My mom was there and my dad was still alive, but he was in a coma. I wished I could have known of some procedure to revive him for just one last conversation, but I had to accept that I couldn't awaken him—ever again.

I went over to the window side of the hospital bed and took my dad's hand. It was nice to feel his warm tone still present, but I knew I had to be ready for his transition into another phase of existence. Since his breathing was heavy, his lips, tongue, and mouth were dry. The nurse in the room gave me a wooden tongue depressor with a moist pad attached to it with a rubber band. I took this handmade instrument and softly pressed it just inside my dad's mouth, moving it across the dry areas. Just before his mouth got dry again, I'd dip the rigged instrument into a glass of water to moisturize the pad. Then I repeated the routine.

The process of keeping my dad's mouth moist became a way of not simply being with him, but silently *interacting* with him. I sensed his semi-conscious participation within the cycle of my refreshing the moisture in his mouth. At times, he seemed to anticipate my next move. His awareness was subtle, but it was unmistakable.

By 1:00 PM, my brother walked into the hospital room, having traveled there from his home in Columbia, South Carolina. He had visited my dad the first weekend in January, but not since then. Peter always had a distant and rebellion-filled relationship with my dad— one that had never been suitably addressed. During the next hours, the physical arrangement of my mom, my brother, and me did not change much: I stayed by the window side of the bed administering that moist instrument in and out of my dad's mouth. My mom sat in an armchair on the other side of the bed. My brother stayed in the far corner of the hospital room, standing many feet away from my dad—and frequently leaving the room for one reason or another. I clearly remember taking note of how we each were relating to my dad: Our locations, postures, and movements followed what had become the structure and functioning of our family.

By late afternoon, my dad began to lose more of his color. On each of his hands, his four fingers were gently curled inward toward his palm, with his thumb tucked deep inside.

Without any forethought, I began breathing—in synch—with Dad's inhales and exhales. Instead of focusing on the previous cycle of interacting with my dad by moisturizing his mouth, I switched to an even more interconnected way of inhaling and exhaling our lives together. As I continued to focus on this hypnotic dance of breath, I began to experience our lives in slow motion.

In a magical synchronization with my dad, I followed the very beginning of our inhale, through the elongated pulling in of air to fill whatever could be held in our lungs. At the end of our inhalation, there was a quiet pause, a brief resting place, when there was no flow of air, either in or out of our lungs. A little while later (again in slow motion), I could then follow the very beginning of our exhale, through the elongated pushing out of air to empty whatever was held in our lungs. At the end of our exhalation, there was a pause, a resting place, when there was no flow of air, either in or out of our lungs. And then we inhaled again—as we continued to replenish the recurring cycles of our experiences together.

This last dance with my dad continued for what appeared to be a very long time. In our connected rhythms of being, we were totally present with one another. It didn't matter in the least that one of us was in a coma and the other was not. All that mattered was that the flow of breath within and between us was perfectly expanded—and then collapsed—with the miracle of life.

And then it happened, the essence of which we mere mortals will never be able to truly fathom: My dad and I were dancing with an elongated exhale, as we gracefully moved toward the pause, the resting place, at the very bottom of the cycle. Then we were together in the huge void—in the supreme stillness—the precious pause that sets the stage for the next inhale. It was a very long pause that didn't seem to end. Finally, I had to inhale—but my dad didn't. At 4:05 PM, it was over. All that remained was the pause that never ends, a form of eternity for the body that once was.

When it was evident that my dad had run out of inhales, my mom, my brother, and I looked at each other. My mom spoke first: "Well, that's it. Martin is now at peace. No more pain." I looked back at my dad, but he was no longer there. His body was there, but it was no longer my dad. I looked at my mom and then at my brother and asked: "Where's Dad? Where did he go?"

Just then I experienced one of the most alien sensations in my entire life. But it did not originate from one of my five senses: Some other, extrasensory perception had successfully found the presence of my dad. It was as clear to me, as any ordinary physical sensation can ever be, that the essence of my dad, the essence that made him whole, was indisputably floating—or hovering—around the room. All my education at CMU and UCLA, all my illustrious degrees and academic achievements, did not prepare me for understanding this out-of-body experience.

Before I left the hospital room, I touched the hand and kissed the forehead of the body. These physical connections were more a symbolic gesture than a real good-bye to my dad. Because of what I'd experienced in the hospital room just moments before, I never *had* to say good-bye to my dad. From that moment on, I could always feel his presence—at any time, in any place.

The funeral and burial for my dad were held two days later, on February 7. The most striking moment of these sacred rituals was at the gravesite in Apple Grove Cemetery. There was a casket with my dad's body inside it, but I could feel he wasn't there. His essence was outside of it. I saw the burial process as purely symbolic, because we weren't burying my dad: The gravediggers were simply putting his remains in the ground. As such, I felt no sadness concerning: "There goes my dad." He wasn't going anywhere beneath the earth. He was staying up here, with me.

I've wondered how many people, who weren't able to be present when their parent (or loved one) exhaled their last breath, actually believe—and therefore have to live with—the agonizing image that the person they love is stuck in the ground or forever lost at sea. I don't know what I would've thought myself, if I hadn't experienced my dad leaving his body at the exact moment of his transition into another realm.

Just as my father taught me how to live my life, his last gift was teaching me how to die. And it turned out to be a very simple lesson: You die the same way as you live: by radiating love, joy, peace, and compassion, and *courageously resolving all your primal relationships and traumatic experiences*. That's precisely what makes living and dying so beautiful, meaningful, and overflowing with gratitude.

During the following years, I've always felt my dad's presence and have had many engaging "conversations" with him. Yet it's the traditional conversations—involving his physical form and mine—that I occasionally have missed the most. Especially during the first few weeks and months after his transition, it was hard not receiving his surprise midday phone calls beginning with: "I miss you." And on February 3, 2005, which would've been my dad's 106th birthday, I said to myself: "It's hard to believe it has been a quarter of a century since I last spoke to my dad." But those natural feelings of missing his *physical presence* don't last long, since I'm blessed with the *spiritual essence* of his pure love and complete understanding.

11

Additional Rounds of Therapy

My first round of therapy—one fifty-minute session per week—took place in Pittsburgh, Pennsylvania, from early 1975 to mid-1979, with a psychiatrist, Dr. Chasin. As noted before, the focus of that therapy quickly gravitated to my four eye surgeries. On the one hand, since Dr. Chasin was a male MD, it might have been easy to focus on my eyes, because my dad also was a male MD, an ophthalmologist who had actually considered being a psychiatrist. (Freudians have referred to this interactive process, through which the patient unconsciously projects his thoughts and feelings onto the therapist with whom he unknowingly identifies, as "transference.")

But on the other hand, perhaps I first had to blast through the illusion of a perfect childhood (which just happened to be created by the ongoing threat of one more eye surgery), before I could hope to examine much of anything else. So Dr. Chasin and I didn't spend time examining my relationship with my mother or with women.

My second round of psychotherapy—one fifty-minute session per week—took place in Pittsburgh, from October 1986 to August 2001, with a psychoanalyst, Dr. Nicole Renning. While there were a few years, now and then, when I took a valuable break from therapy, this fifteen-year span for self-examination, from when I was forty to fifty-five years old, greatly enhanced my understanding of many life situations. But finally, my history with women—and especially the difficult relationship I had with my mom—became the main topic of discussion, now that I had resolved the relationship with my dad and dissolved the illusion of a perfect childhood. During my initial meeting with Dr. Renning, I recall saying to her: "I never had therapy with a woman analyst before." To which she replied: "Well, perhaps you're now ready to work with a woman, and on your relationships with women."

My third round of therapy took place in California, from April 2002 to July 2004, with a psychoanalyst, Dr. Marsha Jellinik. Instead of going to therapy one day a week as I'd previously done, I decided it was time to experience the couch: lying face up on a sofa, but not being able to view the analyst (which, according to Freudian theory, significantly enhances the transference process and the freedom of expression). What was the schedule? A forty-five minute analysis of my ego took place four times a week for over two years—by far, the most intensive therapy I'd undergone. In essence, there's no hiding from yourself with such a daily analysis of your life. I never found myself saying, as I did with my previous weekly sessions: "What was I thinking about last week?" All that I'd discussed during yesterday's session was quickly accessible for today's session—day after day. *Life slows down when psychoanalysis speeds up.*

I also found it virtually impossible to maintain any semblance of a protective wall under such daily self-scrutiny. Thus the allotted time of each therapy session was fully spent on probing myself, not partially spent on defending myself. And because Dr. Jellinik was a *woman*, she and I made very effective use of the transference process to thoroughly explore my recreated patterns with women, at a level of detail and depth beyond any of my previous rounds of therapy.

Some people may wonder: *"Why the need for so much therapy?"* In the beginning, I wished I could discover my unconscious habits in just one or a few sessions. Now that would be extremely efficient! Or maybe I could learn all about myself by going to therapy for just one or two years (the time needed for earning an associates degree in a junior college), let alone participating in therapy for four to six years (which would be like receiving a college and graduate degree from a university).

Perhaps a better analogy than therapy as *education*, however, is therapy as *software and hardware:* Based on what computer tasks you want to do, how well and how fast, and what you then learn can be done even better and faster with the most recent software, you might find yourself upgrading your computer and programs, the same day they become available. However, if you're happy with what your old programs and your old computer can do—you can continue to live your life just by using your tried-and-true programs and processors, without any need for software or hardware upgrades. Now think of your mind/brain as the software/hardware of your being: *How often, and to what extent, will you upgrade to the newest generation of software programs and computer processors—through a combination of mind/body/ spirit modalities—as your journey through life unfolds?*

The life-altering question that every human being addresses— either consciously or unconsciously every day of his life—is simply this: Given your earliest childhood traumas and your ongoing adult challenges, are you willing to do what it takes to make sure you will *continue* to know yourself to the deepest core of your being, so you can live your life to the fullest? More than two thousand years ago, Socrates provided the springboard for this fundamental question in his most famous quote: "The unexamined life is not worth living." Rather, to make sure your life *is* worth living, what investments will you make to know yourself, which provides the underlying basis for doing everything else in life? Asked differently, *how can you possibly make a good decision in either your work life or love life, if you don't know who you are and what brings you bliss?*

As for me, I've often wondered how I acquired my *burning desire* to receive a doctoral education in social systems (and then to remain in a university setting for thirty-plus years), just so I could continue learning about the universe for the rest of my life. I've also wondered how I acquired my *ceaseless determination* to pursue multiple rounds of therapy (and many other modalities to be discussed in subsequent pieces of my mosaic), so I could continue learning about myself.

Why didn't I just stop and say: "That's enough! I'll live out my life with what I already know about myself."

I can only guess that my blessing came during those early years of agonizing confusion—when I was struggling to figure out why I was being subjected to one eye surgery after another, and when this surprise torture might be inflicted on me again. Somewhere within these painful struggles, I had my awakenings.

I've been gifted with my early eye traumas, which, if you recall, may have literally saved my life—by preventing me from attending the Vietnam War. Without my eye traumas, I truly believe I would've remained asleep and lived out the remainder of my life with few, if any, system upgrades. Ironically, I remain extremely grateful for my childhood traumas, precisely because they drove me (unconsciously) to recreate immensely difficult situations, again and again, just so I could discern my self-defeating patterns and then replace them with self-awareness and boundless love.

12

Damaged Boundaries, Damaged Lives

In my rounds of therapy, four related topics help me appreciate ego development: (1) all childhood traumas, no matter what they might be called, share the common ingredient of violating one or more of a child's *sacred boundaries*; (2) these primal boundary violations then prevent a person from developing his individuality—a separate, yet positive and enduring sense of self for effectively transcending life's stream of challenges; (3) these violations then prevent an adult from establishing distinct *temporal boundaries*, which are used for staying present today (therefore not living in the past) and adjusting present behavior to create a better future tomorrow (rather than being stuck in the present); and (4) when two boundary-damaged adults decide to start a family, one or both parents will usually violate the sacred boundaries of their innocent children, which embeds past traumas into future generations.

Regarding the first topic, let's now examine what it means to mindfully manage five *sacred boundaries:* physical, sexual, emotional, mental, and spiritual boundaries. Try to picture these boundaries as concentric oblong spheres, largely invisible, surrounding the gross shape of a human body—much like a person's *aura.* All boundaries surround every person's essence, which encompasses the outer skin and all that emanates from *inside* the visible body to several feet or more *outside* the visible body.

Your physical boundaries comprise your face and body (with all those organs and biochemical systems) and a comfortable buffer around your face and body that includes the larger physical spaces where you live and work. Your sexual boundaries include not only your sexual organs and erogenous zones, but also your sexuality and sexual identity. Your emotional boundaries are how you feel about anything or anyone—especially how you feel about yourself. Your mental boundaries define what you believe, such as your thoughts, assumptions, opinions, and how you think and arrive at decisions— especially the thoughts and decisions about yourself. And then your spiritual boundaries include your soul (why you were born as form in the first place, why you remain in this form for a while, and your ultimate purpose in life) and the ineffable experience of being one with—and a pure reflection of—what's "inside" all beings.

If you are conscious of your sacred boundaries, you will notice when another person crosses what shouldn't be crossed: your body, your sexuality, your feelings, your beliefs, or your reason for being. To get a sense of your physical boundaries, remember a time when another person, a stranger, came up to you and stood so close to you that you felt very uncomfortable (in your face or in your space). You might have taken a few steps away from that person to create a more comfortable physical distance. Your other boundaries operate pretty much in the same way, except that these other boundaries are more subtle than physical—because they concern intentions, innuendos, feelings, thoughts, or spiritual awareness. When other people don't honor your physical space, or when they make inappropriate sexual comments, or expect you to feel what they feel or believe what they believe, you may decide (consciously or unconsciously) whether to ignore, deflect, or absorb these other people's behavior.

Imagine what would result from teaching young children that they're *entitled* to their own physical, sexual, emotional, mental, and spiritual boundaries—and that no one, not even their parents, can inappropriately cross or hijack these sacred boundaries. Aside from being given a *Bill of Rights*, therefore, every child is also entitled to a *Magna Carta of Sacred Boundaries*. With this entitlement, every child is taught that he has the right to his body, his sexuality, his feelings, his beliefs, his own destiny, and a spiritual connection to everyone and everything in the cosmos. Imagine what it would be like for all children, at a young age, to (1) consciously know their boundaries, (2) be actively supported to assert themselves—when they felt their boundaries were being violated or threatened, and (3) courageously know, respect, and protect all other boundaries in the universe.

I'm talking here about what it means to be whole—to be fully human—and the ethical respect of the physical, sexual, emotional, mental, and spiritual boundaries that exist around all beings. When a person's *boundary system* is firmly established and functioning well, it is the person himself who decides what flows in and out of every boundary. Other people's touches, emotions, beliefs, and judgments will be ignored, deflected, or absorbed: The choice, hopefully, would entirely be determined by the person himself, assuming this person is aware, confident, and effective at managing his own boundaries.

Regarding the second topic, let's see how a person's awareness of boundaries then shapes his sense of self: Is my *own individuality*— including my self-identity, self-esteem, and self-worth—dependent on something (or someone) either *outside* or *inside* my boundaries? Naturally, if my boundaries have been violated as a child or if I've been taught that I'm not entitled to my own boundaries anyway, it'll be *other people*—what they say and what they do—who define who I am. As a result, my happiness will be short-lived and flimsy, largely determined by the whims of others or the fortunes of nature. But if I define my essence according to what's *inside* my sacred boundaries (physically, sexually, emotionally, mentally, and spiritually), then I determine how I feel about myself: No other person, therefore, can take my self-esteem or self-worth away from me. *Genuine, deep-felt, long-lasting happiness can only be experienced if a person has crystal-clear boundaries and has learned to define his essence by what lives inside these sacred boundaries.*

Regarding the third topic, let's examine *temporal boundaries* and not just spatial boundaries: As boundary-damaged children grow to become adults, they not only have a difficult time creating spatial boundaries between themselves and most others, but they also are unable to form a *clear boundary between the past and the present.* Thus, their boundary violations from the past are unconsciously projected onto the present. Sadly, not distinguishing the *past/present boundary* prevents you from authentically interacting with the person who is right in front of you; instead, you wind up treating that person in the present—by the unconscious processes of splitting, projecting, and attacking—as you would treat those other people in your past who have violated you. Thus it is crucial to know the difference between now and back then.

Boundary-damaged adults also have difficulty establishing a *distinct boundary between the present and the future.* They unknowingly assume these time perspectives are similar or that no boundary can be drawn between now and sometime later. Yet it's possible to learn that you can draw a *present/future boundary* to "jump into the future" and then look back at what you're doing now—so you can change your attitudes, beliefs, and behavior. Basically, it will be difficult to improve what you are doing in the present unless you recognize the regrets you'll suffer sometime in the future—if you continue down the same path with no thought or feeling about where you're going. When you are behaving unconsciously with ill-defined boundaries, being stuck in the present will prevent you (and the ones you love) from being happy in the future.

Note: It's easy to recast the varieties of mental disorders into the principles of boundary theory. Each type of *psychosis* is just a different way of being out of touch with a consensual reality. And each type of *neurosis* describes another approach for defending oneself against a distorted, fearful, or irrational portrayal of that consensual reality. But the common thread that runs through all the traditional labels for diagnosing a person's mental health can easily be simplified as a person (1) living with crystal-clear boundaries that create a timeless and strong self or (2) stumbling along in life without ever knowing the fundamental difference between what's inside or outside one's being—past, present, and future—and how to continually cope with the fuzzy unreality that has resulted from damaged boundaries.

Regarding the fourth topic, let's examine the profound impact of damaged boundaries on family life: First, there are two adults, an everyday John and Jane, who have remained largely unconscious of their boundaries—because they have not been either willing or able to analyze their childhood traumas. As could be expected, these two adults are accustomed to other people defining who they are: They don't have an *internalized sense of self* that's immune from the whims of other people's words and behaviors. Indeed, their individuality is still stuck in the past, because they never had the chance to establish distinct boundaries across time: For them, their childhood traumas flow smoothly from the past into the present, which interferes with every relationship or predicament they encounter. Meanwhile, these two adults are also unable to draw a distinct boundary between the present and future. As a result, they cannot spend time in the future and see the eventual consequences of acting blindly with artificial individuality in the present. Basically, they're destined to follow the same unhealthy path as time goes by—with virtually no opportunity for ever changing the course of their unconscious lives.

And then, these two unconscious adults have children of their own. Not surprisingly, these boundary-damaged parents are unable to nurture their children's boundaries. Consequently, their children will then become adults who also (1) are unconscious of where they end and someone else begins; (2) define their essence according to other people's opinions of their physicality, sexuality, emotionality, mentality, and spirituality; (3) are doomed to violate other people's boundaries in the same way in which their own sacred boundaries were violated, because they are unable to establish both spatial and temporal boundaries; and (4) will thus neglect to teach their future children about the fundamental importance of the five boundaries and the self-creation of authentic individuality.

As you can see, *the vicious cycle of one generation transmitting to the next generation its inability to manage its sacred boundaries sows the seeds for one generation of dysfunctional families after another.* Stopping this vicious cycle—and all the destruction that stems from damaged boundaries—requires at least one round of therapy or other mind/body/spirit modalities. Through this journey of self-investigation—facilitated by expert practitioners who themselves have crystal-clear boundaries—people become more conscious of their boundaries, learn to assert their right to define and safeguard their boundaries, and develop a deeper respect for other people's boundaries. Further, by engaging in an effective process of self-examination, people can develop a strong sense of self that is based on the innate wisdom of their physicality, sexuality, emotionality, mentality, and spirituality.

In my own journey of reclaiming and re-establishing healthy boundaries, I first had to recognize the physical violations I suffered through those four eye surgeries, which also violated my emotional and mental boundaries. Basically, when I was younger, I didn't own the eyes on my face: I silently walked into scary surgeries because I was told to do so (particularly the eye surgeries when I was sixteen and twenty-three years old). In fact, every time my mother lied to me about the supposed reasons for my next eye surgery, she violated a variety of my boundaries, which made it very challenging for me to define who I am in a secure and satisfying manner. Eventually, I had to establish my own individuality and to decide, for myself, what I would or wouldn't allow to pass through my sacred boundaries into my inner being. In the process, I learned where my mother ends and I begin—and to keep that boundary crystal clear at all times.

By examining my childhood history (especially through several rounds of therapy), I have learned to separate the perpetrators in my past from the people in my presence. Through various mind/body/spirit modalities, I've learned to travel into the future, look back at my present, and then modify my behavior for long-term happiness.

Perhaps the biggest boundary-examining breakthrough took place during my second round of therapy: I can remember the exact moment when, in the middle of a fifty-minute therapy session, it dawned on me that my sacred boundaries were firmly in place and under my personal direction. And then, I instantly realized that the inside of this sacred container was empty. At first, I was shocked by this revelation. Then I felt unbounded joy at the prospect of having an exciting boundary-filling adventure before me: *What should I put inside my boundaries?*

Naturally, I had a choice: I could fill myself with what others have taught me to feel, think, and be. Or I could fill myself with my own physical sensations, emotions, thoughts, images, and my direct relationship with God. I decided that the latter *self-directed process* was the better choice. But how would I do that? During my second round of therapy, I learned for the first time in my life what it means to define myself—by myself.

13

Expanding My Consciousness

Before proceeding with my courageous mosaic, I must acknowledge my heartfelt gratitude for being gifted with the desire, willingness, and resources to illuminate my journey. As I discussed before, every person makes a decision, every day of his life, whether, and to what extent, he will invest in his consciousness. I decided to continually upgrade the software and hardware in my mind and body, with one modality after another, so I could thoroughly examine my life. That ongoing dedication to expand my consciousness never faltered. I'm so grateful I never learned another way of being.

In this piece of my mosaic, I present all the mind/body/spirit modalities that guided my journey to wholeness. In this one piece, I can thus focus on the important interconnections among all these modalities, since the effectiveness of each one is usually dependent on certain others. In subsequent pieces of my mosaic, however, I will provide greater detail—and depth—on those modalities that played an especially significant role in expanding my consciousness.

As a result of my T-group experiences at UCLA (1970 to 1971), my first round of therapy in Pittsburgh (1975 to 1979), and then my second round of therapy in that same city (which began in 1986), I had been diligently examining my *mind* consciousness. Yet by early 1997, a number of people invited me to explore other approaches:

While conducting an executive workshop, one participant told me I have to read a profound book that examines human consciousness within a holographic universe, since I was then using a holographic approach for transforming organizations—based on my 1984 book: *Beyond the Quick Fix*. At that time, however, I merely made a mental note of his suggestion. But after two more people, each in a different workshop, voiced that same urgent recommendation, I bought and then thoroughly examined the illuminating book by Stanislav Grof: *The Holotropic Mind: The Three Levels of Human Consciousness and How They Shape Our Lives* (1993).

I was so captivated by Grof's approach to non-ordinary states of consciousness that I attended his weeklong workshop on Holotropic Breathwork, held near Boston, in August 1997. A few months later, I attended an all-day workshop in New York for another Holotropic journey. I was so impacted by these mind/body explorations across time and space that I participated in an additional one-week retreat on Holotropic Breathwork, held in California, in November 2000.

In a Grof weeklong retreat, there may be as many as 200 people who assemble daily in a gymnasium or a large room. Each person is asked to select a partner: One member of the two-person team is the *breather:* He'll be the consciousness traveler during that session. The other person of the team is the *sitter:* She'll be assisting the breather throughout the Holotropic session. These paired participants switch their roles every day throughout the weeklong retreat.

A typical experience of Holotropic Breathwork starts with the breather lying on his back on a mattress, placed directly on the floor, with the sitter attentively situated by his side. Seeing 100 breathers, lying on 100 mattresses, accompanied by 100 sitters, scattered across a large room, paints a rather striking, never-to-be-forgotten picture. Most breathers cover themselves with a bed sheet or blanket, while they rest their head on a comfortable pillow—as if they were about to go to sleep or were ready to take a long journey into outer space. And they usually cover their eyes with a rolled-up T-shirt, just so the outer light from the room won't distract the inner light during their consciousness journey.

Once Dr. Grof has guided all breathers through a foot-to-head exercise for relaxing the body-mind, the sitters are then requested to synchronize their inhales and exhales with their assigned breather, which creates a sacred space that fosters even more relaxation. This synchronized breathing fosters a soul-to-soul connection between sitter and breather. A few moments later, the consciousness travelers are instructed *to breathe deeper and quicker*—which is the key to the process. Meanwhile, the room is gradually filled with a loud tribal music (rhythmic melodies with spiritual chanting), making use of several large audio speakers that are stationed all around the room. Facilitated by experienced practitioners and also surrounded by the collective energy of all those synchronized breathers and sitters, it doesn't take long for each breather to enter a non-ordinary state of consciousness. Each consciousness traveler is then "transported" to another time and place, although he always remains partially aware of his presence in the room, which depends on the speed and depth of his breath.

Based on Grof's research findings, *since everyone is a hologram of the universe, every person has potential access to any place or time—past, present, and future.* And here's the mystery of Holotropic Breathwork: Once in a non-ordinary state of consciousness, a person's own inner radar retrieves the most significant destination for that Holotropic journey, selecting from his biographical life, his birth trauma, or the transpersonal realm. For most participants, a Holotropic journey lasts between two and three hours.

During several sessions, I learned that my current beliefs and behavior were not just stemming from traumas in my biographical life (for example, from my first eye surgery at age three and so on), but with Grof's method I could travel even further back in time and relive, in my mind and in my body, the challenging, life-and-death experiences right before, during, and after my own birth. Indeed, I learned that the *birth trauma* could lock unconscious patterns into my body and dysfunctional beliefs into my mind that would later shape my developing ego and my approach to all my relationships. Even more radical, I could also travel way back in time, well before my own birth, and discover how my early ancestors, my past lives, or other people's experiences (such as cosmic archetypes and mythical figures) had impacted on the development of my worldview as well as my recreated patterns. *Living an examined life thus involves analyzing not only the biographical material that's usually discussed in conventional therapy sessions, but also the deeper layer of the birth trauma as well as the deepest layer of the "collective unconscious." After having time-traveled to several distant destinations with Holotropic Breathwork, I was now open to trying almost any modality that held the promise of expanding my mind/body/spirit consciousness.*

In late August 2001, I resigned from the University of Pittsburgh and moved to California. Ever since my parents had taken the whole family on an extended vacation on the West Coast when I was twelve years old, I wanted to live there.

Once settled into my new home in Newport Coast, inspired by my first exposure to *body consciousness* with Holographic Breathwork, I found myself drawn to Hatha yoga in March 2002. I gravitated to Ashtanga yoga, which was developed by K. Pattabhi Jois: *Yoga Mala* (2002). I subsequently joined the Pacific Ashtanga Yoga Shala, under the leadership of Diana Christinson. There I improved my practice by regularly attending this studio three times each week for a ninety-minute period of synchronized breath, movement, focus, and guided concentration. My Ashtanga yoga practice further awakened my *body consciousness*, which then enhanced all my prior therapeutic work on mind consciousness.

The vitality of the mind/body connection became even more apparent to me after I studied the classic book by Alexander Lowen: *Bioenergetics: The Revolutionary Therapy that Uses the Language of the Body to heal the Problems of the Mind* (1975). This book showed me why I couldn't be fully conscious of my mind, if I were not equally conscious of my body: In other words, when you have a stuck body, you have a stuck mind. *When your body begins to breathe deeply and flow smoothly, however, your mind expands and your spirit radiates.*

As mentioned before, I participated in a third round of therapy with Dr. Jellinik, between April 2002 and July 2004. But this time, instead of going to therapy once a week, I decided to try the couch: Lying on my back for forty-five minutes, four times a week, for over two years—as I more thoroughly investigated my string of recreated patterns from early childhood. Using this intensive analysis, I made significant progress in further expanding my mind consciousness.

Then in late January 2003, I had a very painful and profound awakening in my body: A sizable stone developed in my right kidney that took twelve days to pass. This strange encounter (compared by women to the pain of childbirth) served to radically rebirth my views of wellness *and* consciousness: Instead of continuing to manage my health through medication and surgery (according to the traditional Western view of the body as a biochemical machine), a wise woman, Laurie, encouraged me to consider using an alternative approach to wellness (based on the Eastern view of the body as a holistic system of subtle energy).

That is how I met Joe Giwoff, a highly gifted healer. With Joe's guidance, I began exploring my mind/body consciousness through its energy frequencies, meridians, and emotions. Through my direct experience, I learned that my body had stored energy patterns from early traumas that talk therapy did not release in my body—even if these traumas were now fully conscious in my mind. But what was most astonishing is that many of the subtlest, yet highly significant events in my childhood had never been exposed during three rounds of therapy. Applying Joe's modality, however, I was now discovering traumas that had been repressed for half a century.

Using the electrical resistance of my skin for yes/no answers to a great variety of mind/body questions, Joe helped me discover the *originating* traumatic events in my life. Based on the pioneering work of Dr. Reinhold Voll (regarding electro-acupuncture) and Royal Rife (on bioelectric frequencies), I experienced Joe's modality as follows: In one hand, I held a moist, metal electrode that was connected to an electro-dermal apparatus, along with a frequency-reading computer program. Using a small electric probe that was attached to the same equipment, Joe touched meridian points on my other hand, thereby completing an electric circuit that ran through my body. By silently asking various yes/no questions and then noting the unambiguous changes in the electrical impedance of my skin, Joe would pinpoint the approximate age (in years) when I had originally experienced a debilitating trauma. Using this procedure of *"electrical reflexology"* for identifying the physical, emotional, and mental information in my body, Joe uncovered the first time in my biographical life when I'd learned shame, guilt, grief, fear, and vulnerability. These originating events were then triggered and reinforced by additional—similar— incidents that took place sometime later in my life, which formed a reactive pattern in my mind and reduced the energy in my body.

Once Joe identified the approximate age (usually between age five and fifteen) when I had first acquired a negative belief/emotion, it was then up to me to retrieve the exact event that had traumatized me. I asked Joe: "How can I possibly remember the exact event that first taught me *grief*, when I was only five years old?"

For each identified emotional blockage, Joe had me sip on a mixture of distilled water with a tincture of brandy alcohol, which had been *electrically imprinted* with the specific frequency of a flower essence: the Star of Bethlehem, which was discovered by Dr. Edward Bach. This particular flower essence helps a person recall unresolved emotional traumas from the past. As I sipped on this homeopathic solution of pure energy and information, my mind wandered back to the time when the original trauma had occurred: To my surprise, as I brought back to life each buried event (for example, when I was only five years old, I first learned grief when a pet whom I cherished suddenly died), the newly released energy rippled through the course of my entire life, changing the energetic and emotional charge to all my stories. Not only did I develop a much deeper understanding of my unconscious patterns, but I also experienced a pronounced surge of revitalized energy. Indeed, I found it much easier to deliberately change my behavior, rather than to blindly react to events or recreate my unconscious patterns.

Since it yet has no name, I refer to Joe's amazing modality as "electro-homeopathy and turbocharged therapy." The *homeopathic* aspect (in which like cures like) involves a procedure for matching the electrical frequencies from a function generator to the identical energy frequencies (or their inverse) that have been depleted in the body. In this way, the body is provided with the vital information it needs to heal its own dis-ease. Assisted by the appropriate energy frequencies, you and the natural healing wisdom in your body can eliminate anesthesia (from past surgeries and dental work as well as non-natural childbirth); parasites; viruses; bad bacteria, mold, and yeast; and a whole variety of allergens and allergic reactions. If such frequency-based chemicals, entities, and reactions remained buried in your body, however, they would continue to drain your energy, tax your immune system, and challenge your liver.

The *turbo-therapeutic* aspect of Joe's modality has to do with the instantaneous release of previously inaccessible emotions that were energetically stuck in the body-mind. Even if these deeply repressed events were accessible by conventional psychotherapy, they would've taken many additional years to retrieve and resolve. While I remain thoroughly impressed with the electro-homeopathic work that Joe is able to do with a person's *physical body*, the real magic in his work, I believe, is that he can discover, by applying his turbocharged therapy, the originating traumas that often remain hidden within a person's *energy body*.

I was especially fortunate that Joe also stressed the importance of releasing the toxins in my body—toxins that have accumulated from our highly polluted environment (such as the creation of more than 80,000 chemicals and metals during the past fifty years). First, I had a dentist remove the metalwork in my mouth, which included mercury amalgam fillings and gold crowns. And I replaced these old dental solutions with new plastics and metal-free porcelain. Why? Heavy metal is especially good at conducting electrical signals, not just through traditional wires and cables, but also inside teeth, which contain energy meridians. In fact, any metalwork in the mouth can disrupt the ongoing, bioelectrical flow of information between your brain and all the organ systems in your body, through the extensive network of meridians that transverse your mouth. Furthermore, all metal is toxic to life, but especially mercury, nickel, and tin, and other heavy metals that are used to harden gold and porcelain. Your teeth, just as any other organ in your body, absorb these metals, which can then create havoc in the body. Human beings haven't yet evolved to naturally cleanse their bodies of these unnatural toxins.

Because I had metal in my mouth for so many years (and had sustained contact with heavy metals, such as moveable type), I went to an institute for integrative medicine. There I underwent chelation therapy for the heavy metals that had been absorbed and then stored in my body. About every week, for more than a year, either my left or right arm received an intravenous "push" of calcium EDTA, which is a synthesized chemical compound for binding and then expulsing metal ions from the body. Guided by bimonthly laboratory tests, it took over a year for the chelating agents to remove the accumulated heavy metals in my body: lead, mercury, cadmium, nickel, thorium, arsenic, uranium, tungsten, and aluminum. With the goal of having an internally clean and vibrant body, I participated in other types of detoxifying modalities: electro-footbaths, infrared-sauna treatments, parasite cleanses, homeopathic cleanses, and hydro-colon therapy.

Although I didn't know it at the time, the year 2004 turned out to be a watershed in my soul's journey to awakening: In late January, while leaving Joe's place, I met another wise woman, Rhonda. As we got to know each other, she gradually introduced me to several more modalities that would greatly expand my consciousness.

On February 18, I started releasing the "armor" in my body (the tightness and rigidity in my muscles, tendons, ligaments, and bones) by a process that might be named *"advanced structural realignment."* The practitioner, Perry, using his own integrated approach to deep bodywork, performed a systemic assessment of the structural blocks in my body. He discovered a zigzag pattern of interconnected areas of extra-hard tissue, going back and forth between the right and left sides of my body—all the way from my toes to my head. My unique *zigzag pattern* was the particular way my body had responded to the physical and emotional traumas I had absorbed during my lifetime. By gradually softening the knots of frozen energy along my "zigzag line," my body eventually reclaimed most of the wide range of free movement it had enjoyed many decades ago.

As Perry used his hands, feet, or a specially fashioned tool to soften my hardened tendons and ligaments, I did experience a lot of pain. But after every hour-long session with Perry, I felt more open, relaxed, and invigorated. Because I wanted to have my physical body actively support my examined life, I participated in Perry's sessions, once a week, for over a year.

On February 25, just one week after I had discovered the many benefits of structural realignment, I began participating in a weekly practice of Network Spinal Analysis (NSA) and Somato Respiratory Integration (SRI). These conjoint mind/body/spirit modalities were developed by a chiropractor, Dr. Donald Epstein, and are discussed in his book: *The 12 Stages of Healing* (1994). Briefly, the lower stages of healing reveal how both your mind and body have become stuck in a dysfunctional pattern of selfhood. Meanwhile, the higher stages of healing enable you to resonate—as a nonself—with the spiritual essence of the universe. Because I so enjoyed these two mind/body/ spirit modalities, I attended many weekend NSA/SRI workshops in Denver during the next several years (with as many as 500 people in attendance) and several weeklong retreats in Mexico and Italy (with about fifty people in attendance).

My weekly NSA sessions helped me reconnect with my body, particularly along my spine: from the back of my neck (starting with the atlas on the top of my spine) down to my tailbone (ending with the coccyx on the base of my spine). It seems the physical, chemical, emotional, and mental traumas of my four eye surgeries had taught me to disconnect from the sensations in my body, so I wouldn't feel pain. But by numbing my body from my eye surgeries (and from my other childhood traumas), I then inadvertently numbed all the *other* feelings and sensations in my body. Even though numbing the body to protect the mind is a fairly common practice in our head-based (not heart-based) society, this fragmented strategy blocked me from gaining full access to all the vital energy and information that was potentially available to me. During my first round of therapy, as said earlier, Dr. Chasin asked me what it felt like when I'd awakened in the recovery room after my first eye surgery. I could quickly *theorize* how most children would experience such an awakening. But I wasn't yet able to *feel* what I had actually gone through at that time—since various parts of my mind and body were still fragmented from one another. But NSA helped me reverse that undesirable state.

While I was lying face down on a special table, my practitioner, Dr. Tony Wilson (a chiropractor with additional NSA certification), asked me to breathe deeply and simply feel the resulting sensations in my body. That's all. He then made soft contacts on my spine, so I would *feel* both my energy and breath move throughout my body. Session after session, it became increasingly obvious that long-ago tensions (accumulated from all my physical injuries and emotional traumas, along with exposure to toxic chemicals) had been stuck in my spinal system, which is made up of all the connective tissue and muscles around my spine, the vertebrae, and the spinal cord itself. Gradually, old tension patterns began disappearing from my body, and also from my mind.

After each NSA session of increasingly feeling my body breathe, move, and flow (including various rhythms, patterns, and phases), I became more relaxed, grounded, and connected, and therefore more aware of all my sensory and energetic information. By my sixteenth session, *my spine began moving on its own*, in the form of a spinal wave moving back and forth between my neck and my tailbone, which is called a *somato-psychic wave* (derived from the word "soma" for body and "psyche" for mind). Eventually, I could feel tingling sensations of subtle energy (also called chi or prana) gracefully moving through every section of my spine, including the rest of my body. *I got to know my central nervous system as a cosmic conduit—a network of gateways for uploading and downloading consciousness, energy, and information.*

On March 27, just one month after I'd encountered advanced structural realignment and Network Spinal Analysis, I began a daily, one-hour meditation to further investigate my body consciousness, while giving me welcomed glimpses of spirit consciousness. A dear friend, Nancy, gave me a book by Bill Harris: *Thresholds of the Mind* (2002). Apparently, when your brain waves are primarily oscillating at a high frequency (well above 13 hertz), you experience yourself as separate, anxious, and agitated, since both the left and right cerebral hemispheres are vibrating out of sync with one another across the corpus callosum. Rather, when your brain is synchronized at a much lower frequency (below 13 hertz), you experience unity, neutrality, compassion, and peace.

From late March 2004 to August 2005, I applied Harris' sound technology, called Holosync, virtually every day to synchronize my willing brain to yogic consciousness: I sat on a comfortable couch, closed my eyes, and listened to the one-hour CD program through stereo headphones. Using this prescribed playback device, *each ear receives a different audio frequency*, even though the actual frequencies are masked by the relaxing sounds of rain, chimes, and gongs. When the left ear hears a frequency of 400 hertz and the right ear hears a frequency of 390 hertz, a specialized part of the brain, the superior olivary nucleus, compares and then calculates the difference between the two frequencies, which, in this case, would be 10 hertz. This sound differential between the left and right ears creates a *binaural beat:* a standing wave that entrains the brain to this differential frequency of 10 hertz. Stated differently, the Holosync CD program stimulates a particular part of the brain to generate a low frequency vibration, which then resonates in sync with the whole (holo) brain's organic functioning across the corpus callosum.

The Holosync program has twelve levels of *increasing* intensity, which is accomplished by *lowering* the carrier frequencies for both ears. (Each level, by the way, is recorded on an hour-long CD.) One key outcome of a person progressing through increasing intensities of binaural beats is that the brain's neural networks spontaneously reorganize to a higher level of complexity. For example, consider a stressful situation in the past that would send a person into a state of anxiety, anger, or depression. But once that person had meditated through several Holosync levels of increasing intensity, *the identical stressful situation would now be met with either indifference or effective action—depending on which response would be more resourceful for the person and the situation.*

A brain wave above 13 hertz is called a *beta frequency.* As noted earlier, when your brain is *primarily* (but not exclusively) oscillating in this range, even though you are fully awake and thus can precisely focus your thoughts and efforts, you are also likely to feel anxiously separate from others. The frequency of 10 hertz, as with the example above, is called an *alpha frequency* (between 8 and 12.9 hertz), which captures the state of consciousness just before falling asleep or just after waking up. To meditate at the lower *theta frequency* (from 4 to 7.9 hertz), which is a dream sleep, or the even lower *delta frequency* (below 4 hertz), which is a dreamless sleep, the Holosync program plays the left and right-ear frequencies at the precise differential: To produce a theta frequency of 5 hertz in the brain, for example, the Holosync program provides frequencies for the left and right ear at

200 and 195 hertz, respectively. Although your eyes should remain closed throughout the one-hour program, the challenge (or trick) is to stay wide-awake while you are meditating to the theta and delta frequencies on the Holosync CD. Why? *Your brain learns to be awake while, at the same time, being in a state of unity, neutrality, compassion, and blissful peace.*

Typically, it takes dedicated yogis many years or even decades of daily meditation in order to harmonize the two hemispheres in their brain to theta frequencies. Holosync was especially designed, however, to produce the same result in just months or a few years, based on scientific research that had studied the functioning of the brain during meditation. In addition, the Holosync program further stimulates the brain to enter the deeper delta region of dreamless sleep, which allows you to experience that void of eternal stillness. Very conveniently, as Holosync expands *body* consciousness through *brain* consciousness, it also establishes the essential neural pathways for *spirit* consciousness, probably faster than alternative practices of daily meditation.

It gradually became clear to me that having a brain that is out of sync across its left/right hemispheres (making you feel anxiously separate from the rest of the world) will surely block your capacity to experience bliss. And having a central nervous system that has been compromised by spinal cord tension and having stuck energy along your spinal column will also prevent you from feeling and flowing with what's going on in your life. Furthermore, having a rigid body that's holding extra tension in connective tissue, muscles, tendons, ligaments, and bones—between the tips of your toes and the top of your head—will certainly limit your capacity to experience an open body and, therefore, an open mind. Furthermore, not knowing how to breathe deeply—and not being able to move your physical form in every imaginable way—will prevent you from experiencing the wide range of likely feelings (and thoughts) in your body-mind. In addition, buried childhood events that initially taught you shame, guilt, grief, fear, and anger, which are still energetically stuck in your body and your mind, will further prevent you from expanding your consciousness. And if your body is still polluted with heavy metals and other accumulated toxins, your energy will be further depleted by your body's own futile efforts to purge these foreign substances.

My friend, Rhonda, and my bodywork practitioner, Perry, both introduced me to the healing power of microcrystals. In September 2004, I attended a two-day workshop that was based on the research of Dr. George Yao: *Pulsor: Miracle of Microcrystals* (1986). Even though first conceived to offset the negative effects of electromagnetic fields on human health, Dr. Yao soon realized that his microcrystals also balanced the energy fields within and around the body—which bear a striking parallel to a person's physical, sexual, emotional, mental, and spiritual boundaries.

Each plastic Pulsor is manufactured in the shape of a donut: approximately two-inches in diameter and a half-inch thick, with a familiar hole in the middle. The millions of microcrystals contained in every Pulsor derive from minerals, gemstones, and semiprecious stones, which are then uniquely arranged in different patterns and layers within the donut form. There are different kinds of energetic donuts, each of which radiates different *pulsating* frequencies (thus, the *Pulsor* name) that attract, focus, and amplify the subtle energies that flow within and around all living forms.

During this two-day workshop, I learned how to pinpoint and then balance the subtle energy fields of another person. The client, who'll be experiencing the energy balancing, has nothing to do but close his eyes while lying on his back (usually on a massage table or another flat surface). The remainder of the balancing process is up to the Pulsor therapist (also called a vortex-energy balancer) *and the mysterious exchange of energy between the millions of microcrystals and the willing client.* Using a small pendulum that's composed of all the varieties of microcrystals, the therapist first assesses the *vitality* and *direction* of the "spin" of every major chakra or energy vortex on the client's center meridian: the root, genital, solar plexus, heart, throat, third eye, and crown chakras.

Choosing from a variety of Pulsors, the practitioner then places a number of these specially tuned microcrystals on different energy centers on the client's head and torso. Using the small pendulum for "spinning out" the identified stuck energies or reversed polarities on the client's chakras (whenever an energy vortex is either motionless or spinning in the opposite direction), and allowing a little time for the microcrystals to work their magic, the surprised client usually experiences some profound changes. After just one or a few Pulsor sessions, the *physical body* feels much more relaxed, which includes the connective tissue, muscles, and spinal system—and thus overall tension is reduced. The *sexual body* experiences safety, strength, and exuberance. The *emotional body* feels calm and at ease with the world. The *mental body* is clear, focused, and ready for creative or corrective action. The *spiritual body* expresses love, joy, peace, and compassion.

Following another workshop on Pulsor balancing and several more practice sessions, I became rather adept at balancing a client's subtle energy fields, while experimenting with various donut-shaped Pulsors on my own body. *Through my hands-on work at the innovative interface of universal energy and human consciousness, I learned it takes energy—both gross energy and subtle energy—to maintain and enhance mind/body/spirit consciousness.* Due to the powerful energies that can be balanced by Pulsor crystals, I found myself rapidly assimilating— and further integrating—all my other mind/body/spirit modalities: T-groups, psychoanalysis, Holotropic Breathwork, Ashtanga yoga, turbocharged therapy, chelation, detoxification, advanced structural realignment, Network Spinal Analysis, and Holosync meditation.

And then, in October 2004, all my mind/body/spirit practices led me to North Fork, California, by Yosemite National Park. I went there to fully experience the ten-day Vipassana meditation, the gift of the Buddha, as best described by William Hart: *The Art of Living: Vipassana Meditation as Taught by S. N. Goenka* (1987). I didn't know whether I could last a whole ten days without talking. But I gave it a try: A loud gong sounded at 4:00 every morning to signal the start of the day. By 4:30 AM, silent meditation began and lasted to 9:30 PM—ten days in succession. There were three light meals a day. But even in the dining room, we were asked not to say a single word or make eye contact with anyone, which also applied to the meditation hall, the dormitories, and the dirt paths. From day one, we were invited to remain within ourselves and observe our physical sensations.

During that ten-day period of utter silence, I gradually learned how to distinguish what is *temporary* from what is *permanent:* (1) by systematically scanning (noticing) the ever-changing sensations in my body, rather than following the distracting thoughts in my mind; and (2) by witnessing the enduring peace that lay below the surface of all those shifting sensations and thoughts. As a result, I learned I could stop my suffering in this world by not only breaking my ego attachments to fleeting sensations (whether painful *or* pleasurable sensations), but also by catching myself whenever I reacted to what would eventually disappear.

There was an unexpected by-product of Vipassana meditation: By systematically scanning the tingling sensations up and down my body, day after day, I learned to capture—and guide—those swirling energies with the sheer will of my mind. I discovered a new world of being that interrelated energy, consciousness, and peace. Obviously, this *silent* meditation was far different from anything I'd ever done before, especially my three rounds of *talk* therapy. Without a doubt, the ten-day Vipassana meditation played a major role in expanding my mind, body, and spirit consciousness.

In December 2004, I tried another modality, Neuro Emotional Technique (NET, for short), which was developed in the late 1980s by a chiropractor, Dr. Scott Walker, and continues to be practiced by chiropractors today (and has similar features to Joe's "turbocharged therapy"). NET uses muscle testing (rather than skin resistance) for answering diagnostic questions about a client's reported symptoms (headaches, anxiety, allergies, pain, and so forth).

NET involves a practitioner asking a question (either out loud or silently) that allows for a distinct "yes" or "no" answer. Using just his hand, he then applies gentle downward pressure on the top of a client's outstretched arm (held off to the side of the body, parallel to the ground) to access if that arm will (1) easily maintain its straight, raised position (hence, full muscle strength in tact, which registers a "yes" response to the question) or if the arm will (2) easily be brought down to the client's side (hence, only moderate resistance offered by the weakened muscles, which registers a "no" response). The yes/no questions are chosen to discover the root cause—the source—of the client's symptoms, whether the root cause is physical, biochemical, mental, emotional, environmental, or some combination. Basically, NET is an alternative diagnostic approach that relies on the innate wisdom of the body to know what is causing its own dis-ease and, once reconnected with that wisdom, to promote its own healing.

On one fateful day in December, I went to a NET practitioner, Dr. Carol Anders, because my skin was having harsh reactions to the sun. During the previous year, starting in August 2003, whenever I went out into the California sun for more than five minutes, my skin (other than my arms and face, which were apparently accustomed to the sun) would turn bright red and begin itching badly. When I went indoors or covered my inflamed skin with clothing, the bright red, itchy skin reaction would usually disappear within thirty minutes to an hour. (Conventional Western medical practice uses such terms as *photosensitivity* or *solar urticaria* to refer to this symptom pattern.)

Dr. Anders asked a series of questions about the source of my sun allergy. As instructed, I held my right arm straight out to the side. While she asked each question, she put a little downward pressure on my outstretched arm to see whether my body responded with a "yes" or "no." After going through a hierarchy of clinical questions, she determined that my skin reaction had something to do with a woman! But who could that be?

To determine which woman had played a role in creating my sun allergy, Dr. Anders proceeded with a number of questions going back in time. But first, she tried the most obvious question: Was the woman pertaining to my sun allergy my mother? Answer: "No."

The next set of questions: Did the woman who helped create my sun allergy enter my life when I was between ages fifty and fifty-eight? Answer: "No." Between forty and fifty? "No." Between thirty and forty? "No." And so it continued, all the way back to when I was between zero and ten years old. After my body answered "no" to this presumed final question about my chronological life, I figured this diagnostic approach had run its course. But that wasn't so.

Dr. Anders continued to go back even further in my past: She proceeded to enter my mother's womb, by asking if my sun allergy pointed to a woman I knew while I was in the last trimester (months seven to nine) of my mom's pregnancy. Answer: "No." What about the middle trimester? Also "No." And then that last question: Was my reaction to the sun related to a woman whom I knew in the first trimester (months zero to three) of my mom's pregnancy? "Yes!"

In utter disbelief, I asked Dr. Anders: "Are you saying that I had a twin sister?" She replied: "That's what your body is saying."

In that exact moment, my whole body vibrated—resonated—with the public truth of that *yes*, which came with my outstretched, but tired arm holding steadfast and parallel to the ground, despite Dr. Anders pushing her hand down on my arm. The other questions about my chronological age had brought my arm easily down to my side with the gentle pressure of her hand. I then asked myself these questions: "What does my body know that my mind doesn't? Could this result be true? Or is this what happens in California after you visit too many hippy healers?"

When I got home from this incredible experience, I called my brother, Peter, who at that time was fifty-nine years old. He was my only sibling—at least as far as I knew—before seeing Dr. Anders. I asked Peter if Mom ever spoke about having twins, wanting twins, or anything having to do with twins. Without a pause, he answered "no." But I did not tell him of my recent experience, since he already thinks I'm odd as it is. We then proceeded to talk about other topics and, in a short while, ended the phone call.

To my surprise, less than one hour later, Peter called me back. After our initial phone call, he'd decided to ask his wife, Barbara, the same questions I'd asked him. Peter and Barbara had been married for twenty years by then and Barbara had become very close to my mom. As it turned out, they'd talked about twins when Barbara was pregnant with her second child (which was ten years before my NET experience). Her first child had been a boy and Barbara had told my mom that she was hoping to give birth to a girl—so she'd have one child of each gender. In response, my mother said that she, too, had wanted to have a girl and that happened with her second pregnancy, but the fetus died. Barbara learned that my mom would have named my twin sister: Rose. Because my ninety-seven-year-old mother had gradually developed Alzheimer's disease, however, it was no longer possible to have a meaningful discussion with her about my twin. Nevertheless, after I grieved Rose's physical loss, I have regularly felt her spiritual presence.

To enhance my journey in consciousness, Dr. Anders suggested I read the radical book by Dr. David Hawkins, *Power vs. Force* (2002). With muscle testing, Hawkins created a logarithmic scale of human consciousness that ranged from the lowest energies of shame (20 on the scale), guilt (30), and apathy (50) to the highest energies of love (500), peace (600), and enlightenment (700–1000). After I studied this book, I concluded that all the intense and long-lasting conflicts between siblings, friends, lovers, families, communities, and nations— and between human beings and the planet Earth—all derive from approaching their differences with the lower energies for living life. In fact, the quintessential challenge for each of us is to participate in numerous modalities, throughout our lifetime, in order to raise our level of consciousness. I was then inspired to read additional works on the evolution of consciousness, including the impressive book by Ken Wilber, *Integral Psychology: Consciousness, Spirit, Psychology, Therapy* (2000), as well as the excellent book by Peter Russell, *Waking Up in Time* (1998).

In February 2005 in Orlando, and again in June in Los Angeles, I took the four-day workshop, "Unleash the Power Within" (UPW), presented by Anthony Robbins. While most of the material during the first three days was already familiar to me (except, of course, for the barefoot walk on burning coals), I was most affected by the last day of the workshop: "The Power of Pure Energy." The focus was on what you take into your body (air, water, food, and toxins) and how you get rid of what you don't need. Since I'd never been exposed to nutrition before, especially with respect to bringing energy into my body, I accepted Robbins' challenge to dramatically change my diet for ten days and then observe how I feel. Naturally, I customized his suggestions according to what I wanted to test with my own body: no sugar, flour, alcohol, coffee, vinegar, table salt, animal flesh, dairy products, or processed fats or foods. In contrast, I drank at least two liters of filtered water every day. I consumed a fresh salad for every meal. I ate plenty of fresh green vegetables and drank green juices. I ingested low-sugar fruits in moderation. I ate *organic* vegetables and fruits, including organic whole grains, whenever possible. I didn't eat starch and proteins together; and I always ate fruits at least twenty minutes before or after other food. I drank water before my meals, but not during or right after. I also supplemented my new diet with vitamins, liquid minerals, essential fatty acids, amino acids, probiotics, and digestive enzymes.

While I was eager to experience what my body felt in ten days, I didn't have to wait that long: By the fifth day, I already experienced being more alive and energized than ever before. At the same time that I changed my diet, of course, I also continued to practice all the other mind/body/spirit modalities I had started during the past few years. So it was certainly possible that all these other changes in my life also contributed to my change in energy. Nonetheless, I couldn't help but notice a new vibrancy in my body, particularly during my NSA work and my yoga practice.

Yes, I had to admit it: *Eating live food makes you feel alive, while eating dead food makes you feel dull.* It became clear to me that proper nutrition, which develops an alkaline, non-acid body, indicated by a urine pH level (potential of hydrogen) at around 7.0, provides the vital energy that feeds mind consciousness and spirit consciousness, and not just body consciousness. Naturally, once I'd completed the ten-day nutritional challenge, I continued—and further refined—my energy-enhancing, dietary intake.

Motivated by the silent stillness I had already experienced with Vipassana meditation, and with the wise encouragement by my high school buddy, Richie, in May 2005, I attended a one-week spiritual retreat by Gangaji, described in her book: *The Diamond in Your Pocket: Discovering Your True Radiance* (2005). The Gangaji retreat, held just outside Yosemite National Park, was silent, except for a few people who got to go onstage to have a one-on-one dialogue with Gangaji, during our hour-long morning and afternoon gatherings. The focus of this retreat, however, was not, per se, on the stream of sensations that would rise and fall in our bodies. Instead, Gangaji invited us to address a variety of introspective questions: *"Who* is observing those physical sensations? *Who* is feeling the pain or pleasure in the body? *Who* is wondering what will occur next?" As it turns out, no matter what question is asked, the answer is the same: Whenever you allow yourself to recognize the "who" behind any of your experiences in human form, you can get a sense of the pure stillness that is always present—that which has no form or substance. This is the ineffable stillness that was always present in the past and will also be present in the future. *This perpetual stillness—or pure consciousness—is who you really are: the Divine Truth of your endless being.*

During the seven-day Gangaji retreat, we learned that trying to be a certain kind of person, attempting to stay in control of our life, aspiring to keep what we have, and getting more of what we do not have—all these cravings will only lead to further suffering. Instead, we can choose to identify with what is always there—and thus never dies. *Gangaji's approach to spirit consciousness is so simple it often eludes us.* We search for enlightenment "out there" and we try to achieve it and then get something from it. And yet, it's always been within us, like a diamond in our own pocket that we continue to ignore, as we try to find diamonds everywhere else. Instead, all you have to do is surrender to the "Truth of Perpetual Stillness," by letting go of your conditioned mind (ego) that would have you view yourself as your body, your thoughts, your feelings, your relationships, your pain, or you possessions. Much like the experience of Vipassana meditation, yet much less physically demanding, the Gangaji retreat invited us to experience the Eternal Truth: the quiet ocean of love, joy, peace, and compassion that permeates everything in the universe—eternally.

From my own direct experience through an increasingly open body and a synchronized brain, I found my glimpses of Spirit to be quite ironic: I recalled how hard I'd worked during three rounds of therapy to develop strong boundaries, within which I could add my own physicality, sexuality, emotionality, mentality, and spirituality. And yet, my expansion into the spiritual realm, especially with quiet glimpses into perpetual stillness, revealed that *all those hard-earned boundaries—all of them—simply evaporated as temporary fluctuations of an illusionary self.* As I pursued spirit consciousness, I thus got to see that *my strong self* and *my open body,* which were rather essential for enabling me to greet Spirit, *aren't really who I am.* Quite the contrary: I am boundary-less at the core of my being-ness, which, with further irony, cannot be explained by theories, thoughts, concepts, or words. I am Spirit: a perpetual mystery and an unsolvable paradox—yet is beautifully captured in Kirtana's Gangaji-inspired song, "I Am," on her 1999 CD, *This Embrace.*

THE COURAGEOUS MOSAIC

After attending Gangaji's weeklong retreat, I discovered a new choice in my life, with profound implications: (1) What would it be like to live my life as a *strong self,* being attached to my boundaries, including my self-identity, self-esteem, and self-worth? Or asking the same question differently: What would I experience in life, and how would I be with other people, if I defined myself according to what would *always* disappear when my body dies? (2) What would it be like to live my life as *Pure Spirit?* Or asking this question in another way: What would I experience in life, and how would I be with other people, if I defined myself according to what would *never* disappear when my body dies? And here's my epiphany: How I define who I am—as either *strong self* or *Pure Spirit*—would fundamentally affect my happiness, what happiness I could add to other people's lives, and the gifts I could give to my children and the planet as a whole. Needless to say, I chose *Pure Spirit* to define my true essence.

My growing participation in mind/body/spirit modalities then brought me to a late February 2006 workshop, based on the book by Karen Kingston, *Creating Sacred Space with Feng Shui: Learn the Art of Space Clearing and Bring New Energy into Your Life* (1997). Proceeding with my energy practices, in early April 2006, I attended a four-day workshop, described in a book by Richard Bartlett, *Matrix Energetics: The Science and Art of Transformation* (2007). In mid-April, I attended a weekend workshop, based on Samuel Sagan's book: *Awakening the Third Eye* (1997). Then, toward the end of April 2006, I participated in a three-day workshop, based on the book by Doreen Virtue and Judith Lukomski, *Crystal Therapy: How to Heal and Empower Your Life with Crystal Energy* (2005).

Essentially, these additional modalities taught me to become aware of the flow of energy not only throughout my body, but also wherever I direct my attention through my third eye: an oval area between the eyebrows (which may have a physical basis in the tiny, usually dormant pineal gland that resides between the two cerebral hemispheres in the brain). In particular, I discovered I could further expand my mind/body/spirit consciousness by (1) focusing on the energy that flows between my inner third eye and my outer world; (2) radiating these open flows of energy in the sacred spaces where I live, work, and visit; and (3) amplifying this internal and external dance of energy through the natural power of crystals.

In the spring of 2006, as a fitting culmination of all my mind/body/spirit practices during the past twenty-five years, I received the *Deeksha*, the Oneness Blessing, as documented in the book by Kiara Windrider with Grace Sears: *"Deeksha: The Fire from Heaven"* (2006).

According to Sri Bhagavan, the divine inspiration behind the Oneness Blessing, the purpose of the Deeksha is to recreate certain parts of the brain that our species originally had thousands of years ago, before we began erroneously evolving into separate selves as a way of controlling the natural environment and then competing for ownership of the planet's resources. It seems we're the only species whose brains have genetically evolved to neurologically sustain an illusion of separateness from the source, which is what causes us so much suffering. However, by channeling divine energy through the Deeksha, our species can rewire its brain. Consequently, all human beings will be able to experience the truth of their oneness with the source of everything—and can then live with joy in every moment.

Giving and receiving a Deeksha is deceptively easy: A *Deeksha giver* places both his hands on top of your head for a few moments, or a few minutes, at the most. During this brief period of time, the Deeksha giver channels a cosmic energy through your crown chakra that can radically alter the neurological functioning of your brain.

After a person receives just one or a few Deekshas, several things begin to happen: Similar to what usually happens when listening to a Holosync program through stereo headphones, receiving a deeksha also synchronizes the left and right hemispheres of your brain. This neurological change allows you to be fully awake with your whole brain vibrating at the lower alpha, theta, and delta frequencies. Such a vibrational change in your brain enhances your sense of unity and peace as opposed to separation and suffering.

It was fascinating to experience the Deeksha giver channeling intelligent energy through his third-eye chakra into my crown chakra. By the Deeksha giver placing each of his hands on either side of my head, he created a "two-point" quantum field that allowed energy and information to enter my brain and body, as I had experienced during my workshop on Matrix Energetics. I realized, however, if my crown chakra had been shut down, it would've been more difficult for me to receive the cosmic energy from the Deeksha giver. And if the other chakras from the base of my spine to my third eye had also been energetically stuck, it would have been more difficult for the Deeksha giver to stimulate the subtle energy flows that run up and down my central nervous system. Once again I discovered: Without an energetically flowing body, a flexibly flowing spine, an already synchronized brain, and a conscious mind that could surrender to a higher level of consciousness, I would not have been able to benefit so fully from the Deeksha, or any other modality.

On a wonderful sunny day in June 2006, I crossed my present/future boundary and time traveled to my deathbed: It was evident to me that the mind/body/spirit practices, to which I'd been magically drawn, were perfect for expanding my consciousness. In the process, I learned *the three superhighways* to consciousness that offer a useful framework for living an examined life: (1) becoming aware that you have been *recreating patterns* that derive from your earliest traumas, including the birth trauma, and your transpersonal traumas (mind consciousness); (2) freely flowing with all the available energy and information in your body, for the purpose of *breaking your patterns* and transforming your beliefs and behavior (body consciousness); and (3) feeling the peace that lives beyond your sacred boundaries and your individual self, for the purpose of *transcending patterns* and thus living love, joy, peace, and compassion (spirit consciousness). *The Courageous Mosaic* is your soul's unique approach for recreating, breaking, and transcending patterns—all of which are illuminated through a dedicated practice of mind/body/spirit modalities.

There appears to be a developmental sequence to greet Spirit: A good dose of mind consciousness provides a solid foundation to establish a strong self with crystal-clear boundaries—so you'll have the safety and fortitude to break into your numbed body. And when you have enhanced your body consciousness, you'll then have the energy, connection, and flexibility to flow with the feelings in your body and the thoughts in your mind. And blessed with a conscious and flowing body-mind, you'll now have the strong self to let go of your conditioned mind, while you'll also have the open body, third eye, and rewired brain to directly experience Spirit.

While other paths to consciousness exist, they are often more difficult by (1) an insecure ego that won't find it advantageous to let go of itself and (2) a body that can't readily feel what it is, in fact, experiencing. In this day and age of wanting it all right now, you can be tempted to jump on the spiritual bandwagon or take the spiritual bypass: Craving a peak experience of Pure Spirit, yet having neither the mind consciousness nor the body consciousness to stay present with the ultimate encounter with your ego—*becoming a nobody after having been a somebody.* If you want more than just a brief encounter or a peak experience with Spirit, then, ironically, a solid foundation of mind/body consciousness will enable you to merge with Spirit— for as long as you like.

14

Revisiting When Time Began

After reading Stan Grof's 1993 book, *The Holotropic Mind*, I became excited by the possibility of taking a consciousness journey, whereby I could revisit my early biographical life, my birth trauma, and the transpersonal universe. So I signed up for Grof's one-week retreat on Holotropic Breathwork, which took place in early August 1997, near Boston, Massachusetts.

About 200 participants showed up for the program. During the first evening session, Dr. Grof and his staff explained the day-to-day activities. When Dr. Grof asked if anyone had a question, I quickly raised my hand. Well he called on me and I expressed the following comment and concern: "I've studied your book and I'm eager to go wherever my body's wisdom will take me. But what if that doesn't happen? Do some people attend these programs and then don't get to go anywhere?" Grof smiled and said: "All you have to do is follow the process. The only time people don't enter a non-ordinary state of consciousness is when they really don't want to explore their body or aren't ready to examine their mind. But that's rare, given the type of people who sign up for these retreats." I then stated my intention: "I really, really want to go on a consciousness journey!" To which Dr. Grof replied: "Well then, just follow the process and you'll have no difficulty exploring the holographic universe."

The next day, all participants assembled in a large gymnasium, which was already filled with 100 mattresses—scattered all over the hardwood floor. We first took a little time self-selecting a partner for the week: Rotating two roles session by session, the "breather" goes on the Holotropic journey, while the "sitter" stays by the breather's side and assists the process. Brody, my partner, suggested I go first. I agreed, but I was still worried I wouldn't enter into a non-ordinary state of consciousness and, therefore, I'd miss out on a Holographic journey. Nevertheless, I diligently tied a T-shirt around my head (so I wouldn't be distracted by all the daylight in the room), pulled the bed sheet over my torso, laid back on my mattress, and relaxed my body from toe to head—all in accordance with Grof's instructions. I next heard Brody's breath synchronized with mine. Grof then asked the breathers to start inhaling and exhaling more rapidly and deeply. And then it happened: Even before one of the facilitators turned up the volume of the tribal music, I was off on my journey.

My first Holotropic trip took me to my mother's womb in early January 1946. For some reason, the wisdom in my body decided that it was important for me to witness the first time my consciousness encountered my father. In my mind's eye, my transpersonal self was traveling side by side with the single sperm that was to become me. As I was swimming along with this one sperm, I noticed a spider on the way to the egg. (If there were other sperm or another egg present, I couldn't tell.) After my dad and I had maneuvered past the spider, I witnessed a very bright, yellow glow, the divine source of love that creates all life, inside my mother's fallopian tube. In a microsecond, the bright glow then fully joined with the egg. I couldn't distinguish the fertile egg from the yellow glow. Thus, I didn't have a chance to actually witness my own conception. That wasn't the main purpose of this transpersonal experience.

Surprisingly, my journey then fast-forwarded to February 1980, inside that hospital room in Manhattan where my father was taking his last few breaths. I saw this closing scene from the same vantage

THE COURAGEOUS MOSAIC

point as when I'd been directly by his side during his transition: He in a coma and I moistening his mouth with a small sponge attached to a tongue depressor. Then I began breathing in sync with my dad's inhales and exhales, exactly as I'd done seventeen years before (and just as I'd done moments before with my sitter, Brody). Although I knew my mother and brother had been in that hospital room with me in 1980, I didn't see them there: All my attention, just as when I was swimming alongside his single sperm in my mother's womb, was on my dad and me. But then my journey ended, right before my father's last exhale, just as the first scene had ended right before my divine conception.

When I returned to an "ordinary" state of consciousness, it still took me a while to sit up from my prone position on the mattress. I was lightheaded and remained in an altered state for quite a while. After I stood up, Brody escorted me to another room, which was next to the gym. In this "drawing room," there were rectangular sheets of paper, each containing a large circle on one side for creating my own mandala: a representation of the search for universal oneness or a symbolic portrayal of the whole self. Next to the stack of paper was a variety of drawing implements: crayons, colored pencils, and pens.

A retreat facilitator then instructed each breather to capture his recent Holographic journey in the form of a mandala—making use of whatever drawings, colors, and words would serve this purpose. The facilitator emphasized that we shouldn't be worried about the quality of our artwork: Anything was fine; this wasn't to be an artistic competition. Nor should a person leave anything out: Even if part of our journey had baffled us, we were encouraged to find some way to capture that mystery in our mandala. Apparently, what did not make sense now might make sense later.

I had no trouble drawing my recent Holotropic trip on a sheet of paper. I purposely included the spider in the womb, even though I had absolutely no clue as to its meaning. I couldn't remember any significant experience that I'd ever had with spiders. But I was most curious to see if another journey or dream would someday explain this peculiar aspect of my first Holotropic experience.

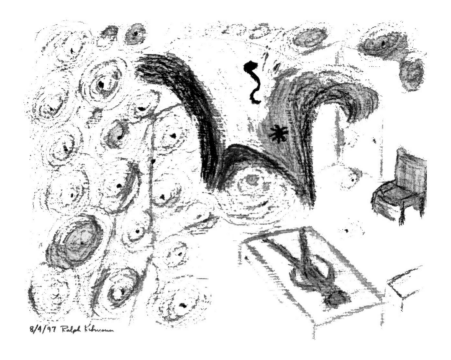

8/4/97 Ralph Kibuann

During the next day, I took part in my second Holotropic trip: I traveled far back in time so I could witness the divine process that created our universe, *before* the big bang set energy and matter into motion. To my surprise, I experienced creation as an act of violence, and not just love. I entertained these questions: Would the universe continue to expand and take up more space? Or would the universe eventually begin to contract, due to the force of gravity, which would transform that big bang into a big crush—an infinite mass/energy within infinitesimal space/time? During this Holotropic journey, I found myself able to float through our entire universe, side by side with galaxies, which was reminiscent of my having been alongside my father—just before my conception and just before his death. But

THE COURAGEOUS MOSAIC

this time around, I was traveling much faster than the speed of light, shepherding matter and energy toward a singularity—a black hole—when the divine source would again decide whether a new universe would be created by violence or, instead, by love.

After my journey, Brody walked me to the drawing room, where I captured my recent journey with a colorful mandala. Through this artistic process, I recognized that my conception and the birth of the universe (the beginning of a cycle) as well as my father's last breath and the potential collapse of our universe (the end of a cycle) were being guided by the same divine source.

8/5/97 Ralph Kihman

A few days later, I was getting ready for my final journey of the retreat. Since I'd enjoyed traveling through outer space, I hoped this third trip might continue where the last one left off. But little did I know that my next Holotropic journey would, instead, be revisiting *inner space:* My body's innate wisdom, not my mind's wishes, would determine where I needed to travel on my next journey.

Once again I was lying on my back on that same mattress. My body became further at ease during Dr. Grof's guided meditation—gradually moving the subtle energy up my body, from foot to head, over the course of five minutes. And then I felt even more safety and peace when Brody began synchronizing his inhales and exhales with mine. I then started breathing faster and deeper as the tribal music became louder and louder. Similar to my first two journeys, it wasn't long before I entered a non-ordinary state of consciousness and then traveled to another place and time: *I woke up in a recovery room, right after my first eye surgery, when I was three years old.* I guess my body had decided that now was a good time to revisit the violence when time had begun for me—not as a detached thought with the mind of an adult, but as a direct experience within the body of a child.

In retrospect, the setting for my journey was perfect: There were all these mattresses in one large room (similar to the children's ward of the hospital). My eyes were covered with a bound T-shirt (which recreated the bandage that had covered both my eyes—not just the right eye). I could hear loud screams in the background from other breathers going through their journey. Indeed, because a significant percentage of the participants tend to revisit the birth trauma, each Holotropic session included loud background screams that replayed traumatized infants and toddlers. Although there were no metal bars surrounding my mattress, I had tucked the bed sheet underneath it, so as to establish a well-defined boundary for my body—since some active breathers tend to move off their mattresses and then encroach on other people's journeys. But little did I know that my three-sided, bed-sheet enclosure would wind up simulating the imprisonment I had experienced after my first eye surgery.

But I did not have to simulate nausea, fear, and anxiety. These feelings were generated through my journey since, in a non-ordinary state of consciousness, my body literally went back to the sensations and emotions I'd experienced in that recovery room. I started to cry, just as I had done when I'd gained consciousness after that 1950 eye operation. I then heard a woman's voice (surely a nurse) say to me: "If you cry, you'll lose your eyes." But despite this horrific warning, I couldn't stop my tears.

Note: A unique feature of Holotropic Breathwork is that your consciousness can be aware of two places at once: (1) in the present time and location where the retreat is being held and (2) when and where your journey has taken you. With chemical or herb-induced trips (such as an "acid trip" with a psychoactive drug), you no longer are grounded in an ordinary state of consciousness. But Holotropic Breathwork enables you to maintain "solid ground" in your present surroundings. The relative proportion of your body-mind that is in the "here and now" (ordinary consciousness) versus with the "there and then" (non-ordinary consciousness) is based on your mode of breathing: The more quickly and deeply you breathe, the more your body-mind will concentrate on your Holotropic journey. The more normally you breathe, the more your body-mind will remain in (or return to) the workshop setting. As a result, the breather can control the extent to which he goes deeper into his consciousness journey or remains aware of his current situation.

After a few sessions, every breather learns to deliberately alter the speed and depth of his breath to work through a primal trauma in the past with the help of a Breathwork facilitator in the present. In particular, breathers are instructed to ask their sitters to summon a facilitator if *Holotropic bodywork* would enhance their consciousness journey. Typically, a trained facilitator applies physical pressure on a section or point on the breather's body to intensify the experience, so the part of the body that has been numb or in pain for years can now be entirely experienced, thereby releasing the trauma from the body and not just from the mind.

If, for example, a breather's journey returns her to a past life when her grandfather had often punched the sides and back of her head, the facilitator would apply additional pressure to the areas on her head where she is re-experiencing those painful violations from another lifetime. This extra pressure allows the person's body-mind to feel each violation, relive that accumulated pain, and then release the stored burden that's been brought from a past life to the present form. Previous to that Holotropic session, the breather might've tried many contemporary modalities to stop her intense headaches (such as medical, psychological, and physical modalities), but to no avail. Yet by discovering the actual source of what the body was painfully storing, as intensified by the facilitator's competent bodywork, the breather's migraines can be healed forever.

Now back to my journey to that 1950 hospital room: It wasn't long before Brody brought one of Grof's facilitators to my bedside. While one part of my consciousness remained on my journey, the other part was very much present in the gym. I was thus able to ask the facilitator to keep my two arms pinned down on the mattress. I let him know I was going to do my best to raise them and rip off the T-shirt that was tied around my head. But I asked him to use all his weight and strength to prevent me from doing that. He repeated my instructions, just to make sure he got it right. Although he might not have known exactly why I needed what I'd just prescribed, he knew enough about Holotropic journeys to comply with my request, with all the energy in his own body-mind. Note: I don't remember how I'd determined what bodywork I needed to release my trauma. But I knew I had to fight back: I was no longer going to be a victim of this violence. I was determined to take command of my body.

In normal consciousness, however, I hadn't reclaimed my body until I was twenty-three years old, after the intense pain of my fourth eye surgery. *But my journey was now giving me the opportunity to reclaim my body almost twenty years earlier—after my first eye surgery.* I've read that victims of sexual abuse often wish they had fought back. Maybe they could've stopped the horror: "Why did I freeze, dissociate, and let it happen? I wish I could've kept my wits about me and found a way to escape."

Now I had a chance to work through that unfulfilled wish in my body-mind to have rebelled against what was being done to me, without my consent or receiving any explanation. Whether or not I could have really cancelled those surgeries wasn't the issue: *I needed to clear my body-mind of its shameful passivity.* Otherwise, I would not have the courage to confront all the other traumas and demons in my life, which would confine my subsequent journey to wholeness, just as the stiff sleeves around my arms had confined my capacity to feel my body.

Returning to my Holotropic session, the facilitator let me know that he was in position, and ready, to use all his weight and strength to hold down my arms. I then started breathing faster and deeper. In a short time, most, if not all, of my consciousness was now back in that 1950 recovery room: I could hear the loud crying of all the other children who were also recovering from their surgery.

I started screaming. As I gave voice to my trauma, I gathered my strength and began lifting my arms, so I could remove my bandage. But the facilitator successfully pushed both my arms back down to the bed. In retaliation, I started lifting my head and upper torso off the bed, so they could reach my two hands, instead of the other way around. The part of my consciousness that was still present in the gym heard the facilitator quickly tell my sitter to push my shoulders back to their original prone position, and to keep them there. Brody immediately did just that. Now the gap between my hands and my bandaged eyes was as wide as ever.

At that moment when the facilitator was pinning my arms as Brody was restraining my shoulders, *immense rage flew out of my body:* Never again was anybody going to tie me down—and blindfold me. Although I had two strong adults confining me, I screamed out my fury with a barrage of shrilling sounds that were altogether foreign to me: I never knew myself capable of such shrieks. They surely filled the entire gym and rattled its tall windows.

My violent screams then summoned my worst demons: I saw familiar faces appear on that Holotropic screen in my mind's third eye: First I saw my dad in his surgical mask hovering over me in the operating room. I shouted at him: "Why didn't you explain anything to me? Why didn't you tell your wife to shut the fuck up when she badgered you about my crooked eye? Why did you pretend to be the head of the household and a licensed ophthalmologist? You failed me! You failed your profession!"

And then that nameless, faceless, manipulating nurse appeared on my Holotropic screen. I proceeded to scream my buried rage at her: "You didn't want to hear me cry—so you silenced me with fear. You are a disgrace to your pledge! I hope you suffer for the sadistic warning you gave to me when I was nauseous, bound, blindfolded, imprisoned, and scared to death."

I continued to scream my rage, as the facilitator and sitter kept my hands far away from my eyes. But I still used all my strength and more to try to counteract their efforts. I felt streams of sweat on my body. I didn't know how I found the strength to continue my primal rebellion. But continue I did.

I next saw my mother visiting me in the hospital room, while my eyes were still bandaged. I vented my longtime rage at her: "How dare you put me through this insane torture, just because you didn't like how my lazy eye looked at you? You have no right to change my body! Except for that first operation, every other eye surgery was all about you, while you were claiming to be taking care of me. I spent my childhood living in fear. I hate you for subjecting me to all that pain. You're not the perfect mother you pretend to be!"

Just when I thought my body was finally done with its ranting and raving, three people appeared at once: my dad, the nurse, and my mom. Their images were overlapping one another, so I couldn't tell which was which. But I used whatever energy I could muster to bring my stretching and straining hands to both bandaged eyes, but my facilitator and sitter were much too strong for me. With my last supply of energy, I let out my most courageous scream: "I take back my life! I've had enough of this bullshit!" At that exact moment, the excruciating tension in my body collapsed into nothingness. My two helpers were no longer needed to hold me down. I had exhausted all my energy. This Holotropic journey was over.

My whole body lay limp on the mattress. I remained exhausted for another ten minutes or so, as I tried to gather enough strength to sit up. Meanwhile, still laying on my back, I chatted a bit with Brody. I remember what he said to me: "When you were trying to bring your hands to your head, it looked like the veins in your neck were going to explode. We had to use everything we had to keep your arms and head down. I'm drained from your experience!"

Brody then helped me to sit up and place my arms around my knees. I just sat there for a while, as my consciousness slowly shifted toward its more normal state. My clothes and bed sheet were soaked with my sweat. The T-shirt around my head was drenched from both sweating and crying. I decided it was now a good time to remove my bandage, so I could get further grounded. But I had no idea of what was in store for me.

As I slowly undid the knotted T-shirt from the back of my head, I remember thinking how I hadn't been able to remove the bandage that was across my eyes in 1950. But now, in 1997, when I removed my makeshift bandage, I was shocked: *The part of the T-shirt that had been on top of my right eye was completely dry, as was my right eye itself!* Although abundant moisture had freely flowed from all other parts of my body, including my left eye, no moisture had come out of my body anywhere near my right eye.

Similar to the previous Holotropic sessions, Brody escorted me to the nearby drawing room. There I gathered colored crayons and a blank sheet of paper. As I looked down on the open white space in front of me, it didn't take me long to decide what to do. I pushed all the crayons aside, except for two: medium charcoal and bright red. In the center of the sheet, using the charcoal crayon, I drew a large mattress that was bound by metal rails all around it. I drew myself, as a three-year-old child, lying face up on that mattress, with my arms and legs laid flat and open. I positioned my head on the bottom of the canvass, so the viewer would see me lying upside down. Indeed, my life at that time *was* upside down. My mandala showed smaller beds with metal rails, representing all the other children who were recovering from their surgery. These smaller beds, with children also drawn upside down, were randomly placed around the open space of my mandala. I pictured no walls or boundaries in this recovery room: It went on indefinitely and forever—much like my concept of space and time when I was only three years old.

All the children and beds in my mandala were drawn in the medium charcoal color. Then I took the bright red crayon and used it for just three rectangular blotches of color: to depict the stiff sleeve on each arm and the bandage across both my eyes. To me, the color, blood red, signified the recurring violence that had been repeatedly inflicted on a boundary-less child. Although I considered sketching those three powerful people who'd appeared during my journey, my stark recollection of the recovery room would forever remind me of everything. My mandala thus said it all to me, and that was the whole point of creating it. After I completed my artwork, I signed my name at the bottom, and dated it: August 7, 1997.

Remaining "under the influence" of my Holotropic journey, I spent the next hour in the drawing room gazing upon my mandala. I remained in awe of the memory in my body: After forty-seven years of life (from age three to fifty), my body still protected me from the nurse's terror-inducing statement: Although I was crying, screaming, and sweating for several hours, my right eye remained dry while the rest of my body became wet—including my other eye. Yet I couldn't help but wonder if my body would ever release the nurse's threat to keep my eyes dry. Indeed, *if only my right eye could fully liberate itself,*

I wouldn't have to waste any more energy on needlessly protecting myself from that nurse's vicious—and erroneous—threat. Maybe someday, I'd be able to find a way of doing just that.

8/7/97 Ralph Kihmann

Still gazing at my mandala, I next remembered the three people who had sequentially appeared during my Holotropic journey: my father, the female nurse, and my mother. I particularly recalled the anger, rage, and hate I had just screamed at these three people. Yet I had never before expressed these powerful emotions to them in any form, in an ordinary state of consciousness. I didn't even know these powerful emotions had been neatly tucked away in the cells inside my body. By the time I became an adult after my last eye surgery, I'd already learned not to express such emotions to anyone—especially to myself: Unconsciously, I couldn't let myself feel the destructive potential of my furious rage, nor could I take the chance of possibly antagonizing other people: They would surely find a way to punish me with more surgery—or worse. That was my biggest fear.

I then reflected on the common theme in my three Holotropic journeys: Was it violence—or love—that guided (1) my conception in the womb and my dad's last few breaths of life before death, (2) the creation of the universe and whether its destiny would be more growth or ultimate destruction, and (3) my parents' decision to put me through those repetitive eye surgeries and whether I retained or released the ensuing emotions in my body? Less than a decade later, I'd learn that such spiritual matters defy either/or questions. Rather, *both* love and violence are divine. And *both* love and violence play a vital role in a person's awakening in our evolving universe.

Just before I left the drawing room, I took one final look at my stark mandala: It occurred to me that now, because of all that I had already released from the violence in my early childhood, I might be better equipped to confront the remaining demon in my past. Even though I'd already confronted my father in the process of resolving our relationship, I had to acknowledge that I had never been able to resolve my relationship with my mom. Perhaps my three Holotropic journeys had finally given me the requisite courage—and strength— to confront the most terrifying person in my life: the ultra-powerful woman who'd nurtured my life and my fears.

15

Resolution with Mom

At the final session of the Grof retreat, I reminded myself that I was getting ready for the third and, hopefully, the last confrontation with my mother. I recalled the first time I'd confronted her in September 1976: I had journeyed to New York for the express purpose of telling my parents what I had learned from my first round of therapy. I chose to meet with them separately. I started with my dad. That discussion became his finest hour. Afterward, we became best friends.

When I then tried to have a similar dialogue with my mother, however, I failed to reach her: She couldn't sit still while I described my childhood experiences. She kept interrupting me to correct my feelings, because they challenged her image of Perfect Mother. When I traveled back to Pittsburgh after that historic meeting—although I was extremely grateful I'd been able to resolve my relationship with my dad—I thought it highly unlikely I'd ever be able to do the same with my mom. I concluded: "One out of two ain't bad."

In the late 1980s, during my second round of psychotherapy, I again tried to confront my mom about the reality of my childhood experiences. But once more I failed. I can still remember the hurtful words she used to justify my eye surgeries: "We couldn't have the son of an ophthalmologist look like that!" Using those words, she again told me there was something fundamentally wrong with the way I looked. But even worse, she now implied I was a walking billboard for my dad's medical practice.

Since that last fiasco, I hadn't confronted my mother again. But now it was late August 1997. A few months ago, my mom had turned ninety. But she was still living alone in an apartment in Manhattan, which was a credit to her mental and physical vitality. Nonetheless, I had to question whether she could survive a major confrontation: Could she withstand what could only be experienced as a full-scale assault on her self-proclaimed image of Perfect Mother? Yet I knew if I challenged her now, it wouldn't be another failed effort. I wouldn't back off as I'd done on those two other occasions. In fact, I repeated this battle cry to myself concerning my forthcoming confrontation with my ninety-year-old mother: "If she dies, she dies. But I'm going to have my say."

During the past years, I've met several people who wished they had confronted their parents—before they passed away. I also recall reading a newspaper article that described an adult son who went to the gravesite where his parents were laid to rest. There he dug a deep hole in the ground, inserted a long tube, and then attempted to have the kind of conversation he hadn't been able to have with his parents while they were still alive. From these recollections, I decided I wasn't going to wait until my mother's body was deep underground before I'd attempt to have a meaningful conversation. But I pointedly asked myself: "Will my upcoming confrontation with my mom be based on love or violence?" Undoubtedly, both were involved: Love was motivating me to reach the same resolution with my mom that I'd achieved with my dad. Violence might help me break through her elaborate web of psychological defenses: her sturdy protective walls.

On August 25, less than three weeks after my three Holotropic journeys, I phoned my mom around 7:00 in the evening. As soon as we exchanged our usual greetings, I let her know I'd been thinking about my eye operations and wanted to ask some questions. I could tell by the sound of her voice that her attitude was along these lines:

"Oh no, not again! *Why do you always have to go back to that subject?"* But I proceeded anyway: "I've tried to discuss my eye surgeries with you on several occasions, but our conversation always breaks down. But this time, I'm not going to let you off the hook. You are going to hear what I have to say—whether you like it or not. If you want to shut me up, you'll have to hang up on me. I don't know how much longer you are going to live. But I'd like to resolve our relationship while you're still alive."

As usual, my mom challenged me: "What's the point of going over that subject?" I responded: "I already answered that question. Are you ready?" I'm sure my mom realized that I was determined to proceed no matter what she said. Perhaps there was a strength in my voice she'd never experienced before. Or maybe she no longer had the strength to combat my challenges. In fact, I might've chosen the ideal time: I was still primed from the recent Holographic retreat to confront the biggest demon in my life. Meanwhile, my mother still had the presence of mind to understand my childhood experiences, but her armor had softened with age.

For the next four days, my mom and I talked about two hours every night. This was the longest and most intense dialogue we had ever tried with one another. I expressed, in no uncertain terms, what it was like to live through that string of surgeries, much as I'd shared with my dad twenty-one years prior. During the presentation to my mom, however, I often stopped to express my genuine love to her. I also implored her to accept my reality: "Despite your love and good intentions, my childhood wasn't the happy and safe experience you wished for me, *because of* those eye surgeries." And then, whenever she defended her right, as my mother, to have put me through one surgery after another, I resorted to violence. *I screamed at her with the new voice I'd acquired during my Holotropic journeys:* "For once in your life, shut the fuck up and just listen to me. I'm tired of hearing your bullshit excuses for putting me through those surgeries. Just shut the fuck up and hear me out!"

I had to give my mother a lot of credit: In those multiple-hour conversations, four days in a row, she stayed on the phone with me, shut her mouth (when instructed to do so), and did her very best to respond to my pointed questions. Conveniently, my brother wasn't around to overhear my violent and vulgar treatment of our mother, and squeal on me to our dad. And my dad wasn't around to beat me up for talking to his wife in that demeaning manner. But unlike the quashed rebellion when I was only ten years old, this attempt, when I was fifty, was entirely between my mother and me.

For the first three days of these phone conversations, there was little progress—mostly yelling and screaming. At the age of ninety, my mother could still tap sufficient energy to support her previous decisions. But on the fourth day, she surrendered to my unwavering insistence that she had to face my personal reality. For the first time in our fifty-year relationship, she began to *listen* to what I had to say. And when she opened her mind and heart to my life experiences, the conversation became smooth. Finally, I was able to walk her through a series of questions that illuminated the root cause of our conflict.

"Did I ever complain to you about my right eye, how I could see, or how it looked?" She said no. "Did any of my friends make an issue of how I looked at them?" She said no, once again. "Did any of our relatives, especially my cousins, ever comment on my eyes?" She said another no. "When you spoke with my teachers in school, did any of them ever suggest I could be a better student if my eyes were straight?" She gave another no. "Did Dad ever complain about how my eye looked?" No, not once. "Then tell me: Who, besides yourself, ever complained about the look or wanderings of my eye?" In a soft and humble tone, she acknowledged the obvious truth: *She was the only one in the universe who had a problem with my eye.*

I next asked my mom if she remembered the rationale she had used to account for my surgeries: To her credit, she admitted she had argued that our family couldn't have the son of an ophthalmologist look like me. But then she surprised me when she acknowledged the insulting nature of her comment: "That was cruel." Then I reminded her: "When I confronted Dad in 1976, he made it clear that only the first surgery had a chance of saving my sight and allowing me to see depth. The next three eye surgeries were strictly done for cosmetic reasons: to fix my physical appearance. So why did you tell me, over and over again, that those last three surgeries were done to improve the quality and depth of my vision—when that simply wasn't true?" She said she didn't know. To me, that was a breakthrough! I'd asked her that same question a few times before and she always had made up some medical-sounding excuse to justify those surgeries.

I then asked my mother the most challenging question so far: "Who decided that I needed that eye operation when I was sixteen years old?" Again, she took some time to remember what had really happened. After a long pause, I heard the ultra-powerful woman cry as she spoke: "I am so sorry for what I did. I became obsessed with how you looked and how I wouldn't have wanted to look like that. Every time your eye wandered off course, I felt terrible for you. But I also felt bad for me. You were my child. Maybe I felt guilty because I'd given birth to a flawed child. I know that wasn't being very kind to you, but it's the only way I can explain those surgeries. Dad told me to leave you alone. But I kept asking him: 'Shouldn't you fix his eye?' I guess he got tired of my constant complaining. So when you were sixteen, we arranged another eye surgery. But it didn't take long for your right eye to become crooked again. Dad said your body, at sixteen, was changing. But then, by the time you were twenty-three, you were done growing. So I nagged Dad to try fixing your eye one more time. That summer, you were switching to another graduate school, so I thought it would be the ideal time for eye surgery. You shouldn't blame your father for those surgeries. I pestered him."

But I couldn't put all the blame on my mother: "Dad should've ignored you. You were the housewife; he was the eye surgeon. Even if you pressured him, he could've told you to mind your own business. I resolved my relationship with my father a long time ago. But I can't pretend he didn't play a damaging role. Whether you nagged him or not, the surgeries wouldn't have happened unless he agreed to make the arrangements."

There was another long pause in our conversation. My mother's crying broke the silence. As she continued sobbing, she moaned: "I'm sorry. I never realized those surgeries would hurt you so much. I feel terrible that you had to live with all that pain and confusion. I can now see you had no idea why this horrible thing was being done to you and when it might be done again. I wanted your childhood to be happy. But instead, I made your childhood miserable. I'm so sorry."

Just when it was evident that I had finally reached my mother's soul, I began sobbing on the telephone. When I could bring myself to speak, I thanked her for seeing my world: "All I ever wanted was for you to acknowledge how I experienced my childhood. You did so many great things for me while I was growing up: You introduced me to classical music, exposed me to fine art, and continually supported my passion for printing and getting accepted by my dream college. But in the background, in between those many great experiences, I was living in fear of my next eye surgery. I know you didn't want to frighten and hurt me, but I never felt safe and secure in our home." Then my mother interrupted me, but this time for a different reason: "If only I had known what those surgeries would do to you, I would have left your eye alone."

But I had to tell her: "There's no need to apologize. I just wanted you to see my childhood as it was for me and stop insisting I had a perfect childhood. It wasn't great. But I've had a great life anyway— despite my early fears, confusion, and pain. But now, maybe we can be honest with one another. Maybe we can now talk to one another without having to make up some phony story about how everything in my childhood was so perfect and wonderful."

I then thanked my mom for having stayed on the phone, even when I swore at her to shut up and listen to me. She said she wanted to end our arguments. At her age, she knew this string of phone calls might've been the last chance we had to make amends.

When I got off the phone, I sat on the couch in my home office. I couldn't believe it: *I had just resolved my fifty-year relationship with my mom.* From that first confrontation in 1976, it took another twenty-one years to achieve what I thought could never be. As much as I'd learned to define myself from the inside out, *it felt good to be seen by my mother.* But I couldn't help but remind myself of the obvious: If it took me four consecutive days of two-hour phone calls (with love as well as violence) to break through my mother's powerful defense shields (with her at ninety and me at fifty), *I hardly had any chance of reaching her when I was three, seven, sixteen, and twenty-three years old.* During my final confrontation with my mom, I got to see—as never before—what I'd been up against all my life. But now, after all those years of family lies and defensive reactions, I felt peace, knowing I'd resolved my relationship with *both* parents, and not just one of them. And I felt especially blessed that both of these resolutions took place with *live* conversations.

During the next few weeks, my mom telephoned me every three to four days. She began each conversation by apologizing, once again, for what I'd experienced as a result of those surgeries. She expressed remorse for having instigated the non-medical cosmetic operations. Each time I reassured her: "Mom, it's okay. I'm at peace with all that happened. You don't have to apologize. I just wanted you to see and accept my childhood." Within a few months, my mother and I started talking about other things.

In November, I attended a one-day program in Manhattan on Holotropic Breathwork. I had so enjoyed the weeklong retreat in early August that I couldn't miss taking another Holotropic journey. There were ten people in attendance, so it was easy to divide into pairs and switch roles as "breather" and "sitter." When it was my turn to go on a journey, it didn't take me long before I entered a non-ordinary state of consciousness. And I immediately could tell where the wisdom in my body had sent me: I was back in outer space!

Astonishingly, I was the commander of my private spaceship; I had the freedom to follow my wishes and travel anywhere I pleased. What seemed very strange, however, was the type of navigation and propulsion system that was under my personal control: All I had to do was think my preferred direction and speed, and my mental waves would direct my spaceship's movement. Perhaps even stranger was the unique mechanism by which my spaceship could quickly switch direction and speed: There were numerous thin sectional extensions surrounding the outer hull of my spaceship. With just the effort of a thought, those lanky extensions would wisp me through space to my imagined destination.

During my journey, I felt so much joy in effortlessly being able to travel wherever my heart desired. And I was so excited about the possibilities. After I had been gallivanting through the galaxies for a while, I eventually approached a huge V-shaped void in the distance. I couldn't tell if it was a rupture in spacetime, a black hole, or a new universe. I felt trepidation, yet I was surprisingly intrigued with what had emerged before me. As I was debating whether to proceed into the unknown, an unusual "object" suddenly appeared: A large hand, with its back toward me, emerged in the center of the void. Through its gentle motion, it beckoned me to come closer. Even though I was anxious about what might occur to me if I were to continue moving toward this anomaly in space, I also felt the hand was reassuring me that everything would be all right. When I finally chose to enter the void, my mind confidently instructed the lanky extensions to move my spaceship forward. Just then, my journey came to its end.

Once I got up from my mattress, I went to the side of the room that had a few tables and chairs, blank sheets of paper, and drawing implements. This time, I used watercolors to capture my recent trip in an art form. It wasn't long before I completed a colorful mandala, showing the deep blues of outer space, the bright stars from distant galaxies, the light and medium grays of my small spaceship, the dark gray extensions that protruded all around my craft, and the very dark V-shaped void I'd encountered in outer space. Inside the void, I used a brown-and-green color to draw the single hand that had beckoned me forward.

Incidentally, I'm not an artist by any stretch of my imagination, but I was able to do a decent job of rendering my journey on paper. I was taken aback, however, when I was compelled to turn my mandala over: The watercolors I'd used to draw an amateur-looking hand had bled through the paper to create, on the other side, an accomplished artist's detailed rendition of that same hand—including fingernails, knuckle joints, and different textures of skin. How was this possible? I was baffled by the transformative process by which the bleeding of watercolors through a sheet of paper had "coincidentally" produced a high-quality drawing that was far beyond my artistic ability. I turned the paper over to the front, signed my name, and dated my mandala: November 8, 1997.

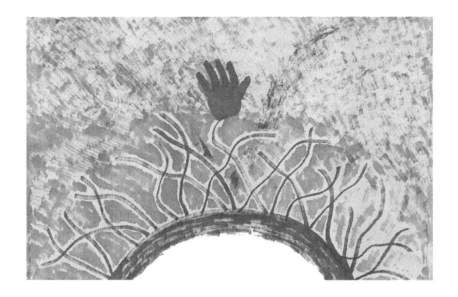

When all the participants had concluded their Holotropic trips and drawings, the ten of us sat in a circle and shared our experiences. When it was my turn to speak, I first displayed my mandala for all to see, while I expressed my joy in having traveled across the galaxies. I then briefly described the unusual features of my private spaceship and how it was propelled by the intentions in my mind. I also shared what it was like to come across that dark, V-shaped void, including my ambivalent feelings when I'd first entered that mysterious space. As I talked about the gentle hand that had motioned me forward, I again displayed my mandala.

It was the specific act of "holding up the hand" to the group of fellow consciousness pilgrims, when I suddenly recalled my mother. I shared with the group that she had studied palmistry for fifty years. Every time I visited her, she would ask me to hold up my hands, one at a time. That was her way of trying to understand me and see where my life was headed. But now my mother's hand was encouraging me to go into the void: *The other side of the darkness, just as the other side of my mandala, revealed a life with greater depth, detail, and texture.* I next disclosed that I'd just resolved my fifty-year battle with my mom. So it came as no surprise to me that she—and her loving hand—would now be guiding my subsequent journeys for becoming whole.

One of the participants then asked me: "What's the meaning of those weird extensions on your spaceship?" I looked at my mandala, but nothing came to me: "I have no idea. But I still enjoyed how my mind could direct their movements."

Since I was done sharing my journey, the next person began to share her journey with the group. But she hadn't said two sentences, when a flash of light hit me straight between the eyes. I was so struck by this sudden epiphany that I exclaimed out loud: "Holy shit!" The woman next to me stopped talking and everyone turned toward me, expecting a justification for my outburst. I apologized, but the group still wanted me to describe what had just popped into my head. So I explained: "Those weird extensions on my spaceship are the legs of a spider. *My compact spaceship is a biomechanical spider*" After I breathed, I continued: "During my first Holotropic journey this past August, I was inside my mother's womb, swimming alongside my dad's sperm that was to become me. On the way to the egg, I saw a spider. But that made absolutely no sense to me at the time."

A woman in the group inquired: "Are you interested in finding out what the spider means?" "Definitely," I said. That same woman offered this invaluable perspective: "I've studied animal symbols. In some cultures, the spider, including its web, represents the universal bad mother: the mother that traps you and thus prevents you from moving forward in life."

As I heard this woman's input about the symbolic meaning of a spider, I felt goose bumps all over my body. Even if other societies interpret spiders differently, the idea of being trapped, blindfolded, and imprisoned in the hospital room by the bad mother, *including a web of lies about my bad eye*, resonated with every cell in my body. But most extraordinary, the spider that I had previously encountered on my journey in my mother's womb had just been transformed into a magnificent vessel for exploring the universe. And whenever I might encounter a challenging "void" in the future, my inner being, actively encouraged by my mother, would see me through to the other side. I marveled at my lesson. Those previous bad aspects of my mother— that spider—were now a living part of me: my expanded navigation and propulsion system. *I never dreamed that a resolution with my mom could have turned our troubled relationship into an expanded body-mind.*

On February 3, 1998, which would've been my father's ninety-ninth birthday, I called my mom to reminisce about my dad. I don't recall how the subject came up, but I recall her assessment: "Weren't we fortunate that Dad was an ophthalmologist, so he could arrange all those surgeries at no cost." Struck by the cavalier fashion in which my mom had brought up my traumatic childhood, I then reminded her of what we had talked about last August. But it quickly became apparent that she'd unconsciously repressed our string of phone calls and her many apologies that followed. *It was as if those conversations— and our resolution—had never taken place.* For a split second, I thought of challenging her memory, but I quickly changed my mind: As far as I was concerned, especially given my recent Holotropic journey with my spider-based spaceship, my mom and I were at peace. Our final attempt at a resolution had been a complete success. Period.

There are few, if any, miracles in awakening: For most people, it takes different portions of love, violence, and a courageous journey, making use of mind/body/spirit modalities, for becoming aware of recreating patterns, breaking patterns, and transcending patterns. By my heartfelt (yet tough) confrontation of my ninety-year-old mom, I'd *briefly* succeeded in getting through her defenses and reaching her soul. Even though she had remained aware—and remorseful—about the realities of my childhood for a short while, she just couldn't live with those same realities in the long run: She *had* to believe she was Perfect Mother: That was the only way she could justify her life.

My mother had been a full-time housewife for fifty-plus years, who'd given up her dream of becoming a concert pianist in her teens.

Afterward, she never held a job, pursued a career, or found any other outlet for her musical and artistic passions. Instead, her entire sense of self became firmly attached to being a perfect mother for her two children. My August 1997 phone calls with my mom had challenged her long-standing view of herself and her ultimate value in life. While these calls allowed me to resolve our relationship, she couldn't adapt to the "new" information: Must she now conclude that her life was, in fact, worthless, because she wasn't the perfect mother in the end? For whatever reason, she'd been unable to use her pain as the fuel to examine her unconscious patterns, so she could awaken to her true essence. Instead, at almost ninety-one years old, my mom chose to re-establish her familiar defense shields and live out the remainder of her unexamined life. She had survived World War I, had escaped certain death in Nazi Germany, and had lived through World War II, but she never learned how to thrive in times of peace.

So I chose to accept—and deeply respect—my mom's decision to retain her old self-image along with her old patterns. But when I woke up the next morning, I asked myself: "What is resolution? And how do you know when you have it?"

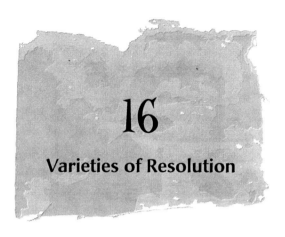

16

Varieties of Resolution

By mid-1998, I became fascinated with resolving relationships and how resolution plays a special role in expanding our consciousness: Why do people need to resolve troubled and difficult relationships? Are there different strategies for achieving resolution? Can peace with another person be achieved through an inner dialogue (instead of a live conversation)? What is the role of truth in achieving resolution, or when does truth not matter? Is there something else that matters more than truth?

All these questions grew out of the varieties of resolution I had encountered in my lifetime—especially regarding my mom and dad. From direct experience, I came to appreciate that how—and to what extent—we resolve our prime relationships in life profoundly affects the opportunity for expanding our mind/body/spirit consciousness and, therefore, our capacity for love, joy, peace, and compassion.

First, I'll discuss three terms that are essential for healing and becoming whole: relationship, truth, and resolution. As we will see, *relationship* is defined in terms of an energetic exchange between two people, *truth* is defined as each person's story of what happened in the past, and *resolution* is defined according to the clarity and vitality of each person's spatial and temporal boundaries. *By resolving all the challenging relationships in your life—based on a shared truth—you can heal your wounded boundaries.* During this process, you can establish a well-defined, strong self for living your soul's purpose—without distractions, distress, or disease.

Second, I'll relate resolving relationships to *energy fields,* which will revisit the distinction between negative energy fields (ego-based needs) and positive energy fields (spirit-based intentions). As you'll see, radiating positive energies makes a big difference in being able to create a lasting resolution, and live your personal and vocational dreams to the max.

Third, I'll examine *three dimensions* for negotiating the truth of what occurred between two people: the integrative, distributive, and protective dimensions. Practically speaking, these three dimensions reveal *five approaches* for negotiating different versions of reality into a shared viewpoint: maintaining, synergizing, combining, isolating, and conceding the truth. These five ways for reaching an agreement on truth are then used within a *nine-stage process* for enabling people to heal their wounded boundaries. The *Thomas-Kilmann Conflict Mode Instrument* (1974), which I developed with Dr. Kenneth W. Thomas, allows people to assess their relative propensity to use the five ways for negotiating agreements.

And fourth, I'll describe *a spiritual-based approach* for resolving relationships, which transcends boundaries. Stated differently, once you have become aware of your recreated patterns and have already had some success in breaking your patterns, you're then free to stop defending your ego and its need to be right all the time. In contrast, you can be happy with all the souls in the universe—no matter what suffering and hurt you've experienced in the past. By transcending your patterns, therefore, you can achieve resolution with everyone.

Let's define a *relationship* as an energetic connection between two people (whether positive or negative) that can be based on any kind of interaction: usually love, violence, or whatever happens to connect people. For the sake of convenience, I will always refer to a relationship—and a resolution—of two people. But every now and

THE COURAGEOUS MOSAIC

then, a boundary violation involves three or more people. Yet even in those more complex social situations, I still think it's prudent to approach the total damage with a series of one-on-one resolutions. Having only two-person interactions will likely prevent any majority from ganging up on the minority.

Moreover, even if we're focused on the same violation, different people undoubtedly played different roles—which can be addressed most effectively with just two people at a time. For example, the first time I confronted my parents with their decisions about my lazy eye, even though the subject was the same for each one, I first had a one-on-one confrontation with my dad and then with my mom. I achieved a resolution in the first meeting—but not in the second. Just imagine what would've happened, however, if I'd confronted both of them at the same time: It's unlikely I could've achieved any resolution at all, since my mother, as always, would have dominated my father—and thus her explanation of why those surgeries were essential would've derailed any chance at achieving peace with either of them.

Let's now discuss "*What is truth?*" I acknowledge the presence of one "Divine Truth" (with a capital "T"), which represents one source, God, Spirit, or whatever word you use to describe pure, holographic consciousness. But there can be many truths (with a lowercase "t"), which reflect different people's accounts of what occurred and why, or whether something happened at all. A consensual reality is when many people share the same truth, which may or may not be the one Truth. And because people often lie to themselves in order to protect their insecure or damaged ego, they unknowingly lie to others: Their spoken or written truths are thus untruths, because of the ingrained self-deception from having grown up in a dysfunctional family.

Of course, lying can also be deliberate, which defines a serious character flaw: If a person knowingly *presents false* information (lies of commission) or *withholds relevant* information (lies of omission), it will be difficult to take anything that person says as his truth (since deception has been deliberately introduced with both types of lies).

Such a character flaw is revealed by this puzzling, paradoxical quote: "Right now, I'm lying to you." Does that statement mean the person is telling the truth about his lying? Or is he really lying about what he's saying, which would then mean he's really speaking the truth (as when a double negative thereby becomes a positive)? In either case, there's no truth to be found in such a misleading assertion and thus there's no basis for trusting the truth of that person's next statements or actions. Consequently, people who lie to themselves and to others (unintentionally or deliberately) are basically preceding everything they say with that same puzzling, paradoxical quotation. *Yet the more a person has participated in a number of mind/body/spirit modalities, the more she can tell the truth to herself with little distortion, and can thus tell her truth to others.*

Let's consider *resolution* as having well-established boundaries and a well-defined self, so you can focus all your time and energy on manifesting your physical health, your sexual being, your passions, your principles, and your soul's purpose. No matter if you are doing something on your own or with others, you can be entirely focused on manifesting yourself—with no distractions from tiredness, stress, confusion, or anxiety. *Having achieved resolution with the key people in your life thus eliminates the typical blockages that prevent you from living your dreams. But unresolved relationships will continue to drain your soul's energy and cloud your mind.*

Basically, it's very challenging to get anything done when your energy and focus are being distracted by negative feelings about your parents, siblings, lovers, spouses, children, relatives, neighbors, friends, work associates, and strangers who've violated your boundaries and thus harmed your sense of self. Indeed, a simple way of defining the significant people in your lifetime is to make a list of those who have enhanced or damaged one or more of your five sacred boundaries. That's how people affect one another, for better or worse. But people who have neither enhanced nor damaged your boundaries won't be experienced as significant.

As I suggested, there are five *spatial boundaries:* physical, sexual, mental, emotional and spiritual. Unresolved relationships have most often created some havoc in one or more of these domains. Certainly, parents (or any guardians) have convenient access to their children's sacred boundaries. Parents also serve as our chief caretakers and role models. Our siblings, especially if close in age (let alone a twin) can also hurt (or enhance) our very delicate boundaries when we're very young and, inadvertently, teach us powerful lessons about what we can expect from other people in the future.

Besides spacial boundaries, we also realized that there are two *temporal boundaries:* past/present and present/future. By establishing distinct temporal boundaries, (1) people's past violations don't seep into the present and (2) they can also travel into the future to see the long-term consequences of their current behavior, so they can travel back to the present and therefore make the required corrections. *But unresolved relationships prevent the formation of distinct past/present and present/future boundaries.* The net effect is that you inappropriately react to present people as if they were the past perpetrators who had hurt you. And you are unable to see beyond your immediate pain to know why you must change your behavior, *and achieve resolution with those who have violated your boundaries,* if you ever expect to have any hope of realizing your dreams in the future.

Based on a holographic universe, always keep this Divine Truth in mind: Whenever you violate someone else's boundaries, *you also violate your own integrity.* The journey to awakening, therefore, requires you to not only resolve the hurt that has been caused by others, but also to heal what you've indirectly done to yourself.

The bottom line: Unresolved relationships are exactly (1) what have derailed your efforts and goals in the past (physically, sexually, emotionally, mentally, and spiritually); (2) what you're carrying into the present that are draining your energy and confusing your focus; and (3) what will prevent you from anticipating the future and thus getting yourself back on course. *You can enhance your boundaries and strengthen your self, however, by successfully confronting the people who've violated you (and also seeking out those people whom you've violated) and then working with them to achieve a lasting peace. You and they will then have more energy for everything else in life!*

Because most violations have both a mental *and* an emotional component, their resolution must be addressed by (1) talking about what happened (with an outer or inner dialogue) and (2) releasing the blocked energy. If your boundary violations also had a physical and sexual aspect, low self-esteem and other negative energies could be stuck in your body-mind, which often require additional healing modalities besides confronting your perpetrator. Thankfully, *various mind/body/spirit modalities can help prepare you—ahead of time—for a successful confrontation with those you are seeking resolution.* In my life, both talk therapy and Holotropic Breathwork helped establish the groundwork for me to achieve resolution with my mom.

Let's next consider the *energy field* that's being radiated by one or both persons, according to their mind/body/spirit consciousness. In a previous piece in my mosaic, I described Hawkins' logarithmic scale of human consciousness (which extends from 20 to 1000, with 200 being the critical point where external *ego* force shifts to internal *spirit* power). Here are the emotions that create a *negative energy field*, since each of these emotions has a frequency below the critical point of 200: shame, guilt, apathy, grief, fear, desire, anger, and pride. Very different emotions generate a *positive energy field*, since they are at or above 200: courage, neutrality, willingness, acceptance, reason, love, joy, peace, and enlightenment. But I don't think that two people who have been affected by violations must both radiate positive energies to promote healing. I am certain that one person's positive emotions can significantly expand both people's consciousness. According to Hawkins, a positive emotion is much more powerful than a negative emotion, which is the reason for the *logarithmic* scale: An increase of one point on the scale represents a ten-fold increase in spiritual power over ego force.

Let's now imagine three scenarios in which resolution between two people would be beneficial: (1) someone's previous decisions or actions have seriously wounded you; (2) you have violated another person's boundaries; or (3) both of you have harmed each other. In these possible scenarios, three important dimensions offer different approaches for negotiating the truth of what happened between the two people: the distributive, integrative, and protective dimensions.

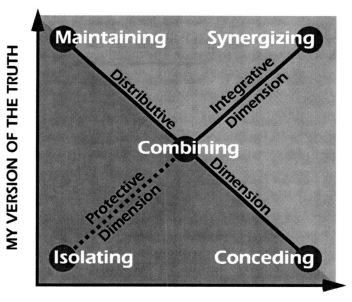

The *distributive dimension*, as its name implies, distributes truth across both people in a relationship, but the total amount of truth is fixed: There is my truth and your truth, which "sums" to 100% of the truth. The only issue is *what percentage* of my version of the truth and *what percentage* of your version of what happened will guide how we resolve our relationship. Three approaches for resolving conflict can be seen on the distributive dimension: maintaining, conceding, and combining/neutral.

At one endpoint of this distributive dimension is *maintaining:* With this approach to negotiating truth, my version of reality will be used to develop our resolution, while your version will not be taken into account: You thus affirm what occurred between us in the past according to my story—or recall—of reality. On the one hand, since most complex relationships involve at least two truths, it might be shortsighted to adopt one version of reality while downplaying the other (which is why there are other approaches to negotiating truth besides maintaining). On the other hand, some scenarios can be the case of *one person having violated the other.* As such, maintaining the victim's version of the truth in the negotiation (while negating the perpetrator's original claim to reality) has a much higher likelihood of achieving a permanent resolution. *And maintaining this imbalance* in whose reality counts, and whose doesn't, is especially appropriate when an adult or parent has violated a child—unless there is sound evidence to believe that a child has falsely concocted a story to hurt a parent. Between two adults, however, there are many situations in which one person has exclusively wounded the other's boundaries: *Maintaining the victim's reality might be the only way to actually achieve a long-term resolution to a one-sided violation.*

At the other end of the distributive dimension is *conceding:* With this approach to negotiating truth, I completely accept your version of reality and totally surrender mine. Basically, conceding is identical to maintaining, except that the roles of the two people are reversed: With maintaining, *my truth* shapes our resolution; with conceding, *your truth* shapes our resolution. It might at first seem ideal to always use maintaining over conceding as an approach for negotiating truth. But that strategy only works when the other person is always the one who violated you. It's worth repeating: *When you were the perpetrator of a boundary violation, maintaining your argument about truth cannot possibly achieve a workable resolution with the victim.* In fact, whenever a perpetrator attempts to maintain his version of what took place in the presence of a victim, such insensitivity only serves to replay the violation, which makes everything worse—which is why conceding is the best approach, under these circumstances.

Between these two endpoints on the distributive dimension is *combining/neutral:* With this strategy for negotiating truth, each of our versions of reality is only partially used to address our relationship. Thus, neither you nor I will feel entirely validated or vindicated for our different stories about what really happened between us. At the extreme, (1) maintaining is 100% my truth and 0% your truth; (2) conceding is 0% my truth and 100% your truth; and (3) *combining/ neutral is 50% my truth and 50% your truth.* That's why the amount of truth on the distributive dimension (also referred to as the total size of the pie) is fixed: The two people just distribute their unique truths (different size pieces of the pie), so the total sum equals 100% (the whole pie). Truth therefore remains stuck inside the proverbial box, which provides rather limited solutions to both people.

The approach of combining/neutral is most evident when both people simply agree to disagree and thereafter refrain from bringing up the subject. They continue, however, to speak about other things, so there is the facade of a relationship. *Although combining/neutral is workable for a time, it's important to recognize that the previous boundary violations have not been addressed—certainly not in any meaningful way.* Each person's story of what happened is only partially affirmed, while both people pretend to have a relationship. Basically, the people have unknowingly eliminated the chance for broadening and deepening their understanding of the situation (enlarging the size of the pie or looking outside the box), which might have led to their achieving a greater peace with what had transpired between them. (The neutral designation for combining/*neutral* helps to distinguish this version of combining with combining/*plus* and combining/*minus*, which will be discussed shortly.)

The *integrative dimension,* as the term implies, has the potential for integrating both versions of reality, by going "outside the box" of truth and thus expanding the size of the pie available to both people.

The integrative dimension has two defining points: synergizing and combining/plus.

At the one end of the integrative dimension is *synergizing:* With this approach, both people actively share their version of reality with one another, with an open mind and an open heart. *With synergizing, both people strive to achieve a lasting resolution, since each separate story is fully incorporated—integrated—into a shared version of what boundary violations took place for one or both persons.* With the synergizing mode, each person's version of truth expands to take into account the other's truth, which *always* results in a broader—more encompassing—story than any single truth. Indeed, the defining quality of synergy is that the whole version is more than the sum of its parts, when one plus one equals three, and when the size of the pie is not fixed. Using a simple calculation for the sake of comparison, the synergizing mode can thus integrate 100% of my truth plus 100% of your truth into an expanded story of what happened between us, which sums to 300%. Synergizing two truths into a more complex story thus expands the size of the pie—from the fixed sum of 100% along the distributive dimension to the sum of 300% on the integrative dimension.

At the other end of the integrative dimension is *combining/plus:* With this approach to negotiating truth, the two perspectives on truth are partially (not wholly) synergized in the resolution. The approach of combining/plus is evident when both people are able to expand combining/neutral by modifying each of their different versions of what happened between them, based on what they learn from one another. The negotiation for truth, as a result, includes *pieces* of both people's separate truths into a workable solution (combining/plus), but the two people do not integrate *all* of their two original versions of what happened into a new—synthesized—version of reality (as in synergizing). Nevertheless, combining/plus starts to expand the pie, which allows both people to achieve a more meaningful resolution, based on a greater percentage of *shared truth* than any approach on the distributive plane. Let's use a simple calculation to illustrate this key distinction: The approach of combining/neutral always sums to 100%, while the mode of combining/plus sums to 110 or 120%.

Lastly, the *protective dimension* is the opposite of the integrative dimension: The latter, as noted, expands the size of the pie. But the former reduces the size of the pie. The protective dimension has two endpoints: isolating and combining/minus.

At one endpoint of the protective dimension is *isolating:* With this approach to negotiating truth, either one person avoids or hides from the other—or both people stay away from one another. But in either case, there's no meaningful contact between the two, whether by e-mail, letter, card, telephone, or face-to-face meeting. As a result, neither person has a chance to share his truth with the other—or to learn more about the other's version of the truth. The relationship remains in limbo and, therefore, royally stuck in the past. Actually, there's no active relationship in this case: Only a pseudo or pretend relationship exists when one or both persons have chosen to isolate themselves—for an extended period of time.

The approach of isolating is considered *protective*, since it serves to prevent people from being further hurt, either out of fear or spite. Fear, of course, can be real or imagined. *When fear is real*, the person staying away is fully justified in believing that she might be further violated if there is contact between her and the other person. *When fear is imagined*, there isn't any solid evidence to justify staying away. Besides staying away from another person out of fear, some people use spite to isolate themselves from a relationship: "If I'm mean to him, he'll leave me alone." Sometimes, spite serves a dual purpose: not only does it keep the other person away, but it also provides an opportunity to vent some unresolved anger, rage, and hate.

Whether driven by either fear or spite, the protective strategy of isolating someone can be suggested with this simple calculation: 0% of my truth and 0% of your truth amounts to 0% of total truth, which amounts to a nonexistent pie. Except when there's actual danger of being harmed, if the two people refuse to meet, don't confront one another, and don't negotiate the truth between them, there can't be any kind of live resolution.

The other end of the protective dimension is *combining/minus*. This combining approach is related to combining/*neutral* mode on the distributive dimension: Both people's versions of the truth are used to resolve their relationship, but only partially, not wholly. With combining/*minus*, however, the resulting sum of the two truths equals less than 100%, let's say 80 or 90%. In this case, some of each person's truth is *withheld* from the negotiation. Why?

Some level of fear or spite is preventing each person from fully revealing his truth to the other. Here are the sorts of inner dialogues that capture combining/minus: "I don't trust you enough to tell you everything, since you might use it against me." "After what you did to me, I'll be damned if I'm going to tell you everything I know." If these negative emotions permeate the negotiation for truth, it is no wonder that the "resolution" will be based on half-truths—*lies based on omission*. That is why combining/minus usually produces an even less effective resolution than combining/neutral. But at least the two people haven't isolated themselves from each another. Sometime in the future, they might establish trust and respect, which will reduce their fear and spite, so they can seek a more satisfying resolution.

The distributive, integrative, and protective dimensions reflect different strategies for resolving relationships—yet they intersect at the point of combining (neutral, plus, and minus). It is fascinating to see that people automatically choose one of these three options: (1) negotiate *inside* the box of truth—along the lines of maintaining, conceding, and/or combining/neutral on the distributive dimension; (2) negotiate *outside* the box of truth—along the lines of combining/plus and/or synergizing on the integrative dimension; or (3) escape altogether from the situation—by using the modes of isolating and combining/minus on the protective dimension. Which dimension a person chooses for negotiating truth is based on his belief system: Is the size of the pie fixed (distributive dimension)? Can the pie be expanded (integrative dimension)? Or should I stay away from that person and the topic (protective dimension)? One thing is certain: *It takes a lot of courage to share your truth and also be open to hear the other person's truth, which might be very different from your version of reality.*

Most of the time, it might seem best to remain silent—whether you are the perpetrator or the victim—rather than challenge another person's truth and then have them challenge yours. *But when a vital relationship has resulted in boundary violations, short-term convenience is no substitute for achieving a long-term resolution.* The former will drain your energy and confuse your mind; the latter has the opportunity to heal damaged boundaries and promote a stronger self. Aside from courage, however, achieving resolution might also take a good dose of violence—in the form of aggressive, unrelenting confrontations— to overcome another person's attempts to silence the truth. *But if the violence is coupled with love, it's possible to transform a silent person into an active participant for healing old wounds.*

Let's now explore how the energy field surrounding a damaged relationship influences which approaches are chosen for negotiating truth: If both persons radiate the negative emotions of shame, guilt, apathy, grief, fear, desire, anger, and pride, they will likely choose the distributive approaches of maintaining, conceding, and combining (or, perhaps, the protective approach of isolating) in order to resolve their relationship. But within any negative energy field, maintaining translates into competing for the truth: winning the negotiation by argument, intimidation, or a show of force. Competing means I win and you lose. If that vibration permeates the environment, then both persons will become locked in an attempt to win the battle on truth, which may have little to do with what really happened between the two people. And having a backup strategy of isolating, "if you don't adopt my view, you won't see me again," will radiate more negative emotion, which usually sabotages any chance for a resolution.

However, *if one or both persons radiate the more positive emotions of courage, neutrality, willingness, acceptance, reason, love, joy, peace, and enlightenment, the negotiation for truth will likely switch to the integrative dimension.* While the mode of combining (the intersection of all three dimensions) may be the correct choice when both persons have hurt one another, since both of their truths will be partially represented in a workable resolution, even the combining/plus approach is only a little beyond the distributive dimension. Within a field of positive energy, however, the two people will be more inclined to muster the *courage* to openly share their different versions of truth, while having the *compassion* to listen to the other person's story of what took place between them. As a result, both people will probably use synergizing to develop a shared truth. They'll then create an expanded story on their prior boundary violations, which will help them achieve peace.

Here are some core principles for successfully negotiating the truth: (1) allow the clearly identified victim to maintain his version of what happened, which means the perpetrator has to concede that his old story only served to protect his sense of self; (2) if both people have hurt one another, combining will generate a workable solution in the short term, where at least both persons can stay in contact with one another, with the potential for greater healing in the future; (3) don't isolate yourself from the person you need to heal your sacred boundaries and reclaim your selfhood—unless you have to protect yourself from future, potential boundary violations; (4) participate in mind/body/spirit modalities so you will radiate positive energies toward everyone; and (5) if positive energies and emotions can be radiated for the other person in the conflict, negotiate the truth with the synergizing mode, so you can transform your conversation from the distributive to the integrative dimension and create an expanded version of truth and a lasting resolution.

The stage of negotiating the truth of what happened is probably the most neglected part of resolving relationships. Because of hurt egos and negative energy fields, people mostly use modes on the distributive dimension (maintaining, conceding, or combining/neutral), or find some protection by isolating the other person, without recognizing they have the opportunity to go outside the box of truth and employ an approach that moves from combining/plus to synergizing. Using a mode on the integrative dimension creates the best outcomes.

Although negotiating truth is key for achieving resolution (and that is why I have given it so much attention), there are a few stages *before* the negotiation for truth begins and additional stages *after* the two people agree on some version of reality. While it would be easy to suggest any number of steps—from beginning to end—to resolve a difficult relationship, I find it useful to organize the whole process into nine stages. These stages start with the foundational Stage Zero, the groundwork, for the remaining eight stages: (0) participating in mind/body/spirit modalities to embody positive emotions and then radiate positive energies; (1) deciding to meet with another person to resolve a relationship; (2) confronting the truth of every person's story; (3) negotiating a joint version of reality; (4) apologizing for having violated the other person's boundaries; (5) taking steps that will prevent another violation in the future; (6) forgiving the other person—and yourself; (7) mourning what was lost for both persons; and (8) moving forward in life.

The underlying Stage Zero (participating in mind/body/spirit modalities) has significant implications throughout the remaining eight stages for achieving resolution. The field of energy surrounding the two people not only influences the choice of which approach to use for negotiating the truth, but also determines whether a spiritual perspective allows both people to transcend their sensitive egos and wounded boundaries. This foundational stage also affects the mood of all conversations (compassion versus competition) and whether forgiveness can be given and received, despite the past hurt.

The first stage (deciding to meet with another person to resolve a relationship) includes your thoughts and feelings regarding which of your boundaries have been most violated by other people. *Of those violations, which ones can be resolved without interacting with the person involved and which ones require a live conversation?* For you to make the best decision, it usually helps to discuss what happened with trusted friends and an expert therapist. But if the relationship still exists and involves your family of origin (parents, siblings, or other caretakers), there are benefits from meeting face to face (before the person is no longer alive), as long as you take steps to protect yourself from being further violated. Moreover, if you expect to have regular contact with this person, it's often best—long-term—to pursue a live resolution.

But if you see the person infrequently or you have valid reasons to believe (from your prior attempts at resolution) that a productive dialogue can't take place, it might be best to resolve the relationship on your own. (See Dr. John Demartini's 2002 book, *The Breakthrough Experience*, for a useful process for "collapsing" lopsided, troublesome relationships into pure love and gratitude—without a live meeting.) From my experience, *if you are attuned to the subtle sensations in your body, you'll know which resolutions must take place in a live meeting and which ones can be resolved on your own.* Besides, whatever you decide, you can always change your mind later. Essentially, the first stage is only meant to get the process started by choosing which boundary violation (and which person), if resolved with a live dialogue, would make a big difference in reversing and then revitalizing your drained energy, confused focus, and battered self.

The second stage (confronting the truth of each person's story) involves setting up a meeting to discuss the boundary violations that allegedly occurred, either recently or, in most cases, a long time ago. A fair amount of courage is usually required for one or both persons to propose such a confrontational meeting in our society, where the prevailing cultural practice is to avoid discussing hurtful and violent behavior. As said earlier, at least one person in the relationship must radiate positive energy (courage being at the vital threshold between ego-based force versus spirit-based power) for both persons to have a chance at healing their wounds. Yet it also helps if the first meeting to address past wounds has been carefully planned in advance, with an agenda and a readiness on the part of both persons to minimize defensiveness and maximize responsiveness. But it's not unusual for spontaneity to work well, whereby the two people just happen to be in the right place at the right time (and in the right mood) when the topic magically appears and the dialogue easily unfolds.

For some boundary violations, it may take several years before one person has the courage to raise the topic, set up a meeting, and confront the other person. After the fact, here's a typical response: "I wish I would've confronted him years ago. We wasted so much time and heartache by avoiding the topic." And yet, here's another typical response: "What was I thinking? I can't believe I brought up the topic and thought we could resolve it. I'll never try *that* again!" In advance, of course, it's difficult—if not impossible—to know how both people will respond to a confrontation. And that's exactly why a good dose of courage is required—the courage to risk a bad consequence for a worthwhile purpose by confronting another soul with a potentially threatening, but highly therapeutic topic.

The third stage (negotiating a joint version of reality) can occur after the two people have already shared their truth: their version of what occurred. Usually, there's a marked discrepancy between who did what to whom—and why. So often it's a question of convenient memory: Each person remembers the events to protect his ego from shame, blame, guilt, and another sort of threat to the person's sense of self. Again that's why it's so important for one or both persons to radiate the positive energies of human consciousness.

During this stage, each person chooses, whether consciously or unconsciously, the approach to negotiate the truth of what actually happened. If both people are relating within a negative energy field, they will probably negotiate truth along the distributive dimension (maintaining, conceding, and combining/neutral). But if one or both of them are radiating a positive energy field, they are more likely to negotiate truth along the integrative dimension (combining/plus to synergizing). Although the mode of isolating the other person seems irrelevant (since both people are already meeting, confronting, and negotiating with one another), it's not usual for discussions to break down. If a positive energy field surrounds the two persons, however, it is unlikely they will resort to isolating one another, since fear and spite are negative energies.

The fourth stage of resolution (apologizing for having violated the other person's boundaries) must, obviously, be based on a shared understanding of what took place and why. If an agreement has been developed on the *distributive dimension* (maintaining and conceding) and is based on one person having violated the other, then a genuine apology can be voiced by the perpetrator and accepted by the victim. But if a competing approach (along with ego-based energy) was used to force an agreement on the truth, then an apology, no matter how sweetly delivered, is still unlikely to be accepted by the other person, even if he receives the apology without external protest. Keep this in mind: *If an agreement on truth has been won through battle, any apology is meaningless.* However, when an agreement on truth has been "won" on the integrative dimension (somewhere between combining/plus and synergizing), each person can fully apologize to the other, since they both recognize they've contributed to one another's pain.

In the case of using the combining approach (whether chosen from the distributive, integrative, or protective dimension), a mutual apology can be extended by both people. However, that apology isn't likely to be genuinely accepted by either person, since it wasn't based on a deep discussion of their two truths nor did it heal their violated boundaries. But at least both persons continue to interact—until the relationship fizzles out from boredom or again becomes alive when the topic is revisited in the future.

The fifth stage (taking steps that will prevent another violation in the future) is a natural progression from apology to forgivingness. Essentially, an apology is more likely to be accepted and respected if it includes a plan to ensure that the previously violated boundaries are now safe from further harm. But in cases when the violation took place in childhood, the immediate adult situation guarantees safety:

The former child can now assert and safeguard his boundaries. Thus no plan for action is needed, unless it would be useful for the victim to know, traveling back in time, how the same situation would have been handled differently, with today's consciousness. (In some cases, taking steps to prevent another violation occurs *before* an apology is offered and accepted. Indeed, there can be a back-and-forth process among *all* the stages for achieving resolution.)

The sixth stage (forgiving the other person and yourself) can be easy or difficult—depending on the mind/body/spirit consciousness of those involved in the situation. At the one extreme is the oft-cited claim: "If I can't forget, I can't forgive." Or, stated in its converse form: "I'll forgive when I can forget." While we never wish to minimize the enormous pain of a severe boundary violation (involving physical boundaries, such as murder, or sexual boundaries, such as rape), if there's no forgivingness, there's little healing. Instead, various masks or addictions are used to avoid the misery of living with a damaged self. Rather than live with such pain, the healthier option is to find a way to forgive—through an internal dialogue and/or a live meeting. Naturally, if the latter is not possible or would create further harm by replaying the violation, that's one thing. But with mind/body/spirit modalities, it's also possible to see the same situation from a higher plane—from the integrative dimension—and then find a synergistic perspective to regard all people as Pure Spirit (especially if they were previously viewed as "perpetrator" and "victim" on the distributive or protective dimension).

But one thing should now be quite apparent: If the two people radiate a negative energy field around their wounded boundaries, it is unlikely that the one who was harmed will really forgive the other, no matter how genuine and sincere the apology. Thus, it's possible to move through the stages toward a workable resolution and then be blocked by the inability—or unwillingness—of the "victim" (and his family and friends) to actually forgive the "perpetrator." If that's the case, everyone's boundaries will remain damaged with little hope of moving forward in the future—*as fully healed souls.* Life will remain ego-based, unhappy, and angry for those who won't forgive because they can't forget. Nonetheless, the ultimate challenge is to forgive the other person—even when a violent crime was committed—without a live meeting or even an apology. As we'll see, the latter is possible with a spiritual perspective: when long-term happiness is viewed as more important than being right (and winning the ego's argument on its truth, its "objective" reality, and its view of "justice").

The seventh stage (mourning what was lost for both persons) recognizes that both people have been living with decreased energy, and poor focus, whether (1) from having their physicality, sexuality, emotionality, mentality, or spirituality stressed or (2) feeling guilty from having caused the hurt and damage. Mourning is a process for *really feeling* the sadness, rather than defending against it—by either pretending "I'm over it" or by denying that anything bad happened. With expanded mind/body/spirit consciousness, however, the body is not numb to the pain of loss, but deeply feels it. In fact, the more the two people can deeply feel what they have lost, the sooner the mourning period will be put to rest.

I have recognized, however, that people often prefer to bypass the mourning stage, because they want to quickly resolve the conflict (and thus not feel the pain of what they lost). But if the seventh stage hasn't been adequately addressed, the skipped stage of mourning will ultimately prevent both people from healing their wounds and then transcending what they've missed in life. Note: It's often helpful to conduct a special ceremony or some ritual that acknowledges what was lost, so the pain can be felt and released from the body-mind of both persons as well as their friends and relatives.

The eighth stage (moving forward in life) is about redefining—and reforming—the sacred boundaries that were violated: to replace what was previously lost with a more solid container and a stronger sense of self. Once mourning has successfully passed, a tremendous relief is usually experienced, a release of stuck energy, whereby each person now feels lighter, younger, more relaxed, and more optimistic about life. *It's only after this powerful experience of relief and release that people can truly appreciate how living with an unresolved relationship was continually decreasing their energy and distracting their mind.* With clear boundaries, a stronger sense of self, and more positive emotions, each person can now move forward in life—and live his soul's purpose.

Often, however, after having resolved one difficult relationship, *another* unresolved relationship springs to the forefront. The healing process then cycles back, once again, to the foundational Stage Zero (participating in mind/body/spirit modalities to embody positive emotions and then radiate positive energies) and continues with the first stage (deciding to meet with another person), and so forth.

In a previous piece of my mosaic, I discussed the irony of first developing clear boundaries and a strong self (primarily the Western view of human development), so these qualities can be transcended into a spiritual realm in which all boundaries are simply an illusion and all that exists is pure consciousness (primarily the Eastern view of spiritual enlightenment). Yes, a healthy ego can pick an approach on the integrative dimension for negotiating truth that's somewhere between combining/plus and synergizing (to see beyond one's own body-mind and thus acknowledge the inner world of another soul). But I think it's easier to use synergizing with a spiritual perspective— after those hard-earned boundaries have evaporated into wholeness and the size of the pie has become infinite. Naturally, radiating those positive energies will sustain the healing process.

Consider another insight from a spiritual perspective: *Is it more important to be right or happy?* Out of habit, our ego fights to be right, by investing much time and effort in trying to prove what happened and why—according to its convenient version of the truth. *But sadly, relationships have often remained damaged and estranged for a long time (or for a lifetime), simply because each person can only accept his limited truth, while he rejects all other perspectives on the truth.* Alternatively, if we can surrender our ego and its relentless need to be right, we can more easily support (or create) a version of the truth that will, in the long run, make us—and others—happy.

A respected example of a spiritual-based approach for healing relationships is called the twelve-step program: *Alcoholics Anonymous* (1939). It asks participants to accept a higher source than themselves (God or Spirit) and, thereby, to transition from an ego-centered life to a spiritual awakening. With a sponsor's help (someone who has already gone through the process), participants make an inventory of the wrongs they have committed against others (as in boundary violations). The participants are then asked to make amends to the wronged individuals, unless additional hurt might be inflicted with a live contact. Prayer and meditation help all parties stay connected with the Divine Truth in all their decisions and actions. Because the twelve-step program was designed for addicts who had violated other people's boundaries (and not vice versa), addicts are primarily taught to use *conceding:* Thus, the addict is the perpetrator and the other is the victim. As the addict surrenders to the victim's story of truth, the door of resolution opens—so both of them can effectively heal their wounded boundaries.

While initially based on addiction to alcohol, the twelve-step program has since been adapted to many other kinds of addictions, which include drugs, gambling, and eating disorders. While defined in a number of ways, *addiction is a person's compulsion to persist with a behavior that is destructive in the long term, but momentarily satisfies his need to avoid the built-up pain in his body, self-responsibility, and feelings of helplessness and hopelessness.* It might be beneficial to add one more addiction to the list: *compulsively living without having resolved primal relationships.* For short, let's call it a "resolution crisis."

Whenever a person lives with damaged boundaries, along with an ill-defined self, she's probably (1) avoiding the pain in her body from her previous violations; (2) avoiding her adult responsibility to heal her relationships with those who violated her and those she violated; and (3) avoiding her debilitating feelings of helplessness and hopelessness that support her damaged boundaries and fragile self. Undoubtedly, *the resolution crisis is the root of all other addictions.* In all likelihood, alcohol, drug, gambling, and other such disorders are the ordinary ways that people compulsively avoid the damaged boundaries and weak self that have developed from physical, sexual, emotional, mental, and spiritual violations, during early childhood and young adulthood. Maybe by addressing the underlying source— the resolution crisis—it'll be possible to reduce the prevalence of all other addictions.

Once I had organized the nine stages for achieving resolution, I became especially drawn to Stage Zero (participating in mind/body/ spirit modalities), since consciousness has such a profound impact on the remaining stages of resolution. But a mysterious event rudely stopped me in my tracks and then conveniently showed me how to combine the ultimate awakening (well beyond my early awakenings from eye surgeries) with my expanding consciousness.

17

My Accidental Death

In the fall of 2003, after I'd been living in California for a little over two years, I experienced a life-changing event. Although it took place after two rounds of psychotherapy, several journeys with Holotropic Breathwork, and many sessions of electro-homeopathy, I'm not sure if any of these mind/body/spirit modalities—or my live resolutions with my mother and father—had properly prepared me for my death on Interstate 405.

It was mid-afternoon on a cool, cloudy day. I had just finished teaching an undergraduate class at California State University, Long Beach. On my drive home, I was passing through the Seal Beach area on the I-405, which has a staggering seven lanes of traffic flowing in each direction. I was headed south, adjacent to the carpool lane, at about seventy or so miles per hour. Strangely, there was light traffic for that time of day. And contrary to my habit, I wasn't listening to music on my car's stereo system—so it was easy to hear the freeway sounds all around me.

The following sequence of events took place in fewer than five seconds, but I experienced them in slow motion. It all began when I heard a loud crash coming from the far-right lane on the freeway— several lanes from me. I next saw metal and glass flying through the air. My eyes then locked onto a large Oldsmobile sedan, which was making 360-degree spins, heading directly toward the front end of my small Honda coupe—with no other vehicle between it and me. There was no way I could avoid this out-of-control car from crashing into me while I was traveling at seventy miles an hour: It was only a matter of how terrible this accident would be—and whether I could survive the inevitable crash.

As I braced myself for a major collision, I shouted: "Oh, God!" But just before the moment of impact, the spinning sedan suddenly dematerialized in front of my eyes. It's fleeting shadow then passed right through me. An instant later, it rematerialized directly behind my car—just before it crashed, head-on, into the next car in my lane. While still clutching the steering wheel for dear life, I looked into my car's rearview mirror and witnessed the crash fade into the distance, as my car sped away from that unworldly sight.

I remained frozen for several minutes, but I continued to drive straight ahead in the same lane. I said no words and felt only dread. After a while, I regained some semblance of thought and then called my son on my cell: "Chris, please meet me at home as soon as you can. Something just happened that I can't explain, but I have to tell you in person. I can't say more just now. Can you be home in twenty minutes?" Naturally, Chris was perplexed and worried about my odd request and state of mind. But he didn't ask me to say more. He just promised to leave his Irvine apartment right away.

During my trip home, I had some free time to ponder my state of being: "I feel more dead than alive!"

After I drove into the garage, I walked into my home. Chris was pacing in the living room and anxiously wanted an answer: "Tell me, so what happened?" I described the unusual sequence of events that remained crystal clear to me. When I finished, Chris reflected: "Well, it's obvious you're still alive, but it might take you a while to recover from a near-death experience." I nodded my head as if I agreed with his assessment, but I somehow knew that much more had happened to me than a "mere" near-death or out-of-body experience. Because

I didn't want to worry him about my possibly being dead, however, I changed the topic. In a little while, we said good-bye and he then returned to his Irvine apartment.

I sat down on the living room sofa and carefully examined my existence. It occurred to me that perhaps heaven is a continuation of life on earth. Maybe everything I was seeing and hearing (including that conversation with Chris) had been magically manufactured to ground me, so whatever was left of me would remain at peace with death. And if the afterlife seems like the real thing, then dying is not so bad after all. Maybe death is analogous to a dream you're having while you're still alive, but only sleeping. Death then appears just as solid and real as any dream you have at night, except you will never wake up—because you are no longer alive.

As these thoughts were racing through my mind, I was getting more confused by the moment: "How can I tell if I'm dead or alive? And what's the difference between the two?"

A moment later, I had the enlightenment of a lifetime: "Maybe life is the same as death! Maybe everything on the outside is simply manufactured so it looks as if it's real, solid, and enduring. If I now experience the artificiality of objects and people, perhaps that is the way it always was, but I was never *aware* of it before." I continued to ponder the possibilities: (1) life is real but death is artificial, (2) life is artificial but death is real, (3) both life and death are real, and (4) both life and death are artificial. My scientific mind then kicked in: "There's no method to empirically (or convincingly) test any of these alternative hypotheses in a laboratory study! So how can I decipher which life/death combination is true? And besides, what does it mean that one thing is real and another thing is artificial? *Who decides?*"

For the next few hours, I walked around in my condo, carefully looking at my surroundings to decipher if they were real or artificial. I then took a casual walk through my neighborhood to inquire into the nature of things, including birds, trees, plants, and people. I then returned home and sat back down on the living room sofa. Slowly, I came to the obvious conclusion that everything outside of my inner experience is unreal, made up, an illusion—and thus a dream. No, I wasn't able to test my hypotheses by using the scientific method, yet I had to accept what rang true in my being: *Given that I had directly— and unequivocally—experienced a spinning car dematerialize right before my eyes, pass through me, and then rematerialize behind my car, it made perfect sense that I'd indeed awakened from my previously sleep-like state for the divine purpose of getting my first glimpse of what is really real.*

And what is really real? It now seemed that only an undivided, unchanging, forever present PURE AWARENESS is the only reality, while a divided, always changing, SEPARATE EXISTENCE (whether inside or outside of me) is an artificial dream. As a result, there is no real SEPARATE ME, as would be apparent to any awakened person who could decipher that only pure, undivided awareness is for real. (In a few years, I'd again encounter this illuminating lesson during a weeklong Gangaji retreat.)

I next realized I could devote the rest of my life trying to figure out who manufactures a dream state for us, how such a thing can be done, and what purpose it serves. But for the time being, it seemed a lot wiser to accept the truth, no matter what its source. Incidentally, from the research of quantum physics, any object in the universe can dematerialize into nothingness and then reappear somewhere else in the same or a different form. Even though the probability of that happening for an object larger than a subatomic particle (such as an atom or a car) is infinitesimally small, it's still greater than zero. But I couldn't rationalize my accident on the I-405 with these quantum possibilities. No. It appeared that a dash of enlightenment had been sprinkled on my life in some inexplicable fashion.

In the weeks and months that followed, I could not find a way to disregard my death—nor could I ignore the apparent unreality of my surroundings, which included other people and myself. So I had to reconsider all my experiences with mind/body/spirit modalities. For instance, what does it really mean to develop a strong self when it's only an illusion? Further, what does it mean to develop a feeling body, since it, too, is just one more artificial construction that merely contains the false self in a dream state? Moreover, what does it mean to meet Pure Spirit (with a strong self and a feeling body), or is that the same as awakening to pure awareness? I also asked myself: Does a person need to achieve a level of mind/body/spirit consciousness *before* she can experience what is really real? Asked differently: What does it mean to recreate, break, and transcend patterns before—and after—the experience of pure awareness?

I can't say I have clear or final answers to these questions. But I will express my beliefs about these metaphysical matters at the time of this writing. But such fundamental questions—and answers—are subject to change, day-by-day and year-by-year.

To begin with, even if Earth and its beings are fleeting illusions (just as the flickering fire created dancing shadows in Plato's cave), the evolution of mind/body/spirit consciousness will surely inspire every person to treat all that appears real (whether in physical form or not) with love, joy, peace, and compassion. Why will this be so? Because when you experience non-dual awareness, illusions are still an undeniable piece of the whole. It's not as if pure awareness (the ever-present ground of all being) should necessarily be treated with any more respect than physical manifestations (plants, animals, and people). By honoring everything and everyone, no matter if they're real or not, you honor Pure Spirit, *since reality and unreality make up the whole: non-dual awareness.*

I also believe that a person's evolution of consciousness (via a sequence of mind/body/spirit modalities) can be somewhat distinct from that person's realization of pure awareness (with an accidental death, or with some out-of-body experience). Indeed, consider these four possible combinations of consciousness and pure awareness: A person (1) has expanded his consciousness but isn't awake, (2) hasn't expanded his consciousness yet is awake, (3) has neither developed mind/body/spirit consciousness nor is awake, and (4) has expanded his consciousness and is also awake.

When a person has expanded her consciousness but isn't awake, she has the capacity to treat other people—and the planet—with great love and compassion, but may become too attached to the reality of her surroundings and thus may needlessly suffer when things do not go as planned. This suffering can then distract from some of the love that could be available for herself and others while in a sacred, yet sleep-like state.

When a person has not yet developed much consciousness but is awake, his ego's ongoing struggle for self-identify and self-esteem, his tension-filled body, and his inability to greet Pure Spirit might inadvertently motivate him to mistreat his dreamlike surroundings (including people), because they easily get dismissed as unreal and thus not worthy of his regard and respect. Ironically, although such a person has already realized the truth of existence (pure awareness), his undeveloped mind/body/spirit consciousness regularly distracts him from compassionately loving those who comprise his non-dual awareness. Maybe he doesn't suffer much, but those around him do, particularly if they tolerate his mistreatment of their sleep-like state. Stated differently, people with little mind/body/spirit consciousness, even if they've awakened to the non-dual reality, can be egotistical, insensitive, and destructive to their fellow beings and Mother Earth.

When a person has neither developed much consciousness nor is awake, she will suffer, as will all those around her: A wounded self will compel her to violate the *sacred boundaries* of other people and the planet. And her attachment to the seemingly real surroundings will also lead her to feel (and radiate) the lower emotions of human consciousness: shame, guilt, apathy, grief, fear, desire, anger, and pride. This combination of undeveloped mind/body/spirit consciousness and not experiencing pure awareness reveals the underlying cause of our society's life-and-death challenges: war, violence, hatred, poverty, hunger, disease, hopelessness—and the destruction of planet Earth.

Interestingly enough, these "realities" would all be viewed as divine with another combination of consciousness and awareness.

In particular, when a person has expanded his consciousness and is also awake, he has merged both the real and the unreal into non-dual awareness. This person will regard pure awareness and his dreamlike existence with identical love, joy, peace, and compassion. This perspective represents what is meant by *spiritual enlightenment*: The "spiritual" part comes from a dedicated pursuit of mind/body/spirit *consciousness* (recreating, breaking, and transcending patterns of behavior); the "enlightenment" aspect comes from serendipitous *awakenings* (which come from the hidden blessings of surgery, rape, prolonged abuse, abandonment, a debilitating illness, a near-death or out-of-body experience, or a real-death experience). I suppose it's also possible for a person to awaken by asking himself, "who am I," while searching for Truth or reading the biographies of enlightened beings. But my own experience tells me that the ultimate awakening usually occurs through a mysterious accumulation of both past-life and present-life events.

As I noted before, it isn't necessary to know the absolute "truth" of your being either a strong ego or Pure Spirit. Which of these two perspectives you choose to *believe*, however, largely determines how you experience your life. Similarly, I find it especially worthwhile to reflect on the practical implications of two radically different belief systems: (1) What would life be like if people were to live every day as if everyone were real and thus subject to real pain and suffering? (2) What would life be like if people were to live as if everyone only existed in a dreamlike state and, therefore, the only true reality were pure awareness?

In the first belief system, I believe that people would focus on what makes them happy, either as a strong ego or as Pure Spirit. In the second belief system, however, I believe that happiness is largely irrelevant: People would experience life simply as it is: They wouldn't be attached to those "things" that artificially cause pleasure or pain.

Rather, they'd embody grace and gratitude for all people and events, since everything in the universe is perfect (and miraculous) in pure consciousness. Questions of happiness versus sadness, right versus wrong, good versus evil, and other such human polarities can all be fully resolved (either experienced in duality or dissolved into unity), depending on whether a person has awakened to the reality of pure awareness as well as the unreality of a dreamlike existence.

In sum, if a person has neither developed much consciousness nor is awake, he is living his life according to the first belief system (as if everyone were absolutely real) and will thereby experience ups and downs. But if that person takes the journey to expand his mind/body/spirit consciousness while he realizes pure awareness, he has chosen to live according to the second belief system (as if everyone existed in a dreamlike state) and will thereby experience unwavering equanimity. Because both journeys are valid and sacred, I honor the *truth* of each person's story of his/her life, as I honor the *Divine Truth* of pure awareness, which includes both the reality and the unreality of human experience. This life-altering question is entirely neutral: *Do you want to become more conscious and awake, or not?* As said a few times now, every person decides, either implicitly or explicitly, what amount of time and effort she'll invest in living an examined life.

Paradoxically, once I had thoroughly pondered my existence, I again asked myself: "Am I dead or alive?" Honestly, I wasn't sure! Yet as time went by, the distinction between being dead or alive became increasingly meaningless to me. Regardless of which is my true state, it's all divine.

18

My Energetic Awakening

Because of my growing interest in mind/body/spirit modalities for expanding consciousness, one of my friends, Rhonda, invited me to visit a chiropractor, Dr. Tony Wilson, who specialized in a modality with the name: Network Spinal Analysis (NSA). She said: "Ask him to show you the wave." Even though I didn't know what was in store for me, it sounded interesting.

On February 24, 2004, I went to Dr. Wilson's office. As my fate would have it, he happened to be standing by the receptionist desk when I arrived. Once I introduced myself, I asked him: "Can I see the wave?" He first seemed surprised I'd asked him that blunt question, but he quickly responded: "Sure. Let's go to the practice room where you can observe several participants on the tables."

I followed him into a nice room that had six chiropractic tables, arranged in pairs. They were all occupied. In each case, a participant was lying flat on his stomach with his face nestled into an opening on the front end of the cushioned table—typically called a *face hole*. Some participants were not moving, but others were breathing deeply and moving their bodies. I saw Dr. Wilson make some soft contacts with his fingers on a person's neck and tailbone. Directly above these points, he then made sewing-like motions through the air. It seemed like Dr. Wilson was pulling strings out of a person's body and then tossing them to the sky. It almost seemed as though Dr. Wilson was dancing with imaginary stars.

(Note: In NSA or Network care, a participating person is called a *practice member*—similar to someone who is participating in a yoga practice. The term "patient" is not used, since it views the person as needing to be treated or fixed, according to a medical diagnosis.)

Dr. Wilson then signaled me to come closer to one of the tables. When I was standing only a few feet away, he again made only slight contact along a woman's spine, followed by those same sewing-like motions. Naturally, since this practice member was lying face down on the table, she couldn't see what Dr. Wilson was doing above her. But the instant that sewing motion began, her body spontaneously began moving like a wave: I could easily see distinct ripples moving back and forth along her spine—from the top of her spinal column (the atlas) to the bottom of her spinal column (the coccyx)—like a wave approaching a shoreline and, shortly afterward, receding back to the ocean. If that spontaneous movement wasn't enough wizardry to mesmerize me, the shape of the wave *changed* as Dr. Wilson made *different* sewing motions. While each person on a table seemed to be at a different level of expressing and experiencing a wave, the more "advanced" practice members evidenced a kind of mind/body/spirit phenomenon I'd never seen before—or ever imagined.

After Dr. Wilson further demonstrated how spines respond to different contacts, he asked me: "So what do you think of the wave?" I answered: "I want it! When can I start?" He brought me back to the front desk and introduced me to Marianne, his receptionist. Without further ado, I made an appointment for the next day.

During my first session on February 25, nothing happened. Dr. Wilson reminded me to breathe deeply and feel the sensations in my body. He encouraged me to allow my body to move and do what it naturally wanted to do. At the end of the session, I asked him: "When will I get the wave?" He chuckled and said: "It could take you a while. Like most people, you probably numbed your body, so you wouldn't feel its pain. But if you continue to breath deeply and allow yourself to feel all the sensations in your body, you'll eventually experience the wave."

During the next month, I was lying on one of Dr. Wilson's tables three times a week—breathing and feeling. On March 29, which was my mom's ninety-seventh birthday, it finally happened: During my sixteenth session of lying facedown on the table, I felt my neck start to quiver on its own. And I then felt the same quivering movements in my tailbone. As I laughed out loud, I said to myself: "It's starting! I'm getting a wave!" And that was indeed the case: A few moments later, I felt a spontaneous connection occur between the quivers in my neck and the quivers in my tailbone. In an instant, a wave began moving back and forth between the top and bottom of my spine. I was amazed—and then rendered speechless!

After about two to three minutes of experiencing these natural waves along my back, I started feeling pain in my right eye. At first, I thought I might've been putting my eye against the right side of the face hole. So while the wave continued, I purposely moved my head away from the table. But the pain in my right eye continued to grow in intensity. I didn't know what to do. Since I'd been waiting for this huge event for a whole month, however, I decided to withstand the pain and continue the wave.

But in another minute or so, when I wasn't expecting anything, I got the surprise of a lifetime: *Moisture started draining out of my right eye.* Even more profound: My left eye remained dry, as did the rest of my body. Recall this sequence: In 1950, when I was three years old and awoke in the recovery room after that first surgery on my right eye, I started crying. A woman (nurse) came over to my bedside and said: "If you cry, you'll lose your eyes." In 1997, when I was fifty-one years old and removed the bound T-shirt from around my eyes after a Holotropic journey, the part of the T-shirt that had been covering my right eye and my right eye itself were completely dry, even though the remainder of the T-shirt and me were soaking wet, including my left eye. It seemed my body had remembered the nurse's words and, after all those many years, still sought to prevent the loss of my right eye. But now in 2004, when I was fifty-seven years old, *a spinal wave allowed my body to release what psychotherapy and Holotropic Breathwork couldn't.* And because of that release, I no longer had to squander my energy by unconsciously honoring the nurse's erroneous warning.

After the wave had subsided, I remained on the table for a few minutes and relished how my NSA wave had released the last vestige from my first childhood trauma. I was also amazed when I realized that my energetic release had occurred on my mother's birthday. Was that a coincidence? Hardly! *It seemed those two female caretakers—one a nurse and the other my mother—had compelled me to numb my body to hide my tears and silence my fears.*

In a little bit, I stood up, reached under the table, and retrieved my wallet, keys, and glasses. Unlike my previous sessions, I noticed that a greeting card had been placed next to my personal items. On the outside, a single word proclaimed: "Congratulations!" I looked on the inside of the card and then saw this printed message: "When the spine begins moving in two places at once, a wave is generated. Waves carry information. The wave is the mind-body processing old information that has been stored in the body in the form of a spinal tension pattern. This phenomenon is known as *retracing.* This is how the body releases the spinal tension patterns and all types of trauma. *Retracing happens as your body re-experiences the stored information that was previously unsafe to experience* [italics added]."

It's important to emphasize: This card was pre-printed. It was not written for my benefit. As such, I was further struck that I'd just demonstrated exactly what the card explained: It'd previously been unsafe for me to revisit the nurse's threat. Through sixteen sessions, however, I gradually became acquainted with what had been stuck in my body ever since I was three years old. Yet it was my own innate intelligence that enabled me to clear out that tension—and its false meaning. Dr. Wilson didn't know anything about my traumas, since

I'd never discussed them with him. But he did, of course, know how to make the physical contacts and sewing motions along my spinal column, which gave my body the necessary permission to release the nurse's frightening information. I should come as no surprise that I left Dr. Wilson's office astonished by how my body's innate wisdom could be activated by a spinal wave.

During the next weeks, I didn't gain any new insights from the release of tension in my body. Dr. Wilson offered this theory: "If the innate intelligence in your body decides you need to know the story behind the release of stuck energy, it'll tell you. While on the table, you'll see images, make sounds, and feel emotions. Or maybe you'll dream about the source of the tension at night. But most often, the body doesn't believe there's any benefit to be had from knowing the storyline. Tension will still be released, but you will not be informed of—or bothered by—its meaning."

By early May, I had another profound experience with a wave: I was again lying on my stomach with my head in the face hole. I was enjoying the general release of tension in my body, as the wave did its thing. But I was puzzled when pain, once again, developed in my right eye. I remember saying to myself: "No, please, not again! Will I ever be done with this trauma?"

During my latest NSA wave, however, no moisture oozed from my right eye. Rather, as the pain increased, I entered a non-ordinary state of consciousness and then traveled back to that awful recovery room after my first eye surgery: Remindful of one of my Holotropic journeys, *I relived the frightening feelings I had suffered when I was only three years old.* Given that young age, however, I didn't have words or theories to explain my surgical experience: No words could properly describe the aftermath of that first surgery, because my feelings *were* beyond words. Instead, upon waking up from the anesthesia, I found myself in a non-verbal hellhole. But here are two simple words that attempt to capture my first trauma: *ultimate terror.* I guess I could also add: *absolute fear.*

During my first round of therapy in the mid-1970s, Dr. Chasin would ask me what I felt when I first awoke in the recovery room. But no matter how many times he asked me to express my feelings, I just couldn't recapture what I'd felt during the biggest trauma of my life: I could only think thoughts in adult terms. *Yet those primitive feelings of ultimate terror and absolute fear were dramatically retraced during that wave in May 2004.* According to Dr. Wilson, my body somehow knew that my journey to healing and wholeness would be best served if I could know the meaning behind that release. And it complied.

When I got off the table at the conclusion of that session, I felt ten years younger and ten pounds lighter. It also felt as if the energy in my body had increased ten fold. In subsequent NSA sessions, my awareness of the sensations and feelings in my body was noticeably heightened. Even my NSA waves produced more free-flowing energy as my vertebrae were able to dance at will, without being in the least bit constrained by the previous, surgery-related tension that had been stuck all around my spine—including the spinal cord itself.

On September 3, after six months of enjoying the wave several times each week, I flew to Denver, Colorado, for a five-day program: "Transformation Gate and the Twelve Stages of Healing." First, the "transformation" portion of the retreat focused on Network Spinal Analysis (NSA) and took place on Saturday and Sunday. The "twelve stages" portion then focused on Somato Respiratory Integration (SRI) and convened on Monday and Tuesday. The whole program started on Friday evening with an introductory talk by Dr. Donald Epstein, the creator of both NSA and SRI.

During the two-day, Transformation workshop, each of the 400 participants (divided into two equal sections) was scheduled for six NSA sessions in the grand ballroom of the hotel, three on each day. In that sizeable area, about twenty practitioners (chiropractors with additional NSA certification and valuable experience) were assigned to five tables apiece. The first time I witnessed 100 practice members lying on 100 tables (with the rest of the participants of that section sitting around the perimeter of the ballroom), I could feel all their bubbling energy ready to flow through one NSA wave after another. This high-energy setting was far beyond what I'd experienced in Dr. Wilson's office, with only six people on six tables: All that collective energy positively stimulated my central nervous system!

While my spinal movement and body awareness of sensations and feelings had improved under Dr. Wilson's care, for every session at the two-day program, I could choose from a pool of practitioners, each with a distinctive style for inducing the wave. By experiencing those six NSA sessions with different practitioners, I was able to learn new strategies for engaging with the world. In fact, *every time I learned a new kind of wave, a new way of life became available to me.* Following the sixth NSA session on late Sunday evening, I was now wide open for new adventures and thus ready to get the most out of the second half of the Denver program.

During the two-day, SRI workshop, approximately 200 people continued their journey of mind/body/spirit consciousness. Adding to those six NSA wave sessions, we learned and practiced "the twelve stages of healing," as described and illustrated in Dr. Donald Epstein's 1994 book by that same title.

The first three stages of healing are (1) suffering, (2) polarities, and (3) stuck in a perspective. These first three stages pertain to *mind consciousness:* discovering a wounded self and learning why that self has been spinning its wheels, repeating its patterns, for years or even decades. Suffering expresses the consciousness of both helplessness and hopelessness, since there doesn't seem to be any way out of the trauma, depression, grief, or addictive life style. The second stage of polarities represents the consciousness of longing for someone else to save you: a physician, teacher, or lover, which usually mirrors the fragmented selves that are stuck within your body-mind. The third stage of being stuck in a perspective expresses the consciousness of having recreated an unhealthy pattern, again and again, and finally becoming aware of it.

The next four stages of healing are named: (4) reclaiming your power, (5) merging with your traumatized selves, (6) preparing for resolution, and (7) resolution. Stages Four through Seven pertain to *body consciousness:* breaking into your body where your old traumas, tensions, and stories have been stored, thus breaking your patterns. The pivotal fourth stage is when you reclaim the power behind your own healing rather than waiting—or wishing—for someone else to save you. It reveals the vital transformation from receiving a fix from another person (physician, psychologist, priest, teacher, and so forth) to now healing yourself from the inside out, using your own innate intelligence. The merging stage represents the process of integrating your fragmented or dissociated selves (especially your repressed or "shadow" selves), which then enables you to develop a stronger ego. Preparing for resolution and resolution itself are the vital processes for discharging the stuck energies that have regularly hampered your efforts to break your patterns, and discarding the parts and pieces of yourself that don't support an empowered life.

The last five stages of healing are called: (8) emptiness, (9) the light behind the form, (10) ascent to the light, (11) descent into the self, and (12) community. Stages Eight through Twelve address *spirit consciousness*: experiencing the wholeness of nothingness (no*thing* as such—only light), visiting Spirit, revisiting the self after an exposure to Spirit, and then serving/supporting people and the planet within a diverse community. In certain ways, these last five stages represent transcending all patterns.

Basically, the first three stages of healing enable you to become more aware of how your wounded ego has helplessly and hopelessly recreated patterns—resulting in both a stuck mind and a stuck body. Being in these first three stages radiates those *lower energies* of shame, guilt, apathy, grief, fear, desire, anger, and pride. The next four stages help you become more aware of how your fragmented pieces can be unified into a strong self, which then enables you to finally release the various traumas, tensions, and stories in your body that you no longer need. Being in these middle four stages of healing radiates the *middle energies/emotions* of courage, neutrality, willingness, acceptance, and reason. Based on this healthy foundation of a strong self with an aware body, the last five stages of healing allow you to become more mindful of the pure consciousness that defines who you really are—which then enables you to approach all people and all situations as Pure Spirit. Being in these last five stages radiates the *higher energies and emotions* of love, joy, peace, and enlightenment. In sum, *the twelve stages of healing represent a person's journey to wholeness—from wounded self (Stages One to Three) to strong self (Stages Four to Seven) and then to Pure Spirit (Stages Eight to Twelve).*

Now back to the SRI portion of the program: Dr. Epstein (now called Donald or Donny by most participants) guided all 200 of us through the twelve stages of healing—using lectures, jokes, videos, and hands-on exercises. Regarding the latter, each stage of healing is accompanied by an "exercise" that requires a particular type of *breath* (inhaling and exhaling through the mouth, nose, left nostril, or right nostril, in different ways), *touch* (arranging both hands on different parts of your body—usually the collar bone, solar plexus, or navel), *movement* (using both breath and muscles to move only the part of your body that's directly underneath your hands), and *energy* (using your conscious intention to bring your life force to the same spot on your body that you are touching with your hands, and moving with your breath and muscles).

There's a very different *rhythm* to each stage of healing, which is created by a unique combination of breath, touch, movement, and energy. Feeling the magical moment (called the "SRI moment") when all four elements connect in unison is precisely what propels you to the next stage of healing. Indeed, to move from one stage to the next, you don't have to do anything—but to create that magical moment: the innate intelligence in your body does the rest. The theory behind this transition is simple: Just as in Holotropic Breathwork, *your body contains the universe, which includes your stressors, struggles, and stories.*

The innate wisdom behind the self-healing process is that your body knows how—and when—to move from one stage to the next one. A unique rhythm of breath, touch, movement, and energy is precisely what signals the body's inner radar to exclaim: "Yes, I feel that stage. Now it's time to experience the next one."

The rhythms of all twelve stages already exist in every being. At any given time and place, however, based on the particular traumas, tensions, and stories in your life, you will be living only *one* of those stages. But by connecting with the unique rhythm of that stage, your body can shift its consciousness to the next stage in the series, which then propels your journey to wholeness (rather than maintaining—living—a limited consciousness within the same stage). In addition, no matter how well you move through the twelve stages of healing, you will eventually cycle back to the earlier stages, including the first stage of suffering. However, each recycling of stages is addressed not only at a higher level of consciousness, but also at a deeper level of experience. The journey for healing and becoming whole, therefore, is infinite and eternal, both in breadth and depth.

Several times during the SRI sessions, Donny asked for one or more volunteers to help him demonstrate the exercise for a stage of healing—its unique combination of breath, touch, movement, and energy. Typically, quite a few people of the 200 in attendance would raise their hands when Donny was prepared to demonstrate the next stage of healing. He would then look across the audience and signal someone to go to the center of the ballroom with him. The rest of us would then gather around Donny and his eager volunteer: Those in the front rows would be sitting on the floor, those in the next several rows would be kneeling, and those in the back would be standing—so we could see the procedures of the exercise. After completing the demonstration, the rest of the audience would divide into pairs and then find an open place on the ballroom floor, so each person could take turns being (a) the practitioner who would facilitate the process and (b) the practice member who'd experience the stage (not unlike the alternating roles of the *sitter* and the *breather* during a session on Holotropic Breathwork).

Since the September 2004 program in Denver was the first time I ever experienced the twelve stages of healing, I felt like the new kid on the block: Many other participants had taken this same program several times before. As a result, I never raised my hand to go to the center of the ballroom with Donny. I was content to watch the more seasoned persons demonstrate each SRI exercise, while the rest of us created the theater in the round. This rational plan worked perfectly well for each demonstration during the first three stages of healing.

The fourth stage of healing is a key turning point. It marks the transition from *mind consciousness* (being stuck in recreating the same pattern repeatedly) to *body consciousness* (breaking into your body to reclaim its power, so a merged, integrated, stronger self will be ready to greet Pure Spirit). In relation to Dr. Hawkins' logarithmic scale of human consciousness, the fourth stage of healing captures the switch between the lower energies and emotions (below 200) and the higher energies (above 200). Dr. Hawkins places *courage* at 200 on his scale, which reflects self-empowerment and the capacity of the ego to risk self-harm by seeing beyond its illusions. To explain Stage Four, Donny first gave a funny lecture on what it takes to reclaim one's power. We then saw a short clip from Norman Jewison's 1971 movie, *Fiddler on the Roof*, to illustrate the rhythm of Stage Four: the scene when Motel, the tailor, develops the courage to break tradition by asking Tevye for his daughter's hand in marriage (and not honoring the matchmaker's recommendation and the father's long-standing right to arrange his own daughter's marriage).

Once Donny had responded to questions about Stage Four, he asked participants to raise their hands if they wanted to demonstrate the exercise with him in the center of the ballroom. As usual, many hands quickly went up, as he gazed across the audience for the right selection. Just as I had done for the previous three stages, I kept my hands close by my sides—since I did not feel ready to participate in this strange activity in public. I remember thinking to myself: "What would my prior colleagues at the University of Pittsburgh say if they saw me in a public setting that was exploring energy and healing—not research and publications?"

Before I had an opportunity to answer that question, however, I noticed Donny pointing his forefinger in my direction—suggesting that he was picking someone right in front of me or just behind me. But the people directly in front of me were not raising their hands. I next turned my head and looked behind me. But no one was raising his hand either. As I looked toward the front once again, Donny was still pointing in my direction. So I made a return gesture by pointing my right forefinger to my chest, as if to say: "Do you mean me?" He obviously read my sign language, because he immediately moved his head up and down to communicate a "yes" response to my question. He then pointed his forefinger to the middle of the ballroom, thereby signaling me to join him there. Frankly, I didn't feel I had much of a choice: In this public setting, I had to accept Donny's invitation. But I recall saying to myself: *Why did he pick me?*

Donny has a reputation for being a master—if not a wizard—at working with another person's energy fields. But Donny is also a very funny person, who enjoys bantering with people, particularly if they are able to trade jokes with him. And yet, to date, I'd only exchanged a few hellos with him—since I had only met him a few days before. Normally, therefore, I would never have chosen this setting to begin joking with him, especially since I was entering unfamiliar territory, in public, with the Stage Four exercise.

But I didn't follow my own sensibilities. Rather, just as soon as I reached the center of the ballroom, I challenged him: "Don't hold back on me, Donny. I want it all!" Oh, my God...I could not believe those words came out of my mouth! Even though I had a smile on my face when I publicly made those comments, he smirked, as if to say: "So, you want it all? Okay then, let's do it!" Immediately, I knew I'd be taken to task for my unnecessary and rather naïve challenge to this wizard of energy, consciousness, and transformation: Had I put *both* feet in my mouth?

Donny asked me to lie on my back with both legs extended on the floor. He then sat down by my right side, so he could instruct me to use the appropriate techniques for breathing, touching, moving, and focusing my energy.

The exercise for Stage Four is quite demanding. The breathing part involves inhaling and exhaling through the nose, which builds up the life-force energy (also called chi and prana) in the body. What makes this approach to breathing especially difficult, however, is that a full inhale and exhale begins with the right nostril. The following cycle of breath then takes place just through the left nostril. The next breaths continue back and forth from right to left nostril, after a full inhale and exhale in each case. But here is what makes this breathing a bit challenging: The right/left nostril breathing is accomplished by holding both the thumb and forefinger of the right hand alongside the bottom portion of the nose. Pushing the forefinger down on the left nostril allows a complete cycle of breath to take place in the open right nostril. For the next cycle, the forefinger is released from the left nostril (thus opening the air passage), while the thumb pushes down on the right nostril (thereby closing the passageway). Yet to build up the chi—and synchronize the left and right brain—it is necessary to breathe faster and faster, while effectively closing and opening each nostril by rapidly alternating the pressure of the forefinger and the thumb. For most, it's a challenge just to master the proper breathing technique for Stage Four.

But the breathing is only one component of the exercise. While the right hand is busy with alternating nostril breathing, the left hand is positioned on a specific spot of the torso, *which was experienced as stuck in Stage Three.* This is an area on the body where the connective tissue is tight and the person experiences tension, anxiety, or distress while touching or holding that spot (which might be the collarbone, the solar plexus, the navel, or anywhere else).

Besides touching the stuck area with his left hand, the person is also asked to *twist* his palm or fingers on that area, either to the left or right in a circular motion (whether counterclockwise or clockwise), depending on which direction offers the most resistance. The reason for choosing to move *against* the resistance is to increase the tension in the tissue that's stuck in the body, thereby addressing what's stuck in the mind. For Holotropic Breathwork, the facilitator also applies *additional* pressure on that part of the body that is feeling pain or in need of restraint. In that way, the trauma can be re-experienced, so it can then be released.

Once the breathing, touch, and movement are all in sync, the participant is asked to move (and focus) his life-force energy, which has been accumulating from that rapid nostril-to-nostril breathing, to the precise area that is stuck. Stage Four of reclaiming your power, therefore, intends to mobilize and then focus the chi to blast through the exact spot that's been holding the traumas, tensions, and stories in your body. That energetically stuck area stores the body's cellular memory of unhappy events (Stage Three), especially events that have created prolonged suffering (Stage One) and false hopes to be saved by another person or an external force (Stage Two). *At that magical, SRI moment—when the rapid breathing with the right hand energetically connects with the twisting touch on the stuck area with the left hand—the rhythm of the stage ripples through the person's body, which then sends him to the next stage of healing.*

After a few minutes of working with Donny (and doing a few practice rounds), I knew how to coordinate the key elements of the Stage Four exercise. Then the hard work began: I used the forefinger and thumb on my right hand to rapidly switch my breath between my right and left nostrils—so I could mobilize the life-force energy in my body. At the same time, I used the fingers on my left hand to twist an area of resistance near my collarbone in a counterclockwise direction, which allowed me to gradually approach the sought-after alignment of breath, touch, movement, and energy. Just as I reached the peak of my energetic focus, Donny instructed me to scream at the top of my lungs: "I take my fucking power back!" Right afterward, I collapsed from exhaustion—with my limp arms spread wide on the ballroom floor. (I think it is fascinating that I had shouted a similar declaration of self-empowerment at the conclusion of my Holotropic trip in August 1997, just after I'd revisited my first eye surgery.)

Once I had regained my stamina, I looked up at Donny, as if to say: "Well, I did it!" But he looked back down at me and said: "That was good—maybe a 92 out of 100. But I know we can do better. Let's do it again!" My facial expression must have said: "You've got to be kidding! I don't have enough strength left to do it again." But Donny wasn't kidding, as he proceeded to put my right hand to my nostrils and my left hand to my collarbone. My ego then decided that I was going to show Donny that I could live up to my own challenge—by not holding anything back on my next round of Stage Four. I then went through the same breath, touch, and movement, as I mobilized my chi directly underneath that same stuck spot. Just when I reached that magical point of perfect alignment, Donny had me scream: "I'm not going to take it anymore. I take my courage back!" I gave it every ounce of energy I had—and then collapsed for the second time.

In a few moments, I looked up at Donny for some affirmation that I'd now succeeding in demonstrating Stage Four. But he looked down on me with a huge smile on his face and announced: "Better. But we need to do it again. You got 94 out of a 100. You still have to hit 100. Don't hold anything back!" In these words, I learned *never* to challenge Donny's motivation or mission, certainly not to his face. I was now paying the price for my stupid arrogance. At that moment, I didn't know how I'd find the strength to proceed with the difficult alignment of the Stage Four exercise. When I later collapsed after my third attempt, Donny gave me a 96 out of 100: "Better. But you still didn't make it to 100."

I had no energy left. I was also losing my voice: I wasn't used to screaming so loudly in a grand ballroom with a tall ceiling. And now

I was getting angry! With 200 fellow participants lying, sitting, and standing around Donny and me, however, it didn't seem as if I could easily walk away from this public setting—and its high expectations. What did it matter that I had nothing left to give? I was being asked to reclaim my power—and maybe everyone else's power—with this Stage Four exercise. So when Donny told me to proceed, I looked at his smiling face and said: "Okay. Let's do it!" As before, he guided my hands to their correct position on my body and encouraged me to synchronize the key elements to the unique rhythm of Stage Four.

Since I'd already expended all my energy (and voice), I had no idea how I could complete this exercise for the fourth time in a row, let alone reach 100 on Donny's magical scale of outright perfection. I really don't know how it happened, but a huge amount of energy began accumulating in my body as I increased the pace and depth of my nostril-to-nostril breathing, with the adept use of the forefinger and thumb on my right hand. Simultaneously, I used my left hand to twist that same spot near my collarbone to the left, because that was where I was most stuck. I then had to move my life-force energy and focus it exactly below my left hand—*and nowhere else.* I did not want my energy to be squandered on any other place on my body. *But this time, as I approached the unique rhythm of Stage Four, I was miraculously transported to another world.*

A little later, I would equate this "out-of-body" experience with what had taken place during my sessions of Holotropic Breathwork, when I began breathing faster and deeper. But now, instead of lying on a mattress in a gymnasium with my sitter by my side, I was lying on the floor in a ballroom with Donny by my side. *I am sure that my non-ordinary state of consciousness—from all that rapid nostril-to-nostril breathing—was exactly what enabled me to mobilize my energy and voice from another time and place.* How do I know this? At that SRI magical moment when I manifested the unique rhythm of Stage Four, I had access to much more energy than I had ever experienced previously. This surge of energy was surely sourced from another lifetime.

Just then, Donny asked me to scream out, as loud as I could: "I take my life back!" Just as I started to scream those exact words, two things happened: (1) A huge wave of energy, emanating from within my chest, with the eye of the wave directly over the spot where I had been stuck, rippled and radiated throughout the universe; and (2) I heard a voice come out of my mouth I'd never heard before: It had a deep resonance and an immense volume that vibrated everywhere. I felt some of those energy waves bounce off the four walls and tall ceiling in the large ballroom and then come back to greet me. I then collapsed in exhaustion. But this time my body continued to pulsate that same wave. It seemed as if I was experiencing the accumulative effects of a Holotropic trip, an NSA wave, and an SRI moment—all in one unified experience of time and space.

While my *non-ordinary* consciousness was swirling around the globe, my *ordinary* consciousness heard Donny ask me if I'd permit participants in the audience to touch my heart. Since my body-mind was embracing the universe at that time anyway, I naturally said yes. One participant after another then made his way to me to kneel by my side and touch my heart. I heard Donny's assessment: "His heart has turned to gel. It is pure energy. Do you feel that energy radiating from his body?"

In a little while, I regained my ordinary state of consciousness and looked up at Donny. His face was beaming from ear to ear. So I asked him: "Well, what number do I get for that one?" He didn't say a word, but his delightful laugh told me I had transcended numbers. *My Stage Four experience gave me a persuasive glimpse into a new way of being: connecting with people energetically and spiritually—and not just physically and psychologically.*

Since that demonstration of Stage Four took considerably more time than anyone had expected, Donny announced our lunch break: We were asked to meet back in the ballroom in ninety minutes. This gave everybody enough time to walk outside and enjoy one of the nearby restaurants. I went to lunch with a group of friends, including the woman who had introduced me to Network care: Rhonda. Once we were seated at a local restaurant, several participants came up to our table and asked me only one question: "Can I feel your heart?" I didn't know what to say, so I stood up, let that person feel my heart, and then gave him a hug. That must've happened five or six times in one hour. I didn't know what to make of this unusual event: I knew what *I'd* felt during that grueling SRI exercise, but I couldn't fathom how *other* participants had been affected by the waves of energy that had come out of my body.

After lunch, Rhonda and I took a short walk around the hotel. We had twenty minutes before the afternoon session would begin. I remember the exact place in the parking lot where she stopped and said: "I have a really bad headache. I might have to take some Advil to get rid of it, but I don't like to take any medication. I don't know what to do." I looked her straight in the eyes and these weird words made their way out of my mouth: "Do you want me to get rid of your headache?" She was as surprised as I was, upon hearing a new voice speak with such conviction. But right away, Rhonda said: "Yes. Please do whatever you can. My head is killing me!" Without thinking about anything, I intuitively placed my two hands on her head, as I entered into a non-ordinary state of consciousness.

In this out-of-body healing zone, I could feel Rhonda's energy flows and blockages. Using the chi inside my own body, I consciously channeled that energy through my two hands directly into her head. There our energies flowed and danced together—which then released her blockages. I cannot describe it any other way. (In the next year, I would learn how to channel my healing energy through Dr. Richard Bartlett's Matrix Energetics, Dr. Samuel Sagan's third-eye meditation, and my Ujjayi, throat-friction, nostril breathing in Ashtanga yoga.)

After just a few minutes of feeling different areas on Rhonda's head, I removed my hands. She had a puzzled look on her face. She next moved her head from side to side, rather slowly and cautiously. Not saying a word, she then quickly shook her head back and forth.

A few moments later, she declared the results: "I can't believe it! My headache is gone. How did you do that?" There wasn't much I could say: "I have no idea. Something happened all on its own." That day was Tuesday, September 7, 2004, and my life changed forever (which I didn't think could happen again, so soon after my accidental death on Interstate 405).

In October, I found my way to North Fork, California, where I participated in Vipassana meditation. *For ten days in a row*, I silently mediated from 4:30 in the morning to 9:30 in the evening. During this silent retreat, I had plenty of time to get further acquainted with the life force in my body and how it connects with universal energy. In one radical experiment, I took the energy of my right forefinger, put it into my body, and laid it directly against my spine. By moving my finger back and forth, I could feel the nice physical sensations of something rubbing gently on each consciously selected vertebra. In another daring moment, I took the energy of my right forefinger, put it through my right eye and then gently touched the visual cortex in the rear portion of my brain. Moving that finger here and there then created the most spectacular—psychedelic—light show I'd ever seen.

Vipassana meditation was an unexpected setting for practicing my conscious intentions to channel subtle energy, besides breaking patterns in my conditioned mind by transcending patterns into Pure Spirit. By the conclusion of that ten-day retreat, I fully accepted that my former intellectually driven life within a mostly numb body had evaporated for good.

19
Energy, Healing, and Soul

As mentioned previously, during the summer of 2003, I developed a harsh allergic reaction every time the sun shone directly on my skin: The itchiness and burning didn't occur on my face or arms, but only on those parts of my body that weren't usually exposed to sunlight. I first visited an allergist and then a dermatologist to learn what the medical community had to say about my condition. Independently, they agreed on the same diagnosis: I'd acquired skin photosensitivity or *solar urticaria*. Although there's no cure, there *is* a way to control it: "Stay out of the sun." That treatment plan was unacceptable to me.

Even though I tried all different kinds of sunscreens, including a variety of over-the-counter histamine blockers, nothing was able to prevent my skin from reacting to the sun. Every time I wore a bathing suit on the beach, it took about five to seven minutes before my skin turned red and I experienced sharp, burning pain. I therefore had to get out of the sun as soon as possible. It then took from thirty to sixty minutes for my allergic reaction to subside.

Since my medical community didn't have a workable solution for my solar urticaria, I began exploring other possibilities, including electro-homeopathy, turbocharged therapy, removing metal dental work, and chelation of heavy metals. After I'd tried each modality, I tested my skin's reaction to the sun: Nothing changed.

One of my yoga teachers recommended I see a chiropractor who practiced Neuro Emotional Technique (NET). In December 2004, I had that historic conference with Dr. Carol Anders. Using a series of yes/no questions with muscle testing, she identified the likely cause of my sun allergy: I hadn't "resolved" the relationship with my twin sister, Rose, who'd died while we were co-mingling in our mother's womb. Despite this novel diagnosis, however, my skin allergy was as bothersome as ever. So I asked myself: "Will I have to deal with this annoying ailment for the rest of my life? *How can I get rid of it?*"

In early January 2005, I attended a weeklong retreat in Mexico (an advanced mind/body/spirit exploration for sixty people) led by Dr. Donald Epstein. It was called: "Ultima." About fifty participants were NSA/SRI practitioners, while the rest were practice members.

During the seven-day program, each participant received twelve NSA sessions with Donny, about two per day. As the week progressed, we also went through the twelve stages of healing, also about two per day. In between these NSA and SRI sessions, Donny delivered several lectures on his latest theories about the five energy fields around the human body: life-force, emotional, mental, soul-based, and spiritual. I found it fascinating that these energy fields apparently overlap with what I had learned about the five sacred boundaries: physical, sexual, emotional, mental, and spiritual. There are only two exceptions: (1) the physical and sexual boundaries both comprise life-force energy and (2) the spiritual boundaries make up both the soul and spiritual energies. Never before had I considered the *substance* of those sacred boundaries. Yet it now seems obvious they'd consist of *subtle energy*, rather than anything material.

But the big revelation of Ultima was the underlying theme that tied together the sessions and lectures on energy fields: *knowing and living your soul's purpose.* During this weeklong program, participants were asked to describe, in one sentence, their reason for having been incarnated into a living form, review it with Donny and others (so it could be clearly described and additionally refined), and then recite their soul's purpose during the rest of their NSA sessions. Just as two identical tuning forks will vibrate to the same frequency whenever a mallet strikes only one of them, your energy fields become *entrained* to your life's mission when you proclaim your soul's purpose aloud, as somato-psychic waves move through your body.

What's the benefit of clearly knowing your soul's purpose and then having your body-mind, within its surrounding energy fields, entrained to your reason for having been born into form? Given my recent struggles to get rid of that sun allergy, I was further awakened by Donny's enlightened answer: *"All disease, illness, and discomfort— whether physical, sexual, emotional, mental, or spiritual—is actually caused by not living your daily life according to your soul's purpose."* Obviously, this perspective on health and wellness was in sharp contrast to my exposure to the medical establishment (and my dad's vocation) on the subject of pathology: Rather than some microbe (virus, bacteria, fungus, or parasite), a weakened digestive/immune system, or some other degenerative process afflicting your physical body, Donny was presenting a rather unconventional stance on the soul's primary role in creating—and healing—disease.

The Ultima retreat seeded a shift in my consciousness: *Perhaps my chronic sun allergy was a signal that I wasn't living my soul's purpose 24/7.* Instead of trying "to get rid of" my ailment, maybe I should be grateful that I was being given an opportunity to learn from my skin condition. As a result, my soul wouldn't have to manufacture a more serious signal (a debilitating disease) to get my undivided attention.

Most of the people in the Ultima program had already explored their soul's purpose during other such programs with Donny. Indeed, many of the NSA and SRI practitioners encouraged their back-home practice members to do the same kind of soul work. But this was the first time I attempted to discover and document my unique calling.

To speed up the process, I interviewed several practitioners to learn how they'd identified their soul's purpose. After a number of these interactions, it dawned on me that I could travel back in time and learn why I was created: By activating my third-eye chakra with throat-friction breathing (analogous to Ujjayi breathing in Ashtanga yoga), I intended to enter a non-ordinary state of consciousness so I could learn my destiny. My two soul-searching roommates, Michael and Peter, who had already been to several NSA retreats, suggested I build my soul's purpose around an archetype or metaphor, one that resonated with my body-mind. They gave me some useful examples: fearless warrior, gentle healer, nurturing angel, loving teacher, bright star, cosmic light, and courageous supporter.

Back in my room, I spent several hours in a non-ordinary state of consciousness. My first revelation was the spontaneous emergence of an old memory: On my tenth birthday, October 5, 1956, Cecil B. DeMille's masterpiece, *The Ten Commandments,* was released in movie theaters around the country. With my third eye entirely operational, I remembered seeing that movie more than ten times within a month of its debut. I then wondered why a ten-year-old boy would want to experience such a "religious" movie so many times, *all on his own.* As I pondered why I'd been so enthralled by this movie a half-century before, *I saw the burning bush.* That sight of God on Mt. Sinai stopped me in my tracks: "Who is God? Why did He speak to Moses? Will He speak to me? What does He want from me?" As I returned to a more ordinary state of consciousness, I remembered that this movie, *The Ten Commandments,* has remained my all-time favorite—because my first exposure to Pure Spirit began with the burning bush.

During a few meditations, I wrote several trial phrases for my soul's purpose. After revisions—based on conversations with Donny and others—I discovered the perfect combination of metaphor and phrase that fully resonated with my body: *I am the burning bush that joyfully ignites, lights, loves, and heals.*

In my remaining NSA sessions, I regularly exclaimed my soul's purpose aloud, while Donny aligned the energy fields surrounding my body with a variety of waves from my neck down to my tailbone. In between these NSA sessions, all of us were diligently progressing from Stage Eight to Stage Twelve of healing: the void of emptiness, the light behind the form, ascent to the light, descent into the self, and community. In essence, the higher stages of healing encourage you to realize your special gifts, as captured by your soul's purpose, so you can serve others on your journey to healing and wholeness.

When the Ultima retreat ended on the seventh day, we rested. Everyone there now had a much better idea of why we were created and what we had to do with our life—from this point onward. The closing mantra for the retreat, which didn't need to be spoken, was quite apparent to all: "Live your soul's purpose around the clock. If you do, you'll shine brightly! If you don't, you'll get sick!"

During the next few months, I continued to examine what my soul required of me and to make sure I was doing it very well. In the process, I had my first taste of astrology, when I had my natal (birth) chart analyzed by Avery in Laguna Beach. I purposely didn't tell him anything about me, so I could see what he'd reveal by knowing only my date of birth, October 5, 1946, my time of birth, 8:55 AM, and my place of birth, Manhattan, New York. Although I already knew I'm a Libra, I now learned I'm a Scorpio rising with my moon in Aquarius, and I also found out which houses my planets call home.

Avery then described my ideal occupation, based solely on my birth chart: a university professor who would integrate theories and methods by drawing upon the physical sciences, the social sciences, and the philosophy of science. He then described my likely research interests, which perfectly captured the ingredients of my most recent book. If, before my session, I'd given Avery my last name, I would've concluded he'd found my biographical information on the Internet and then, prior to our meeting, he had studied my publications. But that wasn't the case. As a result of this astrological analysis, I had to acknowledge that the position (and energetic vibrations) of the sun, moon, and planets at the precise moment of my birth had, in some mysterious manner, shaped my work life. But at fifty-eight years old, I was already retired from my university career. Consequently, I now wanted to know what astrology had to say about my soul's purpose for the next years of my life.

A few months later, I had the good fortune to have a *progressed chart* analyzed by Amber in Aliso Viejo. By computing a secondary progression for my age in the current year, she was able to pinpoint my special gifts *for the future*. Without knowing anything about me, other than my astrological facts, she predicted the following: "You're a spiritual teacher and an energy healer. You'll help people expand their consciousness. You will then write a book about what you have learned." Now looking back on that astrological prediction, it seems this book, *The Courageous Mosaic,* was never meant to be focused on me. From the beginning, it was intended to inspire—using my own story only as a case study—how *all human beings* can accelerate and deepen their awakening and journey to wholeness.

In the spring of 2005, I came across Dr. Mark Thurston's 1984 book: *Discovering Your Soul's Purpose.* In it, he suggests five common themes that most people express in their reason for being born: (1) an expansion of consciousness; (2) service to others; (3) closeness to God or Spirit; (4) a view of purposefulness in life; and (5) joy in life. Dr. Thurston suggests that a soul's purpose isn't choosing a vocation or hobby to manifest your talents. Rather, *it is a consciousness—a way of being—that you infuse in all aspects of your life.* When I reviewed my soul's purpose according to the five themes, I was pleased to see I'd already included them during my numerous meditations in Mexico: As a burning bush, I'd bring light, love, and healing—with joy—to everyone in my life.

The weeklong Ultima retreat, including my additional efforts to uncover the nature and meaning of my soul's purpose, radically transformed my old worldview. Indeed, I had to know: If aches and pains appear whenever you fail to live your soul's purpose, will the physical and emotional symptoms then disappear after you get back on track? *Wouldn't it be remarkable if living your soul's purpose were the ultimate treatment for healing all types of disease, disorders, and ailments, while, at the same time, enabling you to enjoy a long, happy, meaningful, and productive existence?*

In this piece of my mosaic, I'll present the crucial links among consciousness, energy, healing, and soul. I'll start by distinguishing two vastly different approaches to healing: diagnosing and treating (1) the physical body and (2) the energy body. After focusing on the oft-neglected energy body, I will then consider how the seven major chakras along a person's central nervous system are the key avenues for channeling energy—and healing the body-mind. This emphasis on the energy body will also include the Tantric concept of *Kundalini Shakti:* gathering energy in the base of the spine and then moving it to the higher chakras (thus, not releasing it through the lower ones), so a person can live his life from a higher level of consciousness.

Next, I'll examine the ongoing struggle between your ego and your soul for the truth: *What dedicated path is in your best interests?* To answer this far-reaching question, you must remember this principle: The conflict modes you use for negotiating the truth (maintaining, conceding, combining, isolating, or synergizing) will determine what resolution you'll achieve and, therefore, what path you'll follow.

Finally, by combining a homeopathic concept from Germany with an Ayurvedic interpretation from India, I will suggest how three varieties of chronic disease—a Psoric miasm, a Sycotic miasm, and a Syphilitic miasm—are the three strategic signals from your soul to your ego that boldly exclaim: *"You're not living your soul's purpose. Get back on track—or your health will deteriorate in predictable ways."*

Let's first consider the *physical body* versus the *energy body*, which define two different approaches for healing disease, awakening, and becoming whole. Regarding the physical approach, conventional—Western—medical practice views physical symptoms as having been caused by physical things that can be diagnosed by various physical devices (for example, thermometer, blood pressure meter, x-ray, MRI, CAT scans, blood-work equipment, ultrasound, electrocardiograph, and electroencephalograph). Once the biochemical—mechanical—

physical form is given some disease label, a physical treatment plan is recommended: medication (to activate, block, fool, or bypass the biochemical functioning of the physical body) or surgery (to repair or remove the defective or diseased part of the physical body). Some more drastic measures include chemotherapy, radiation therapy, and organ transplants. Regardless of the diagnosis, *a physical intervention is made on the physical body.*

As has become obvious to many scholars, the physical approach to healing is based on seventeenth-century science (Newtonian physics and Cartesian philosophy), whereby the various pieces and parts of the universe are physical objects with no soul. All the systems in the universe (including human beings) are considered as a mechanical arrangement of moving parts: If the system doesn't work properly, a part must be fixed, replaced, or removed. With this Western medical approach to healing, even emotional and mental distress are treated with synthetic chemicals that are intended to alter the neurological parts, pieces, and processes in the brain. Thus, psychiatric disorders (including sexual, emotional, mental, and spiritual) are addressed as physical problems—not as challenges to the soul.

But several thousands of years before the development of the physical approach to healing, the *energy* approach gradually evolved from Eastern philosophies and practices (notably Ayurvedic, Tantric, and Chinese traditions). Strange as it seems, these ancient practices are aligned with twentieth-century science (quantum mechanics and Einstein's general theory of relativity). In fact, the transmutation of gross energy—and subtle energy—into matter explains not only the beginning and evolution of the universe, but also the creation and unfolding of life itself.

With respect to the energy approach, every person is viewed as having seven major chakras alongside his central nervous system. As noted in a prior discussion, each chakra can mobilize, channel, and spin a person's life-force energy. Specifically, the lower chakras (root, genital, and solar plexus) embody the ego-protective frequencies of shame, guilt, apathy, grief, fear, desire, anger, and pride—*which then deplete energy by blindly recreating dysfunctional patterns.* But the higher chakras (heart, throat, third-eye, and crown) radiate the spirit-based energies of courage, neutrality, willingness, acceptance, reason, love, joy, peace, and enlightenment, *which then enhance energy by breaking and transcending old patterns.* Just as the chakra system mobilizes and uses energy on the inside, every person also radiates an energy field on the outside: physical, sexual, emotional, mental, and spiritual.

Instead of seeing only physical causes for physical ailments in a physical body, the energy approach views all disease, distress, and discomfort, as deriving from (1) depleted or deflected energy in your internal chakras and (2) diminished energy in your external fields—both of which make it much more difficult for you to live your soul's purpose. Energy balancing modalities—using either natural crystals or Pulsor crystals—can diagnose, redirect, and align the spin of each chakra along your central nervous system as well as harmonize your inner chakra system with your outer energy fields. (For an integrated discussion about the evolution of the physical body and the energy body, see Dr. Amit Goswami's excellent book: *The Quantum Doctor: A Physicist's Guide to Health and Healing.*)

During my healing experience with Donny in September 2004, I learned to channel my life-force energy up my body—by using my breath, muscles, and intentions to move my chi toward an area near my collarbone, while I touched the same spot with the fingers of my left hand. That spot was *physically* stuck (because of rigid connective tissue), which meant I was *energetically* stuck. Said differently, I moved the available life-force energy from my root, genital, and solar plexus chakras to a stuck vortex somewhere between my heart chakra and throat chakra. In this process of first mobilizing and then releasing the life-force energy through that stuck spot, I reclaimed my power: *my will to serve my soul's purpose.*

Some Eastern traditions speak of this same healing experience as building up the serpent-like energy, Kundalini Shakti, in the lower chakras, but not enabling it to escape or radiate at a lower level of consciousness. Instead, that gathered energy is kept in the body and moved up the spine, until the buildup of energy arrives at one of the higher chakras. When Kundalini Shakti is freed via the heart, throat, third-eye, or crown chakra, your life-force energy radiates outward—at a higher level of consciousness. This process of building and then releasing Kundalini Shakti is the divine—feminine—manifestation of *love and violence*, which is the same love and violence that creates universes, gives birth to all beings, and resolves relationships.

Whether using the language of SRI (rhythmically progressing through the twelve stages of healing) or the language of the Eastern traditions (releasing Kundalini Shakti through the higher chakras), the intention behind the containment, movement, and expression of energy is identical: *becoming aware of your mind/body/spirit and then radiating your energy at a higher level of consciousness.* In so doing, you are more likely to discover your soul's purpose—and live it.

But if your life-force energy remains in your lower chakras and cycles through the lower stages of healing (suffering, polarities, and being stuck), you will probably experience aches, pain, distress, and disease. Why? *Your soul is here to evolve, become awake, connect with its source, and achieve its purpose.* But if you choose to ignore its strategic signals that you're wasting vital energy on the wrong pursuits (such as your self-serving needs or some other tempting addictions), your body will eventually receive a devastating message: *Deconstruct your biochemical systems and cells, so your matter and energy can be used more effectively for some other being, at some other time.*

Making use of the varieties of resolution I explained in a prior piece of my mosaic, instead of negotiating truth with someone else, however, *imagine your soul negotiating truth with your ego.* (Please note: When I speak of *your* soul and *your* ego, the "you" is consciousness—Pure Spirit—that transcends and includes all aspects of your being and existence, including your body-mind, ego, and soul.) Consider the case when your ego *maintains* its view that you should recreate your patterns (since that is safe and familiar). Meanwhile, your soul *maintains* its view that you should pursue your destiny (since that is your prime reason for being alive). This life-altering polarity resides on the distributive dimension, a zone where your ego and soul agree to disagree about what's in your best interests (combining/neutral). Unfortunately, with such a superficial, simplistic solution, your ego and soul will remain in a deadlock with one another, without much hope for a genuine resolution.

Now consider the two extremes on the distributive dimension: If your ego wins the argument, your soul loses. You will thus remain off course and experience distress and disease. But if your soul wins the argument, your ego loses. You'll now lose your need to acquire what your mind desires. Being on the distributive dimension means your ego is likely suffering from wounded boundaries, disconnected left/right mini-brains, physical tension, a frozen spine, and an acidic body. As such, *since your body-mind isn't ready to break and transcend its patterns, your ego will find creative ways to undermine your soul.*

Undoubtedly, the worst-case scenario is when your ego *isolates* itself from your soul, which switches the negotiation for truth to the protective dimension. Such a split between your ego and soul (based on fear or spite) will lead to a spiritual emergency, mental anguish, emotional distress, sexual dysfunctions, and physical degeneration. This rather unhealthy state of affairs often stems from keeping your life-force energy trapped in the lower chakras. Focusing on survival and self-protection will surely dominate your time and effort. Sadly, when the soul is prevented from navigating the course of your life, your body-mind loses its will to live.

But a best-case scenario can be realized once you have reached a critical threshold of mind/body/spirit consciousness—so you can radiate your life-force energy through a higher chakra. Under these circumstances, your ego and soul can approach their differences by using *synergy* on the integrative dimension: to find a creative way to coexist in your body-mind for the best of both worlds. As your soul experiences fulfillment in how you use your focus and energy, your ego will find gratification by satisfying its needs and desires. Such a win-win resolution further expands your consciousness—since your ego and soul can jointly create a new journey for living in service of Spirit. Indeed, *only a synergistic approach for negotiating truth between ego and soul will enable you to become whole in this lifetime—so you can radiate positive energies and emotions where you live, work, or visit.* Any other approach to resolve the life-altering polarity between ego and soul (via maintaining, conceding, combining, and/or isolating) will block your path and erode your vitality.

Let's explore this basic question about negotiating Truth: What are your soul's and ego's differing stories about why you were born? *Because a soul never loses contact with Spirit, it always speaks the Truth.* But is the ego listening? Most often, it is the ego that gets attached to patterns, thoughts, and things—and then no longer realizes that it's fooled itself into believing it actually knows who you are. The ego's worst self-deception might be named the *Ultimate Lie:* "I know my soul's purpose and I'm already living it." Maybe the most insidious version of the Ultimate Lie is whenever the ego exclaims: "I have no soul!" And yet, without having devoted substantial time and energy to mind/body/spirit consciousness, it's unlikely that a person knows the difference between his ego and his soul. As for me, even after I had benefitted so much from therapy, breathwork, meditation, and several other modalities, I still hadn't devoted any time and energy on exploring my soul's purpose. Once I was exposed to this valuable quest, however, it didn't take much time to discover why I was born, because I had already established the vital threshold of mind/body/spirit consciousness.

But beware: If your ego has succeeded in dominating your life despite your soul's warnings (with one symptom picture or another), and has been doing that for a long time, it won't be easy for you (or someone else) to challenge the Ultimate Lie. After a while, your ego has so much invested in running "the ship" that it'll fight to the end to stay in control of your life. In particular, your ego will defend its navigation plan (which includes recreating old patterns) by one of these defensive strategies: (1) denial, delusion, or distortion of the classic conflict between your ego and soul; (2) splitting, projecting, and attacking your soul's wishes (and warnings) on another person; (3) rationalizing or intellectualizing that your ego truly knows what is best for you, by using an elaborate justification for your life's work or your last romantic relationship; or (4) repressing or suppressing the ego/soul conflict, so it goes away and leaves you alone.

Maybe the overriding obstacle to surfacing the ego/soul battle for your life's mission is the pain of shame: After years of living the Ultimate Lie, a person might experience shame that he's been living so many years off course, in direct opposition to his inner calling. It may be this brief exposure to shame, in fact, that creates a defensive reaction to the ego/soul dilemma—rather than pushing through the pain to live a soul-focused life for the remaining time. Recall: Shame vibrates at the lowest frequency on David Hawkins' scale of human consciousness. Perhaps that's why so many people, who haven't been able (or willing) to expand their consciousness, continue to let their ego run their life, while keeping their soul's purpose fully repressed in their unconscious mind. Sometimes, it takes a severe health crisis (with a real threat of a devastating or terminal illness), before people consider whether their intimate relationships or vocational choices have worn their body down. But it also takes a huge dose of *courage* (which resides at a much higher frequency than shame) for anyone to overcome his self-loathing and confront the Ultimate Lie.

As mentioned before, however, if the diseased-labeled person has been indoctrinated into a mindset that physical symptoms are generated by physical causes, she'll select a health-care practitioner who affirms this view, and will then use physical-based modalities (as in medication, chemotherapy, or surgery) to suppress, eradicate, or remove the disease. While these treatment plans can temporarily remove the symptoms of your dis-ease, the root cause remains: *Your life is off course.* Indeed, it will only be a matter of time before other signals—physical and emotional illnesses—will appear.

But it's also possible that a health crisis could propel a person to search for alternative approaches for healing. In desperation, in fact, she might choose a practitioner who'll see that same symptom picture as based on a misaligned and depleted body of energy. With the latter diagnosis, a completely different treatment plan would be recommended: (1) bringing to light her recreated unhappy patterns and resolving wounded boundaries that continue to overwhelm her ego's best intentions; (2) establishing an alkaline body with a mostly green diet; (3) detoxing heavy metals, anesthesia, parasites, viruses, bad bacteria, and an overgrowth of yeast; (4) removing the tension patterns that hamper the flow of energy/information in her central nervous system and throughout her physical body; (5) harmonizing the two hemispheres in her brain, so she'll experience bliss, joy, and stillness; (6) moving her Kundalini Shakti along the higher chakras, so she will radiate the higher energies of human consciousness; and (7) discovering her soul's purpose and then aligning her beliefs and actions to manifest that reason for being, which could lead to radical changes in her personal and vocational life.

While some of these energy-based treatments are attending to the physical body, they are intended to establish a well-functioning infrastructure, so the life-force energy—and its divine purpose—can gather and release at will. The modalities listed above *aren't* intended to numb or remove parts of the physical form, which is the case with medication and surgery. Instead, the energy approach makes use of several body-based modalities *to heighten the physical sensations in the body.* In so doing, the soul is freer to express itself—and can then be heard by the ego.

As with most complex endeavors, however, you do not have to choose the energy body over the physical body, or vice versa: It's not an either/or choice. *Both* approaches can be used together (especially for acute traumas, including broken bones and flesh wounds). And some of the physical remedies can buy some time before the energy remedies can produce their beneficial effects, since it doesn't take as long to administer the physical-based treatments (prescribing drugs, resetting bones, or suturing skin) as it does to develop higher levels of mind/body/spirit consciousness and live your soul's purpose. But if using any medication overly numbs the body and dulls the mind, this could inadvertently undermine a person's efforts to expand his consciousness and align his life-force energy with his divine calling. Typically, intense or prolonged pain (as instigated by the soul's plea for attention) is essential to initiate a dedicated journey that honors Pure Spirit.

In Dr. Donald Bakal's comprehensive book, published in 1999, *Minding the Body: Clinical Uses of Somatic Awareness,* he exposed the limited mindset for treating chronic disease in a physical body. He noted that thousands of people have been able to maintain a healthy life long after they'd been diagnosed with terminal cancer and were given a grim prognosis of only a few months to live. Such prolonged survival is labeled a *spontaneous remission,* since there is no physical explanation for a dramatic reversal from a terminal illness. Indeed, the medical community tends to view any such case of spontaneous remission as a fluke: It just doesn't fit with a physical process in a physical body. But Dr. Bakal detected a common theme among all those patients who had defied the poor odds: These "terminally ill" patients had become aware of their core values, their soul's purpose, and then made radical changes in their daily life. Receiving a death sentence apparently shattered their ego's dominance over their soul, which then allowed a synergistic strategy that dramatically changed how they used their energy. *What is labeled as a spontaneous remission in a physical body becomes a highly plausible outcome in an energy body.*

A German physician, Dr. Samuel Hahnemann (1755–1843), is credited with having created homeopathy—in which like cures like. Hahnemann began studying chronic disease when the symptoms of many patients still returned, even after they'd received homeopathic treatment for their acute illness. To rectify this unacceptable result, he developed a new theory about the types of symptoms that linger or return. In his classic 1828 book, *The Chronic Diseases*, Hahnemann defined three *miasms*, referring to a polluted or noxious atmosphere: (1) *Psoric*—a miasm of deficiency or underproduction, often revealed by a nagging condition that erupts on the surface of the body, as in itchy or irritating skin; (2) *Sycotic*—a miasm of excess or some kind of overproduction, often affecting the passageways in and out of the body, often showing up as excessive drainage of mucus membranes; and (3) *Syphilitic*—a miasm of self-destruction, often destroying the tissues and processes inside the body, including the degeneration of vital organs and the collapse of the immune system.

The first miasm, Psoric, while annoying, its symptoms are not devastating. The second miasm, Sycotic, is much more troublesome, since it affects what goes in and out of the body, such as absorbing nutrients and discharging toxins. The third miasm, Syphilitic, is the most problematic, since it can result in death, as the body begins to decay—and then self-destructs. Although Hahnemann believed that miasms are delivered from one generation to the next via bioenergy fields, many homeopaths have continued to debate why the miasms appear and how the three types of chronic disease can be remedied. (Note: Additional miasms have been proposed during the past two hundred years since Dr. Hahnemann's time, including *Tuberculinum*, a miasm of restriction, and *Carcinosin*, a miasm of suppression. But the original three miasms are sufficient for our discussion.)

Dr. Rudolph Ballentine, a respected expert in psychiatry, yoga, meditation, homeopathy, and Ayurvedic medicine, has made a vital connection between the chronic miasms and the soul's purpose. In a 1999 book, *Radical Healing: Integrating the World's Great Therapeutic Traditions to Create a New Transformative Medicine*, Dr. Ballentine gives three corresponding reasons for the appearance of the three chronic miasms: (1) The Psoric miasm appears when your ego wishes to be doing something else, besides living your soul's purpose. While you continue to stay on course, you energy is nevertheless distracted by desiring (and thinking about) activities that are not relevant to your calling. The result? You might suddenly experience a skin condition that generates itchy, irritating, or burning sensations. (2) The Sycotic miasm slowly appears after you've proceeded to act on your wishes, by spending your divine energy and time on doing something other than pursuing your soul's purpose. Although you're fully aware your activities are off track, you continue anyway, whether it's working at a job that pays well but doesn't serve your soul or not resolving those relationships that would heal your wounded boundaries, strengthen your selfhood, and then gift you with more energy to service others. The outcome? You'll develop a disease that bypasses your skin and targets the passageways—the mucus membranes—in your body. (3) The Syphilitic miasm manifests its self-destructive process once you have been living off course for so long that you no longer remember your soul's purpose. You've lost your rudder, your compass, and your reason for navigating your ship. In this case, your soul—making use of both love and violence—might dismantle your prized vessel and then salvage its parts for others.

In terms of the varieties of resolution, when your ego and soul are joined on the *integrative dimension,* but occasional daydreams or senseless regrets distract your ego from its agreed-upon mission with your soul, you'll likely manifest a Psoric miasm. Even worse, if your ego and soul are having their battle on the *distributive dimension* and the negotiation is stuck on polarizing your needs and passions, you'll likely experience a Sycotic miasm. Worst of all, however, if your ego and soul are alienated from one another on the *protective dimension,* and shame and denial keep you oblivious to the Ultimate Lie, you'll likely suffer a Syphilitic miasm, which will destroy your body.

But to literally save you from yourself, your soul will do its best to get your ego's attention, by infesting your body's vulnerabilities with a disease process. Regarding the Psoric miasm, your soul's wake-up call might appear as scabies, itchy skin, dry skin, or *solar urticaria.* For the Sycotic miasm, your soul might let you know of its dissatisfaction with your dysfunctional relationships, off-course vocation, mindless hobbies, harmful addictions, or environmentally harmful consumption and investment decisions, by gifting you with some breathing disorder, digestive problems, elimination problems (constipation or diarrhea), diabetes, or sinus infections. But for the Syphilitic miasm, your soul's last-ditch efforts to grab your ego's attention will probably result in a major health crisis, by gifting you with ulcers, carcinomas, cardiac attacks, gangrene, depression, or autoimmune diseases.

As discussed before, if you're inclined to see yourself primarily as a *physical body*, where physical symptoms can only be remedied by physical solutions (medication or surgery), you are prone to enlist a practitioner's help in cutting off—literally—your soul's messages to your ego. In sharp distinction, if you view yourself as an *energy body*, where the identical physical symptoms can be handled by applying various energy approaches (NSA and SRI, chakra balancing, crystal therapy, homeopathy, and acupuncture), you're more likely to work with a practitioner who will honor your soul's purpose: *What's good for your soul is good for your body.*

If Dr. Hahnemann were alive today, he would surely diagnose my chronic allergic reaction to the sun as a Psoric miasm. Although Dr. Ballentine would acknowledge I've paid attention to my soul by switching from academic research to expanding consciousness, he'd probably ask me if I was still involved with (or even thinking about) my previous interests—which might be squandering my energy and diverting my mission. Based on this self-assessment, by May 2005, I doubled my efforts to stay on course: (1) I decided I'd no longer get involved in research projects or consulting contracts that would be based on my previous career; (2) I would only attend workshops on consciousness, energy, healing, and soul; (3) I would do my best to acknowledge the radical shift in my life, and stop worrying if I would develop any regrets in the future from having abandoned a tenured professorship for the risky life of a burning bush; and (4) I wouldn't get involved in unhappy and energy-draining relationships, whether platonic or romantic.

By early June 2005, I was looking forward to going on my next NSA journey, once again in Mexico, and just a few weeks away. This four-day retreat, "Healing in Paradise," would include NSA sessions for about fifty participants. Again led by Donny, we would continue exploring our soul's purpose and experiencing our energy fields. But this time, I wanted to thoroughly enjoy the sunny beach in Mexico, without having to remain fully clothed (or having to sit on a lounge chair with towels wrapped all around me). But the big question to myself: "How can I heal my allergy?" I'd already received my soul's message and transformed my daily life. But my *solar urticaria* was as chronic as before. (And I could no longer accept that I had to endure such discomfort in the sun—because I now was a "burning bush.") Even though I'd stopped taking antihistamines in hopes of getting rid of the burning sensation on my skin, I began wondering if some other approach might reduce my painful reaction to the sun's rays— *without eliminating the divine communication that had been established between my soul and my ego.*

Just two weeks before that June retreat in Mexico, I decided to use a synergistic solution to integrate my ego and soul for their joint mission: My soul was asking me to be a burning bush, while my ego was still partially stuck on being a university professor. Poetically, in a reply to my soul's message to my ego, "feel the solar urticaria," my ego sent a response back to my soul: "Please pay attention: I'm about to use divine energy, based on *your* divine calling, to heal myself."

I went to the local swimming pool, put on my bathing suit, and laid down on a lounge chair in the bright, noontime, California sun. Typically, my skin would react to this exposure in five minutes. But I immediately closed my eyes, focused on my third-eye consciousness, and began breathing deeply through both nostrils—making a sound, as I pushed air passed my slightly constricted throat. In a short time, I entered a non-ordinary state of consciousness. With a deep inhale,

I mobilized my life-force energy, moved it up my spine into my third eye. From there, I slowly exhaled and sent my energy outward—as a wide spiral of cascading radiance and then had it return and blanket my whole body with a self-soothing embrace. On my next inhale, I again mobilized my Kundalini Shakti, sent it up my spine and, on a prolonged exhale, I sent it out of my third eye on a return voyage to my receptive body. I must've repeated this inward-and-outward flow of healing energy for about five minutes. That was when I began to feel that familiar burning sensation on my skin.

Typically, at the first sign of this symptom picture, I would have stood up in frustration, quickly grabbed my clothes, and gone to the locker room to get dressed—having again failed to heal my allergy with another promising modality. But this time, I continued to cycle healing energy—inside and outside my body. I said this affirmation in silence, repeatedly: "Expel the negative energy in my body; receive the loving energy of the sun." During this process, I felt the burning sensations on my skin stabilize. As I continued this ongoing cycle of breath, energy, and affirmation, the sensations on my skin began to fade. My best guess is that it took me thirty minutes to neutralize my reaction to the sun, using this self-administered healing process.

After I returned to an ordinary state of consciousness, I opened my eyes and examined my body: There was no indication of redness or burning and I had no need to get out of the sun. I remained on the lounge chair for another ten minutes—in total disbelief and awe of what had just happened. It was apparent that healing energy can be focused on yourself as well as others. Gleefully, my ego then sent this transmission to my soul: "I got your earlier message. Obviously, you got mine."

Before I got out of the sun—because I *wanted* to, not because I had to—I prayed to God: "If I should ever long for doing something that doesn't suit my soul, let my skin itch and burn from the sun. Let me never make decisions or take actions that'll put me on the wrong path—away from my soul's divine purpose. And let me never forget why I was born, who I am, and what I'm here to do."

During the June retreat, I enjoyed the sun, beach, and ocean in Mexico. I continued to explore the meaning and purpose of my soul, which, during seven NSA sessions, was joyfully entrained to the gross and subtle waves along my spine. As expected, I became more aware of the life-force energy that flows in my body and how my third-eye consciousness could move it to any internal chakra or external field. By the end of "Healing in Paradise," I'd not only learned more about the relationship between energy and healing, but I also felt extreme gratitude that my soul would always know what was best for me. All my ego had to do was listen—and then respond synergistically.

20

Society, Systems, and Souls

Because I learned so much from the "Ultima" retreat in January 2005 and the "Healing in Paradise" follow-up in June, I returned to Mexico in late July for another weeklong, NSA/SRI program: "Ultima II."

Again I must declare: I feel exceedingly privileged that I've been able to invest so much time and thousands of dollars on expanding my consciousness through one program, retreat, and modality after another. Indeed, I feel compelled to ask these moral questions: How can humankind ever hope to resolve its most devastating challenges (war, violence, hatred, poverty, hunger, disease, hopelessness, and the destruction of our Mother Earth), when so many people do not have the resources to examine their lives and expand their consciousness? Further, since our most complex problems are deeply embedded in our social systems, how can we also bring greater consciousness into organizations and institutions?

For decades, I researched, taught, and consulted on improving the *efficiency, effectiveness, and adaptability of large organizations.* When people used to inquire why I spent my time with organizations, I'd present my perspective: Our society functions through organizations (families; communities; religious organizations; schools; hospitals; businesses; financial service institutions; and our national, state, and local governments). Designing, managing, and then improving these social systems is precisely what distinguishes human evolution from animal evolution. For humans, *organizational evolution* (the survival of the most effective systems for overcoming our human limitations) has replaced *biological evolution* (the survival of the most physically fit individuals who pass their genes to the next generation). In the long run, *those societies that are best at expanding consciousness through their organizations and institutions will awaken people around the globe—which will enable all species to survive and thrive.*

Due to their communication, specialization, coordination, and cooperation, organizations make possible what individuals cannot achieve on their own. That's why I'm still surprised that virtually all mind/body/spirit modalities are primarily intended for *individuals.* Either a solo person visits a practitioner's office or attends a healing retreat on his own or, in only a few cases, with his significant other. But rarely would an entire family be present during a consciousness retreat. And I never saw an entire department from an organization attend a retreat as one unit—so all members could later apply in the workplace what they'd learn from expanding their mind/body/spirit consciousness.

I experienced the same problem with consciousness retreats as I did with management programs, which I have playfully designated the *three-day, washout effect:* After only three days back on the job (or back at home), it's as if the retreat never happened. Instead, it's back to business as usual—enacting the same old behavior, based on the same old patterns, with no relief in sight. Unless members of society are encouraged to first expand and then use their mind/body/spirit consciousness in the workplace, society will thwart its citizens from seeing themselves as Pure Spirit and living their soul's purpose.

In this piece, I'll first discuss the mysterious interplay between soul and Spirit by imagining a wave in an ocean: Just as a particular wave is an expression of the entire ocean (but not separate from it), the soul is an incarnation of Spirit. With this useful metaphor, I will consider how people become the mirror for Spirit to see itself evolve.

This divine impulse to evolve is the primary reason to accelerate—and deepen—everyone's journey to awakening. I'll then consider the relative power of organizations over individuals for bringing about a revolution in consciousness and then spreading this awakening to everyone. Rather than bemoaning the fact that many organizations (from our families to the United Nations) have never been designed to expand consciousness, I'll discuss what changes in organizations (such as public schools, religious organizations, health-care systems, and workplaces) will allow a wide-scale awakening. From organized change efforts, all people—not just a privileged few—will be able to enjoy a healthy, happy, and meaningful life as society, systems, and souls align with Spirit.

Regarding the relationship between Spirit and soul, I affirm an Eastern philosophy: I believe the number of souls in the universe is as infinite as the number of waves in the ocean. Furthermore, just as each wave will never again be the same as it was before, each soul is also unique: It will never again be the same reflection of Spirit. Thus, each soul does not stay intact in the ongoing process of incarnating into form, returning to Spirit, reincarnating into another form, and so forth. For instance, I don't believe a soul travels through time and gets one new body-mind after another, with the same, identical soul. Rather, each reincarnated soul carries the experiences of all previous souls that ever existed in human form. How does this happen? Each soul first returns back to that undifferentiated ocean of Spirit—where it assimilates the life experiences of all the other waves/souls before it becomes part of a new incarnation of Spirit in some other body. In a similar way, a soul in one lifetime can be diffused into many souls in subsequent lifetimes. Moreover, since past, present, and future all mingle together in the ocean of Spirit, souls also have easy access to knowing everything that ever was—and everything that will be.

As I learned during my experiences in Holotropic Breathwork, anyone can have transpersonal journeys with distant ancestors, past lives, and cosmic entities. *Indeed, I believe the eternal interplay between*

Spirit and soul, as the wave expresses the ocean and the ocean experiences the wave, creates our holographic universe. Thus, rather than searching largely for *physical forces* to explain the evolution of the universe and life, I believe the continuous ocean/wave interactions of Spirit/soul, *spiritual forces,* help explain the evolution of consciousness and the union with Spirit. The material universe and the physical body are only the incidental—illusionary—venues for awakening: The actual substance of life, ironically, takes place in the spiritual universe and in the energy body.

I believe the process by which souls become aware of Spirit is the only way Spirit evolves. While we may define Spirit as static and absolute, I define Spirit as *dynamic:* The wrathful, semi-present God in the Old Testament, for example, slowly evolved into the loving, omnipresent God in the New Testament. As God witnesses himself through the experience of all souls, whom He created exclusively for that purpose, He enhances pure consciousness.

Spirit thus creates forms to see itself evolve—and perhaps that explains the mysterious duality between what's really real and what's artificial (as I first discovered on the I-405). There's no other reason for the reality—or the illusion—of the material universe. It's in Spirit's best interest, therefore, to accelerate and deepen each soul's journey to awakening. Moreover, the more souls that evolve to see Spirit, the more the ocean of Spirit absorbs these journeys, which then enables new waves (with the inclusion of previous souls) to experience their life with much greater depth. When these deeper waves of spiritual experience later return to the ocean, *the evolution of Spirit accelerates.* I believe that any mind/body/spirit modality—*or organization*—that accelerates this evolutionary process for all souls in the universe thus honors Spirit. But any method—*or organization*—that blocks or slows down the advance of evolution dishonors Spirit. Essentially, *the more that society, systems, and souls (which define the integral universe of "we," "its," and "I") pursue their divine purpose, the more that Spirit fulfills the impulse to see itself evolve.*

Let's revisit the question I posed at the start of this piec⸱
mosaic: What can be done to give everyone a greater opportₗ
expand her consciousness in this lifetime—no longer relying on an
individual's privileged status (money, time, or flexibility) to pursue
her destiny? The evolving answer is along these lines: Organizations
must empower and encourage its members to discover—and live—
their soul's purpose, which ultimately fulfills Spirit's impulse.

I recall an unpublished experiment that revealed the immense
power of the organization—its systems—over its members: College
students were randomly assigned to one of two vastly different kinds
of organization: a pyramid and a circle. In the *pyramid organization,*
fifteen students had to work on a number of mundane tasks. Within
a hierarchical structure, the many students at the bottom could only
ask questions and receive answers by going through a boss, who then
had to communicate with his boss, and so on. When the one student
at the top of the pyramid received a question through this chain of
command, he'd then make an *autocratic* decision and communicate
it through the same chain of bosses to the workers below. For every
question, in fact, the students had no choice but to accept the rules,
procedures, jobs, and bosses in their pyramid organization.

But another fifteen students had been randomly assigned to a
circle organization. Sitting in a big circle without any pre-established—
bureaucratic—procedures, they could accomplish the same tasks by
talking to whomever they pleased, at any time, without having to go
through a slew of bosses: Everyone in the circle was fully involved in
making *democratic* decisions on their most crucial topics. But if these
students *wanted* to design specialized jobs and/or specific procedures,
they could do that, which is referred to as *self-designing systems.* And if
these students *also wanted* to design coordinating mechanisms among
their specialized jobs, they were free to do so, which is referred to as
self-managing systems.

After having completed a few rounds of work, one member in
the circle organization was switched with a member in the pyramid

organization. Fourteen of the fifteen members in each organization still knew their system, while that new member only knew how the *other* organization got things done. After a few more rounds of work, however, the two new students had learned the new system, with the help of the fourteen other students in their assigned organization. In fact, this procedure for assimilating the culture, "how things are done around here," is pretty much the same whenever new people join an established organization, and then learn "the rules of the road" from the more experienced members.

A little while later, another two "originally assigned" students (who had participated in the same organization from the start) were asked to switch to the other organization. Again, it didn't take long for the switched students to learn the culture and procedures in their new system. The same process then continued: switching two of the original students, proceeding with additional cycles of work (so the switched students could learn what was required of them in the new system), then switching two more of the original students, and so it continued. Eventually, *all fifteen students who were initially assigned to the pyramid organization were working in the circle organization, and all fifteen students who were initially assigned to the circle organization were now working in the pyramid organization.*

It was the *system* that predicted how the students functioned in their organization—regardless of their prior experience, personality style, or work preference: One at a time, pairs of switched students easily learned the autocratic or the democratic process of their newly assigned system. Even if those students who'd been initially assigned to the circle preferred that free-flowing, decision-making process, once they were switched to the pyramid, they quickly learned and adapted the more regimented way of working together. And if those students who were initially assigned to the pyramid preferred such a top-down, decision-making process, once they were switched, they learned how to function within the loosely structured, circle organization. By the way, if there'd been only two or three members in each organization, it would have been natural for these few students to discuss whether they wanted to redesign their structure—on their own. But once there were at least eight to ten members involved in each organization, as a critical mass for ensuring cultural indoctrination, the new students accepted the system and followed its procedures.

It is worth emphasizing: The pyramid and circle organizations both remained fully in tact—even though each was entirely replaced by new employees who had previously experienced a very different system of work. Therefore, an organization can survive its founding members—and their particular gene pool—as long as it adapts to a changing environment. Meanwhile, *an organization's systems (how they are designed and managed) will significantly influence the daily lives of its current members.*

Yet it's so natural to blame separate individuals—not systems— whenever something goes wrong: If someone is asked to define the root cause of a complex problem, at least eighty percent of the time he'll point to an individual: *"He* made that decision. *She* didn't keep her promise. *He* dropped the ball." Since individuals have physical form, it is so easy to use our ordinary senses to see them, hear them, touch them, and smell them. *But how do you focus your five senses on a system?* You can't! A system is a configuration of department goals, group structures, work processes, reward systems, cultural norms, past decisions, and unresolved conflicts, within which individuals make decisions and take action. A system is between the lines, behind the scenes, below the surface, and between/among the people. In a sense, *the difference between a person and a system is like the difference between a physical body and an energy body.* In each case, the former is tangible while the latter is subtle. But research has consistently demonstrated that the root cause of a complex problem is eighty percent the subtle system and only twenty percent the tangible person, even though, as noted, most people routinely implicate individuals, not systems.

Perhaps it's now easy to see how a subtle system is flourishing whenever participants return from consciousness retreats: A new way of being may not be accepted by those back home (whether family members or work associates), because they are deeply embedded in their pyramid systems. Indeed, these *other* members (similar to what happened in the experiment) may expect the returning members to surrender to the cultural norms and practices of their organization (which creates the three-day, washout effect). Those returning home from consciousness retreats may soon learn not to openly share their experiences with others—which certainly makes it more difficult to break old habits and practice new patterns of behavior.

Frequently, the returning participants are badly ridiculed if they share what others judge as being "crazy" or "bizarre." In fact, on the last day of the weeklong retreat on Holotropic Breathwork, Dr. Grof cautioned us not to discuss our consciousness journeys with family members or work associates, for at least a week later. Otherwise, our abundant enthusiasm for what we'd just learned at the retreat might cloud our judgment as to what would be safe to share back home in the "real world." Consciousness retreats and work organizations, of course, are equally real or unreal: They are simply governed by two different systems—flowing circles versus regimented pyramids.

Let's continue to deepen the initial question at the start of this discussion: If human evolution is more affected by the functioning of its organizational systems than by the biological transmission of its individual genes, what can be done to expand consciousness for subtle systems—and not just for privileged persons? Can systems be changed—transformed—so their members will invite each other to (1) participate in mind/body/spirit modalities and (2) apply in the workplace what their expanded consciousness allows them to do?

I will now comment on the nature of most organizations today and how to transform them into conscious systems that can nurture conscious living. Regarding extended families, most adults share that their family of origin was dysfunctional: In one way or another, their sacred boundaries were violated, which made it impossible for them to establish a clear and strong sense of self during their childhood.

Depending on how these terms are defined and then measured, the percentage of all families that are dysfunctional might be as high as eighty percent. Or as one witty observer put it: "Ninety percent of all families are dysfunctional. But no one has ever found the remaining ten percent." Notwithstanding different reports of the prevalence of dysfunctional families, it's evident that most people's first exposure to a formal system of communication, specialization, coordination, and cooperation—wasn't a good one.

Since most families can't afford mind/body/spirit modalities, one might consider that an expanded social services system (through state and federal agencies) could provide a wider range of financial and psychological support to more families. But if the percentage of dysfunctional families is really as high as has been documented, then working family-by-family (and community-by-community) not only will consume an inordinate amount of tax funds—but will also take forever. Furthermore, because of the private nature of these *informal* organizations, it may be quite impossible to reach all the millions of dysfunctional families that suffer in silence (due to denial, delusion, and other defenses): Most dysfunctional families can't acknowledge their pain or won't ask for help (which, naturally, keeps them rigidly stuck in their patterns). But *our formal* organizations (public schools, religious organizations, health-care systems, businesses, and so forth) can reach thousands of people at a time. Furthermore, these formal organizations can invite—and encourage—their members to expand their mind/body/spirit consciousness, which, in time, will positively impact on their *family* life, in addition to their *work* life.

I'll now examine a formal organization that exists outside the extended family: Most children in progressive nations suffer through compulsory education, most often in the form of public schools, but also in the form of private schools that must satisfy the same federal and state requirements. From research surveys by UNESCO (United Nations Educational, Scientific, and Cultural Organization), almost fifty nations have formally instituted compulsory education. Students are subjected to this learned helplessness—beginning when they are between five and seven years old and ending when they are between sixteen and eighteen.

While there are good reasons to force children's attendance at school (as a substitute for child labor, to keep children off the streets, and to help families who cannot afford tuition payments), I believe the long-term costs of compulsory education may far outweigh the benefits. And what are these costs? *The travesty of education begins by assembling a diverse collection of creative children who have very different learning needs and styles (because of their distinctive human qualities as opposed to the uniformity in the animal kingdom). The travesty continues by subjecting these diverse children to lockstep, standardized, homogenized, mass-produced, autocratic schooling by teachers who'd also been subjected to dysfunctional families and compulsory education.*

In the worst case, compulsory education is an opportunity for nations to produce their obedient citizens, good soldiers, and docile workers. (The U.S. approach for public schooling is historically based on the same model of compulsory education that was established by the Napoleonic and Prussian Empires in the nineteenth century. It may be that the nationalistic propaganda in Prussia's public schools made it easy for Hitler to rise to power in the twentieth century with the multi-generational support of Germany's educationally molded citizens.) Although the U.S. was formed by the separation of church and state, it hasn't done the same with school and state. The danger is this: Public schools can easily be used to develop an unconscious and controlled citizenship, making use of *pyramid organizations* that prefer cultural indoctrination over self-learning and self-discovery.

Although this book is not the place to specify—in detail—how to radically redesign educational systems, I can briefly offer the seeds of transformation: I suggest that all children should be encouraged by the state (through invitations and opportunities) to learn the three R's: reading, 'riting, and 'rithmetic—as the vital skills in any literate society. But all other course subjects and direct learning experiences should be offered through democratic communities of students and facilitators. What renders these circle organizations democratic and not autocratic? *Students and facilitators work together to self-design and self-manage live learning experiences that are supported and blended with online explorations of human knowledge.* The purpose of these learning communities is to encourage the growth of each student's particular talents and interests. Moreover, if children can be guided to expand their mind/body/spirit consciousness in a *circle organization,* they'll discover—for themselves—what they must learn and experience in order to become awakened adults and healthy parents.

For just a moment, let's imagine an adult who has successfully survived the public school system (and thus didn't rebel against his compulsory education by becoming a loyal gang member, juvenile delinquent, or high-school dropout): How can he conceive the best decisions about love, work, and the planet if he suffers—physically, sexually, emotionally, mentally, and spiritually—from still having (1) wounded boundaries, (2) a weak self, (3) a numb body, and (4) no idea of his soul's purpose? Essentially, *if most adults are still recreating the same unconscious patterns that they learned during their dysfunctional childhood, the traditional system of compulsory education has totally failed humanity—regardless of test scores and fancy diplomas.*

If our society is still entrenched in the belief that children must be forced to learn (and must do so in a mass-produced fashion that suppresses their unique calling), I extend the following compromise: At least twenty-five percent of the learning activities in our primary and secondary public schools should be based on mind/body/spirit modalities—which should be made available to students, teachers, and administrators. If these consciousness-enhancing modalities are designed and conducted to be playful and meaningful, there will not be any need to force people to attend: *Creating and then maintaining an engaging community for self-learning and self-discovery will, by itself, attract participation.* Furthermore, designing circle organizations that involve students, facilitators, and experts in the local community will engage each person's innate wish to become whole and discover his soul's purpose. Some useful examples of circle schools include A. S. Neill's democratic learning community (Summerhill School), Maria Montessori's self-directed learning environment, and Rudolf Steiner's Waldorf School, which offer their children integrative, imaginative, creative, spiritual, and soul-searching activities. And charter schools, which actively involve key stakeholders (parents, students, teachers, administrators, community leaders, public officials, and others) in self-designing and self-managing public education—also have great potential for creating circle organizations.

I did not experience a self-directed learning organization until my first year in UCLA's Ph.D. program, when I was twenty-four years old. I chose to major in social systems, which required me to take a twenty-four-credit course *(meeting nine hours per week for six months)* with ten other doctoral students. This course was instructed by five professors, each exploring a different perspective on organizational systems and individual consciousness. For three hours each week, we learned behavioral science knowledge by inviting faculty members and visiting scholars to meet with us and discuss their professional journeys. For another three hours every week, we shared the progress of our self-selected research study. And for the remaining three hours a week, we sat in a circle and became a laboratory for learning about our beliefs, attitudes, and interpersonal behavior.

This circle organization for enhancing consciousness is known as a T-group (sensitivity training group), which is presented in the 1964 book by Leland P. Bradford, Jack R. Gibb, and Kenneth Benne: *T-Group Theory and Laboratory Method: Innovation in Re-education.* For the first T-group meeting in my Ph.D. program, the facilitator began the learning laboratory with these words: "We're here to learn about ourselves by exploring what takes place in this group." That was all! Since not one of us doctoral fellows knew what to do with this vague instruction, someone asked the facilitator to explain how we should proceed. The facilitator merely repeated, word for word, his initial statement to us. After we exchanged glances in a dumbfounded way, there was a long pause. Then another student asked the facilitator to explain the theory behind the T-group and how some *other* T-group had dealt with those same instructions. But the facilitator didn't take the bait: He once again said we were here to learn by exploring what takes place in *this* group—and *only* this group.

After a few false starts, we gradually learned how to express what we were experiencing in *our* T-group: chaos, frustration, and anger—because there was no central leadership, no articulated goals, and no specific procedures for engaging in this learning process. *We were so used to being told exactly what to do, based on twelve years of compulsory education and many years in other pyramid organizations, that we did not know how to self-design—let alone self-manage—our learning laboratory.* Week after week, we struggled with creating our own leadership, our own goals, and our way of learning about our behavior. During this process, we gave specific, constructive feedback to one another. As a result, we discovered how each of us deals with a leadership vacuum (just as we'd responded when our parents hadn't supplied what we wanted or needed). We further learned how each of us responds to affection and the fear of rejection (and what we must own ourselves, rather than project on others). And we learned (and practiced) how to get things done when someone else doesn't tell us what to do (by getting in touch with our needs and then collaborating with others to self-design and self-manage our own learning process).

During many T-group sessions, we shared our personal stories about why we were anxious, frightened, or blocked about designing our own learning experiences. In our small community, we laughed and cried as we revealed (and deeply felt) the parts of ourselves that our dysfunctional families and compulsory education had expected us to deny and suppress. I'm not exaggerating: This T-group process was the most exciting educational adventure in my entire life. It was my first exposure to (1) being a participant in a circle organization, (2) self-designing a small community, learning experience, and (3) exploring my unconscious patterns in interpersonal behavior. By the way, *this T-group also was my first mind/body/spirit modality.* It predated my first round of therapy by more than four years.

Inviting children and adults (and facilitators) to participate in learning circles (funded by the federal government, but administered by local communities) would help millions of people pinpoint their unconscious patterns—so they could then break and transcend them (making use of mind/body/spirit modalities). Such a modification to the curriculum in primary and secondary schools could help our citizens radiate a high level of human consciousness. Consequently, we'd have a much better chance of resolving troubled relationships, resolving global challenges, and improving the quality of life for all members of society.

But let's bring this core subject much closer to home: *Children who are able to expand their mind/body/spirit consciousness during twelve years of consciousness-based education (from when they are six to eighteen years old) will be more likely to create functional families and communities when they become young adults—precisely because they'll have overcome their unhealthy patterns.*

At this time, let's consider another organization besides public schools: Religious organizations also give children both primary and secondary school education (including Catholic and other types of parochial schools) to the children in the community. Naturally, this schooling includes religious instruction. Yet the children who attend public schools can also receive religious instruction from a weekend or after-school program. Through this religious instruction, students are exposed to the supernatural realm of the spiritual universe (other than what they learn at home). But it isn't clear who'll help children integrate this faith-based approach with the scientific-based study of the material universe that's provided in public schools. *By separating church and state to ensure religious freedom, have we confused organized religion with spiritual development—and thereby unnecessarily fragmented children's daily life from their spiritual life?*

Individual spirituality should be distinguished from organized religion. With spirituality, there isn't a member versus non-member distinction: Every person on the planet is viewed as being on a path with Spirit—in his own way and at his own pace. The primary issue concerns what barriers (whether imposed by self, others, or systems) may block a person from examining his existence beyond his skin-encapsulated ego. With an organized religion (Christianity, Judaism, Islam, Hinduism, Buddhism, and Chinese folk religions), there are members and non-members, which are easily identified by religious rites, rituals, ceremonies, customs, clothing, and shared knowledge of the religion's origin, deity (or deities), and sacred texts.

Moreover, spirituality is above all concerned with an individual having a personal relationship with the divine source—without the need for an intermediary—other than books, retreats, and teachers who expose participants to modalities for connecting with Spirit. In contrast, organized religion, as the title suggests, uses organizational systems and sacred places—such as churches, synagogues, mosques, temples, or ashrams. Formally sanctioned practitioners—including priests, ministers, pastors, rabbis, monks, imams, and other clergy—then lead parishioners through religious services. While spirituality uses such neutral terms as pure consciousness, eternal stillness, and the divine source, organized religion usually expects the worship of one or more deities (God, Allah, Brahman, and Tu Di Gong).

When an organized religion has a pyramid system, many more people will be exposed to its discussions and practices—because of missionary efforts to spread the word. *But proselytizers or converts will not necessarily develop a deeper relationship with Spirit.* In fact, perhaps the chief criticism of organized religion is that its members regularly attend religious instruction, study religious texts, and participate in religious ceremonies, but the rest of their daily life is conducted as if those religious instructions and practices never took place—perhaps another version of the three-day, washout effect. By thus keeping the development of spirit consciousness far removed from non-religious organizations only widens the gap between knowing those religious principles and living them. Note: I fully agree with the separation of church and state, so government doesn't control the religious beliefs of its citizens (whether due to the insular or the aggressive nature of organized religion). But there must be a way of bringing spirituality into all organizations—*so long as the modalities for spirit consciousness are both meaningful and playful for all members.*

But an individual-focused approach to spiritual consciousness (for example, Vipassana meditation) can easily evolve into *organized spirituality*—even if it began (just as most religions) by emphasizing a direct, one-to-one, connection with Spirit. If a pyramid system is used to organize and spread that approach to spirituality, however, the usual deficiencies might materialize: The organization—with its practitioners and procedures—could become excessively focused on ego conflicts, office politics, publicizing dogma, retaining members, and recruiting new ones. But if organized spirituality is developed as a circle system (thus ensuring that members continue to self-design and self-manage their organization), it's more likely that no one will lose sight of the mission: to accelerate—and deepen—every person's immediate and direct connection with Spirit.

And recall: A spiritual approach, whether organized or not, is meant to be all-inclusive. It merely asks *all* children and *all* adults to experience themselves as being something more than their physical bodies and mortal minds, which will surely radiate a higher level of human consciousness. Usually, spirituality doesn't rely on worship, symbols, dogma, uniform clothing, attendance, certificates, degrees, or decorated buildings. Such accoutrements and practices can easily distract from *experiencing* divinity and letting that experience change how people live their life—which then allows Spirit to see itself. But as the awareness of spirituality spreads (by making far greater use of consciousness-expanding circle organizations), many more children and adults will yearn for a direct, intimate relationship with Spirit— without intermediaries or memberships.

Just as there are many dedicated, conscious teachers in public schools, there also are many dedicated, conscious clergy in religious organizations. And these generous souls do the utmost to serve their students and parishioners, respectively. But never neglect the system within which these heroic individuals try to contribute their special talents: If those schools and temples are organized and managed as autocratic, bureaucratic, unconscious pyramids, it will be incredibly difficult, if not impossible, even for courageous individuals to fulfill their mission in these organizations. Yes, there are some courageous individuals who buck the system—and succeed. But those instances are relatively rare. In most cases, the system succeeds by squelching the offender, transferring him to a remote location, or terminating his employment/service in the organization. The expelled deviant is then replaced by a new person who'll follow the cultural norms and customary procedures—just like everyone else.

However, if both organized religion and organized spirituality are self-designed and self-managed within a circle system, everyone will have the encouragement to expand his spirit consciousness. But if an insular pyramid system is used to deliver religious propaganda to an exclusive membership, the lower energies—and emotions—of human consciousness will prevail: Instead of spiritual growth, there'll be religious wars, whether among neighbors, nations, or continents. But it is the system, not the participants, that'll determine who'll be served or who'll be harmed in the name of religion or spirituality.

There's another set of organizations that also have a significant impact on human evolution: health-care organizations and health-insurance companies. Based on the history of the American Medical Association (AMA), accredited medical schools, the federal Food and Drug Administration (FDA), state licensing boards, and the lobbying efforts and media campaigns of big pharmaceutical companies, *this country continues to focus on the physical body.* Disease and distress are diagnosed as physical causes—and treated with physical modalities (primarily medication or surgery). Almost all heath insurance plans (public and private) only reimburse members for treatments that are sanctioned by the medical establishment—and address the physical body. Of the many mind/body/spirit modalities I've included in this book, only two modalities were (partially) reimbursed by my health insurance plan: (1) talk therapy by a licensed analyst and (2) spinal adjustments by a licensed chiropractor.

Modalities that diagnose and treat people as an *energy body* are usually defined as *alternative* modalities in the U.S. and elsewhere— since insurance companies do not support them. Worse yet, in most states it's against the law for a non-medical practitioner (not licensed by a medical board) to diagnose and then treat anyone's symptoms of disease and distress. Treating a person as an energy body (except by *medical* acupuncture) is outside the usual realm of conventional health and healing.

As noted previously, even though the U.S. has legally separated *church and state* (to promote religious freedom), it has not done the same for *school and state* (which severely limits the freedom for most parents to pick which approach to learning would be best suited for their children). In the same manner, the U.S. has, de facto, failed to separate *health and state*. The U.S. Government, therefore, insists that not only can it make far better educational choices for children than their own parents, but it also can make far better decisions for every citizen on how to heal disease and distress. The federal government has chosen to educate and heal its citizens in an autocratic, pyramid manner—thus treating them just as the totalitarian societies against which our forefathers had fought for our freedom. *Besides the Bill of Rights and the amendments to the U.S. Constitution, what could be more precious to the citizens of a free nation than the right to choose modalities for education, health, and consciousness?*

Perhaps in the near future, health insurance plans (private and public) will offer reimbursement for many other modalities besides emergency care, prescription drugs, surgeries, radiation therapy, and chemotherapy. Instead of chronically paying for the medical care of

THE COURAGEOUS MOSAIC

chronic disorders (which could imply a *societal miasm* of backwards thinking), maybe it would be much cheaper (and more humane) to subsidize the many mind/body/spirit modalities that enable people to discover—and live—their soul's purpose. As a result, fewer people would get sick, which could radically reduce health-care costs.

Besides giving citizens the freedom of choice for learning and healing, we must also realize that adults spend most of their waking hours working for one or more organizations. *Do workplaces support or thwart expanded consciousness?* Just like the Napoleon and Prussian Empires set the standard for compulsory education in the 1800s, those same governments also promoted a pyramid system—*bureaucracy*—for all other types of organizations. Perhaps it's no surprise why the facilitators of consciousness retreats caution the participants not to expect their back-home workplace to understand, let alone support, mind/body/spirit modalities. The cultural norms in today's pyramid organizations are typically mandated in these unwritten rules of the road: "Keep things the same; don't make waves; don't rock the boat; don't introduce new ideas; don't talk about your feelings; don't talk about your dreams; get back to work."

Sadly, bureaucratic, autocratic, pyramid systems split a person into (1) the parts that are expected to be present at work (physical, mental, social, and technical skills for performing all assigned tasks) and (2) the parts that should always stay at home (mind/body/spirit consciousness deemed non-essential for getting the job done). As a consequence, most adults fragment themselves into work and home: the former being a necessary evil, while the latter becomes a crucial sanctuary from a frustrating work life. As discussed earlier, however, if that work life isn't aligned with your soul's purpose, you'll get sick (with one miasm or another). Maybe when our business executives and political leaders take a careful look at the costs for absenteeism, tardiness, accidents, lackluster performance, and poor morale (partly resulting from disease, distress, depression, and fragmentation), they will transform their systems to further expand the mind/body/spirit consciousness of their employees, who are referred to, ironically, as their "most valuable assets."

The most courageous mosaic for our society, therefore, is to transform our pyramid organizations into circle organizations, which include schools for self-directed learning, religious communities for spiritual development, health-care organizations for integral healing, and workplaces for soulful living. And if school, religious, and health-care organizations can be designed for the pursuit of consciousness, many more self-directed, self-aware, and healthy people will be working in our organizations. If a transformation of unconscious pyramid systems into conscious circle systems can also spread to local, state, and federal governments (including the United Nations or perhaps an even more empowered World Federation), human societies will be able to solve their most pressing challenges from the higher levels of human consciousness. (See my 2011 book, *Quantum Organizations,* for a series of eight tracks for expanding self-aware consciousness throughout organizations.)

The mindless alternative that will keep people in their place is to (1) continue compulsory education in public schools, which will stifle the unique soul in each child; (2) continue to relegate spiritual matters to organized religion, thus fragmenting children (and adults) into their everyday self and their spiritual self; (3) continue to treat disease and distress with only physical remedies for a physical body, which will fuel chronic disease and therein escalate health-care costs; (4) continue to use pyramid systems in workplaces, which prevents people from living their soul's purpose and will thereby bring about additional distress and disease; (5) continue to manage our national governments as pyramid organizations, which will further block our species from reversing its projected path of self-destruction; and (6) continue to deny how *today's* dysfunctional families create *tomorrow's* dysfunctional families, which are perpetually nurtured by autocratic/ bureaucratic pyramids: public schools, religious organizations, health-care systems, governments, and workplaces.

Always keep this principle in mind: Systems in society have the dominant say on whether the masses will accelerate—and deepen—their mind/body/spirit consciousness. *Pyramid systems* will make it possible for only a few privileged people to embark on their journey to awakening, healing, and wholeness. *Circle systems,* by bringing the whole person into an organization, will allow millions to live their soul's purpose, which will bring much more happiness to the world and will fulfill Spirit's impulse to see itself evolve.

21
Transitioning with My Mom

On July 7, 2006, I traveled twenty-four hours from my hometown in Newport Coast, California to the Island of Formica, just off the coast of Sicily. I went there to attend another "Healing in Paradise" retreat on expanding consciousness. Although I'd seen many pictures of this heavenly destination and been given verbal accounts of what it was like to be there, all my preconceptions were meaningless: As soon as I stepped foot on that island, I experienced an undeniable vortex of surging energy that had been created by the ageless and history-rich Mediterranean Sea.

Following the four-day retreat, I traveled to Tuscany in northern Italy with my friend, Amy, and experienced the countryside and the charming villages, especially Siena. We then drove to Florence. There we walked along the Arno River and enjoyed the delightful shops on a famous bridge: the Ponte Vecchio. Seeing Michelangelo's "David" in the Accademia di Belle Arti and Botticelli's "The Birth of Venus" in the Galleria degli Uffizi left me amazed. But my time in Florence was way too short for enjoying all its wonders. On Monday, July 17, I had to make my journey back to California, which required a brief stopover in Philadelphia to clear customs and change planes.

Because my cell phone plan didn't have international service, I hadn't been able to retrieve any voice messages from my answering machine while I was in Europe. So when the plane touched down in Philadelphia, I called home. I was shocked to hear two messages from my brother, which had been recorded during the previous week: My mom was in a coma. And she wasn't expected to live much longer. I immediately called my brother in South Carolina. I was relieved he answered his cell. After hearing that Mom was still alive, I told him I'd find the quickest way to Columbia, even though my suitcase was on the way to California. I said I'd call him back as soon as I knew my flight information.

After much effort, I was able to book a flight to Columbia that was scheduled to leave in sixty minutes. By the time I got to the gate, I only had a few minutes before boarding. I quickly telephoned my brother to let him know I would take a taxi from the airport to Mom's nursing home, so I could get there as soon as possible. Knowing her condition, he appreciated the urgency.

I then called my dear friend, Sunshine. I knew she'd appreciate what I was about to experience in Columbia. But I received an added bonus: She gave me some examples of how I could help my mother make that transition to a new phase, even if she remained in a coma and never regained (ordinary) consciousness. I told Sunshine that I hadn't considered such ideas before, but I'd keep her suggestions in mind. In the next instant, I heard a loud public announcement that the boarding process was about to begin. So I got off the phone and proceeded to the Jetway.

Once I was settled in my airplane seat, I then used the next two hours to reflect on "Life with Mother." I started by reminiscing about our resolution, just a few years before—a resolution I'd never thought would ever happen. I also relived all the decades that it took for me to resolve this primal relationship. At 35,000 feet above sea level, it was easy to see the big picture.

In what seemed like just moments, the captain announced that the plane was making its final approach to the Columbia airport, so we would be arriving very soon. I now had to brace myself: not only for planting my feet on solid ground, but also for transitioning with my mom into the spiritual realm.

With only a carry-on backpack, it didn't take much time to exit the airport and get a taxi to my mom's nursing home. I arrived about 6:00 PM. When I walked into her room, I noticed she was attached to an IV and sleeping soundly. She had lost a lot of weight and her face was very pale. A nurse then entered the room and informed me that my mom had been in a coma for almost a week. Her pulse rate was very low: thirty-seven beats a minute. The nurse then told me that the attending physician had made his rounds earlier in the day and had provided his prognosis: "She won't last much longer." I thanked the nurse for her update. After she'd closed the door behind her, I moved a chair to the left side of the bed. My mother was lying on her back, somewhat leaning on her right side, with her head and torso slightly raised with the adjustable bed.

I took my mother's right hand and then rubbed it gently with my two hands. Out loud, I said: "Hi Mom. It's Ralph. I'm here now. Everything's fine." It then struck me that the last time I had seen my dad alive, he also was in a deep coma. In that era, I had to accept the situation—since there was nothing I could do about it. But that was twenty-six years ago. Now, however, it occurred to me that my Pulsor crystals were still inside my backpack. I bent down and opened one of its zippered compartments and found an embroidered pouch: It contained my crystal pendulum and some fifteen crystal donuts that mobilize, amplify, and focus subtle energy.

The pendulum—a pointed object, roughly two inches long and a half-inch thick, connected to a short metal chain—is infused with millions of microscopic crystals that resonate with a wide variety of frequencies. Before I did anything with the Pulsor crystals, I engaged my third-eye consciousness and began my throat-friction breathing. Next, I dangled the pendulum from my right thumb and forefinger, while I placed it by the left side of my body. I nudged the pendulum to swing in a vertical plane. Slowly, it began moving *clockwise*, all on its own. When I performed the identical procedure for the right side of my body, the pendulum began moving *counterclockwise*, also on its own. These results determined that I was energetically balanced along both my left and right meridians, which is a necessary precondition before attempting to assess another person's chakra system, let alone attempting to *change* a person's energy flows.

In this aligned state, I then proceeded to assess the vitality and direction of my mom's chakras along her center line—including her left and right meridians. When a person's chi is abundantly flowing, the crystal pendulum will vigorously swing in the correct direction: When energetically balanced, a woman's crown, third-eye, heart, and genital chakras spin *clockwise*—whereas her throat, solar plexus, and root chakras spin *counterclockwise*. A man's chakras, however, spin in the opposite direction.

As I checked my mom's chakras, I discovered that most of her energy vortices were barely moving. Worse yet, *her third-eye and crown chakras were spinning in the wrong direction*. In retrospect, this finding wasn't all that surprising: My mom had been in a coma for a week—which was surely the cause and consequence of her depleted energy state. Meanwhile, her soul's consciousness (currently residing in her third-eye chakra) was struggling to leave her physical body (seeking exit through her crown chakra). Apparently, my mother wasn't ready to make that leap into the next realm. Maybe she needed some help on two fronts: *resolving her soul and opening her crown*.

I reached into my embroidered pouch and retrieved nine Angel crystals. Each set of three colors—red, green, and blue—is tuned to a different frequency. I put the three blue crystals under my mom's left shoulder, hip, and knee. I did the same on the right side of her body with the three red crystals. I then positioned the three green crystals on her throat, heart, and navel. My fully conscious intention for this particular arrangement of crystals was to create a "burning bush" of healing energy—which would then replenish her dwindling supply of flowing chi.

I retrieved four more crystals from my pouch: I chose Theta and Delta crystals to calm any chatter in my mom's mental energy. I next selected the Five-Element Stabilizer to help calm any turmoil in her emotional energy. Lastly, I chose a Thunderbolt crystal to jump-start the subtle energy in her central nervous system. I placed these latter crystals on the side of the bed. With my right hand, I then swung my pendulum back and forth in a vertical plane, as I mindfully focused my consciousness on the Theta crystal. Silently, I asked Spirit: "Where would this crystal best serve my mom?" I then scanned my left hand very slowly above her motionless body—from her crown to her root chakra. Just as the pendulum started swinging clockwise, I observed the exact place on my mom's body that was directly underneath my left hand. That was where I positioned the Theta crystal, having been spiritually guided by a "yes." I followed the identical procedure for the Delta, Five-Element, and Thunderbolt crystals. In a few moments, my mother's comatose body had been energetically decorated with a variety of donut-shaped microcrystals.

Then I used my right hand to spin my dangling pendulum in a clockwise direction, just an inch or two above my mother's heart (in accord with the proper spin of her heart chakra). While I continued to spin the pendulum, I gradually moved my right hand farther away from her body, but still directly over her heart. At the moment when my arm was stretched to its limit, I had traversed all her energy fields. I concluded this chakra-balancing maneuver with a sudden flick of my wrist, which brought the swinging pendulum to an abrupt stop. I then performed the same procedure for my mom's other chakras— spinning the pendulum, clockwise or counterclockwise (depending on the desired spin for each chakra), across each energy field.

In the midst of this rather peculiar dance, the nurse re-entered the room. I moved my gaze and caught the bewildered expression on her face. It was as if she were saying: "What the hell are you doing to that poor woman?" Before the nurse had an opportunity to express her opinion, however, I said the following: "This is my mom. This is what we do together. You don't need to understand it, but I ask you to respect it." The nurse nodded compliance and remained silent as I resumed my crystal work. A few minutes later, I heard the door close. Hopefully, she was going to honor my request.

Once I had "spun out" my mother's stuck energies, I next used my pendulum to re-assess the strength of her chakras, including the direction of their spins. Every chakra that had previously been stuck was now strong. Regarding the two chakras that had been spinning in the wrong direction, I could tell they had switched direction, even though they were barely moving. Using my pendulum with my full conscious intention, I spent a few more minutes further energizing my mom's third-eye and crown chakras—which would facilitate her soul's return to the ocean of Spirit.

And then the miracle of crystals materialized: First, my mother started breathing more deeply. Next, color returned to her face. And then she opened her eyes. A few moments later, she looked directly at me. There was instant recognition. Although she was too weak to speak, she was able to slowly, but surely, reposition her arms. I put down my pendulum and caressed her right hand. With my eyes glued on hers, I repeated my greeting: "Hi Mom. I'm here now. Everything's fine." Her eyes twinkled. I could also feel the slightest movement of her hand in mine. My mother was no longer in a coma.

Just then, I heard the door to my mom's room open. This time two nurses entered the room. If they had arrived to comment on my crystal work, their agenda soon changed: They noticed that my mom was awake, so they checked the monitor that showed her vital signs. One of the nurses exclaimed: "Oh my God! Her pulse is fifty-nine! How could her pulse rate have gone from thirty-seven to fifty-nine in only thirty minutes?" In response, I said: "My mom's doing fine. I'd like to have some alone time with her—for at least an hour. So please don't disturb us." The head nurse replied: "Take all the time you need!" With the distinct look of disbelief still frozen on their faces, the two nurses left the room.

I returned my attention to my mother and continued to caress her right hand. As I looked into her eyes, she lifted her left hand and brushed away the hair across her forehead. As usual, my mom wanted to look her best for every social occasion. And her last conversation with me would likely be one of the most important occasions in her life. Although my mother was too weak to speak, I could tell that all her energy was being used to understand my words. During our last conversation, aside from adjusting her hair every now and then, her eyes remained glued on mine. We never before had such an intense eye-to-eye connection—not even when she was breastfeeding me as an infant. But a lot had changed in sixty years.

The first part of our conversation began without saying a word. I just looked into my mom with all the love in the universe. From a sitting position, I leaned forward and kissed her hand several times. I then returned my gaze to her eyes. I continued this cycle a few times until the room became a sacred place in which to honor that divine relationship between mother and child. And then I spoke.

"I'm so grateful for all the amazing things you've done for me. I'm so blessed. I especially remember how much you supported my printing hobby and then my professional career. You helped me get into my dream college: In my senior year in high school, you brought me there, just so I could see the campus and speak to the director of admissions. You've always supported my world of work. Eventually, I studied systems—so I could understand the larger forces that shape our society. But my work life has always been about seeing, writing, and printing the letters of the alphabet on sheets of paper. As such, *I must thank you for inspiring me to publish all my articles and books.*"

I then took a brief pause with a deep breath. But my mom was ready for more. So I continued.

"But of all the things you've done for me, I'm most grateful for how you handled my lazy eyeball. Without those four eye surgeries, I couldn't have become the person I am today. We both know those surgeries were painful. And many times, I was mad at you. But given what I know now that I didn't know then, I wouldn't erase those eye surgeries even if I could. Their early brutality awakened me to who I am. They served to teach me love, joy, peace, and compassion. I'm a better person *because of* those surgeries. Even though you might not have planned them for a divine purpose, those surgeries ignited my journey to wholeness. *I know it may seem strange, but I must thank you for the consciousness those surgeries gave me.*

"You and I have previously struggled with what it means to tell the truth. I've often thought about the different ways a child can be taught honesty and integrity. You probably never purposely planned it, but there were some lies during my life that enabled me to learn about truth: I learned valuable lessons whenever you lied about the reasons for those eye surgeries: I've spent my life challenging people to tell the truth, so they can be good to other people, including their children. *So again, it may seem very strange, but I must thank you for the consciousness those lies gave me.*

"I am aware of how I got here, who I am, and where I'm going. Even if I could, I wouldn't change a thing, because, if I did, I wouldn't be sitting here with you right now. And that's why I'm so grateful for the mother you've been to me. Although I criticized you a lot in the past, I now realize how perfect you've been for my becoming who I am: *You inspired me to live an examined life.*"

For every word I spoke, my mother kept direct contact with my eyes. I could sense the fulfillment she was experiencing, while I was affirming the value of her soul, which then served to resolve her life. And she could see my words were carefully chosen—and genuine. I wasn't placating my mom on her deathbed. Rather, I was telling her the truth, because that's what she had taught me to do.

I bowed down and kissed her right hand a number of times. I then looked up and continued our final conversation: "I'm so happy with my life. I'm so happy with my work.

"When you and Dad made your escape from Nazi Germany to America, you set in motion generations of free and happy offspring.

All of us thank you for the many sacrifices you made in moving to a new country, learning another language, and also adapting to a new culture. You made sure your children went to college. And now we're making sure your grandchildren will have that same opportunity. If I can give Cathy and Chris even a small fraction of what you've done for me, I'll have lived a noble life.

"Your family is happy and healthy. You no longer have to hang around anymore for our sake. When you are ready to leave, imagine you are wearing the most elegant evening gown you have ever worn. Unzip the dress and let it slowly slip off your body. Then look up to the stars in the sky, because that's where you're going. You'll reunite with all the other souls in the universe. You'll be with Dad. You'll be with everyone."

I stood up, kissed her forehead, peered right into her eyes, and then declared in the most heartfelt—and authentic—manner: "I love you very much, Mom. I always will." Even as dehydrated as she was, she still had enough moisture left in her body to produce a tiny tear in her right eye. Slowly, it tricked down her pale face. It was a tear of ultimate resolution, pure joy, and inner peace.

A few moments later, I released her right hand and picked up my pendulum. I checked her third-eye and crown chakras: Both were spinning vigorously in the correct direction. When her soul was ready, it would gracefully slip off that elegant evening gown, the beautiful body that had served her for ninety-nine years.

There was nothing else to say. I spent the next hour looking at my mom. A few times, I would focus on her third eye and then shift my gaze to the stars and then I'd repeat the cycle. I wanted to remind her where her soul was going, whenever it was ready to leave. Every now and again, she would close her eyes and then drift off to sleep. But her breath remained strong. A few times, I checked the monitor: Her pulse rate remained in the high fifties. It was evident, therefore, that she didn't fall back into a coma. She remained fully alive in her body—for the time being.

As I watched her sleep, however, it didn't seem to me that she'd transition that night. I sensed she was savoring our conversation. So I kissed her forehead and said I'd be back the next morning. Before I left her room, I said good-night. But I didn't say good-bye.

At 8:00 AM the next day, I re-entered the nursing facility. When I walked into my mother's room, she was still sleeping. I did a quick assessment with my pendulum and found that all her chakras were wide open and flowing. I then sat by the side of her bed for a while. When I took her right hand, she opened her eyes. Although she was still too weak to speak, she was delighted to see me. For the next few hours, we mostly looked at each other.

Even when she fell into a deep sleep, however, I knew she wasn't going to die while I was in her immediate presence (or even while I was in town). For an old-fashioned lady like my mom, that wouldn't be a dignified thing to do. Instead, I felt that she wouldn't transition until I returned home. So at noon, I called the airlines and booked a 2:15 PM flight back to California. Afterward, I told my mother that I was leaving. I kissed her face and then looked right into her eyes for the last time: "Thank you for everything. You're the best mom in the whole wide world. I love you. Good-bye, Mom." I then strapped on my backpack and began walking toward the door. But I looked back one more time, knowing I'd never see her alive again. I smiled, gave her a little wave with my right hand, and walked out of the room.

The very next day, back in California, I received a call from the nursing home: Mom had fallen back into a coma. So I was glad that she knew what to do when she was ready to leave: Unzip the elegant evening gown—her physical body—and free her soul. Her third-eye chakra (the seat of consciousness) along with her crown chakra (the doorway to heaven) were primed for the occasion.

Two days later, Friday, July 21, I momentarily awoke in the wee hours of the morning. I felt my mother's presence—her radiant spirit. Still groggy, I wondered if I was dreaming. But in a little while, I fell back asleep for a few hours. Right after I got out of bed, I received a phone call from my brother: Mom had transitioned during her sleep at 7:25 AM, Eastern Daylight Time (4:25 AM, my time). I was at peace with the news: She had passed into a new phase on her own terms, in a lady-like manner. I was so happy for her: Earlier in the week, I'd been able to spend an evening and the following morning with her in Columbia. And I was so grateful she'd come out of her coma for our final conversation. After more than sixty years together (starting in her womb), our souls had finally connected without hesitancy or fear. Her spirit would now be with me at all times—just as my father and twin sister are always there and always will be. I now have three spirit guides to keep my soul on course!

Later that day, it was time to consider the funeral arrangements. Fortunately, I knew exactly what my mother wanted. Sometime back in 1990, when I was visiting Mom in her Manhattan apartment, we happened to be chatting about my dad's funeral. I remember being taken aback by her comment: "I hope he was pleased with the way I arranged the service." Even though she and I had never spoken about her eventual death, I gracefully asked my then eighty-three-year-old mom: "When you die, how do you want the funeral and burial to be handled?" She wasn't a bit surprised by my question.

We then proceeded to discuss the key details: She wanted to be cremated—even though her religion did not support this procedure. When I asked her how she had come to that decision, she explained: "I don't want to be eaten by worms!" Since she still had some doubt about her decision, however, we agreed that she would let me know if her preference changed in the years to come.

My mom then told me that she didn't want a public service in a funeral home. Instead, she wanted to have a private gathering at the cemetery, only attended by family members and her closest friends. When I asked her who should conduct the ceremony at the gravesite, she responded: "I do *not* want a rabbi. I want a nondenominational minister who's religious, but isn't biased toward any religion." After all those years of living with my dad (who was much more spiritual than religious), I guess my mom had grown beyond her Jewish roots. But just to be sure, in another visit to my mom in 1996, I once again reviewed her funeral preferences, and she confirmed all that we had previously discussed.

The day after my mother had passed, I phoned Peter to let him know about her preferences for cremation—and a gravesite service. Although he was surprised I had those two conversations with Mom (and had kept detailed notes), he easily accepted those arrangements. Since he lived only a few miles from the nursing home, he agreed to handle the cremation process and then have my mother's ashes sent to our parents' cemetery in Kew Gardens, New York. I'd manage the burial process, which meant that I also would contract a minister to conduct a gravesite service. Since my mom's closest friends and two sisters had already passed away, however, the only remaining family members were Peter and I, our children, and our three cousins (and their spouses) in New York City.

Peter then shocked me with his decision: "I'm not going to the funeral, nor are my children." Even though I briefly questioned him about his decision, it was quite evident that he didn't want to attend the gravesite service—either with or without his children.

Regarding the service, Peter said I could make all the decisions myself, since he would not be there. Obviously, I was saddened that my only brother wasn't going to join me in honoring our mom and putting her to rest. But I accepted his decision.

During the next days, my brother made the arrangements for cremating our mother's body and then sending the filled urn to New York. We chose Saturday, July 29, at 11:30 AM, for Mom's service. My son, Chris, would travel with me to New York. My two male cousins would attend the service with their wives. Everyone else was unable to be there, including my daughter, Cathy.

I then had to decide on the service itself. What would give my mom the most pleasure? In my discussions with her on the subject, she had asked for an unbiased minister, not a rabbi. I knew it would not take much time to find a suitable person to conduct the service. In fact, I was sure the office staff of the cemetery could suggest a few names. But instead of taking that route, I thought of someone who could provide the most personal and meaningful ceremony: Me.

I considered this option very carefully: Would I be able to lead the service by my mother's grave, without being overwhelmed with deep-felt emotion, given all we'd been through together? And could I keep my composure, knowing that my dad's remains were buried right beside her urn? I could not have performed the service for my dad. But now, twenty-six years later, I was not only more confident, but also more conscious: "It'll be difficult, but I know I can do it."

On Wednesday, July 26, I reviewed what I planned to say about my mom at her burial: I'd summarize her history of growing up in Germany—going through World War I as a child and her obsession with playing the piano, hour after hour, day after day. At fifteen, she was the youngest woman to drive a car in her town, having received a special license from the mayor himself. Mom met my dad in 1926 and they got married in 1929. I'd next recount their struggle getting out of Nazi Germany, arriving in New York, and eventually starting a family. I would then mention a few family traditions and tell some family stories. Toward the end of the service, I would ask my cousins to share their special experiences with my mom. Since they had both been living in New York for decades, they'd visited her periodically (before she moved to that nursing home in Columbia in 2003).

Because my mother loved music so much, I put together a new playlist on my iPod and titled it: "Mom's Ceremony." By the time it was complete, the playlist showcased ninety minutes of her favorite musical selections, starting with her signature piano piece, Sinding's "Rustle of Spring." Aside from other piano pieces she used to play, I also included selections of her favorite orchestral works. Using my portable speaker system, I intended to play these musical selections at the gravesite service. But I also listened to my playlist daily, which kept my mom's spirit close by my side.

On Friday, July 28, Chris and I traveled to New York and stayed in a hotel just across from LaGuardia Airport. The next morning, we rented a car and journeyed to the Apple Grove Cemetery. We arrived around 10:30 AM. Before we drove to the gravesite, we stopped at the office: I had to sign a number of legal papers for the burial. While I was signing the documents, I was distracted by a powerful presence. One member of the staff had placed a marble urn on the counter: It contained my mother's ashes. I was quickly taken aback by the stark reality of that container. It was the first time I'd been that close to an urn, let alone *my mom's* urn. The cremation process had shrunk her five feet, four inches of physical matter into a small box. Chris and I looked at each other: We were affected in the same way.

When I finished the paperwork, the cemetery staff asked if one of them should bring the urn to the gravesite. I said: "No thank you. I'll carry it myself." Chris watched as I put my hands on the bottom of the urn, picked it up, and held it against my chest. We then walked out of the office to our rental car. Once there, Chris opened the back door and helped me delicately position the urn in the car. He asked: "How did it feel to carry Oma in your arms?" "It was very strange in one way," I said, "but very special and warm in all other ways."

As we approached the Kilmann gravesite, I said hello aloud to my dad. His first name, middle initial, and lifespan (Martin H. 1899–1980) were shown on the right side of the tombstone, and his body was just below that marker. The gravediggers had already fashioned a suitable place for my mother on the left side of my father, which is exactly how they slept in their marriage bed. Mom's name and birth year (Lilli 1907–) had already been carved into the tombstone, more than two decades before. I'd always wondered what year would bring closure to my mother's inscription. Now I knew.

As I got out of the car, I told my dad I'd brought him his wife. I then opened the rear door, picked up my mom's urn, and carried it across the road to the gravesite. I set her body down by her prepared resting place. I had ordered several bouquets of lilies—which I now repositioned to embrace the marble urn. I then placed my iPod and portable speakers off to the left of the tombstone. To test the sound, I sampled a few musical selections. Using my pocket camera, I took several photos of this carefully prepared scene.

I looked at my watch: It was 11:00 AM. The other participants in this gathering would be arriving in the next thirty minutes. So I had a little time to relax. It was a typical summer day in New York City: The temperature was already in the low 80s, at least 50% humidity, mostly cloudy skies, and hardly a breeze. It was going to be another hot, muggy day. But this weather was, in a sense, perfect: My parents had selected a gravesite that was fully covered by the dense branches and leaves of a large oak tree. My parents didn't want to be too hot during the summer months. Their wish was fulfilled: That same tree would now be shading the attendees at the final funeral service for my mother and father.

I wondered aloud to Chris: "Now that we're here, I hope I can conduct this service without getting all choked up." Chris gave me this sound advice: "Precisely enunciate each word. Keeping your left brain occupied will be the easiest way to get through the emotional parts of the ceremony."

In a short while, my two cousins arrived at the gravesite. Steven brought his wife, but Richard left his at home. I hadn't seen them in many years: They had definitely aged a bit. I wondered if they thought the same of me. A few minutes later, my dear friend Robin appeared. Now everyone was present.

I began the service by asking for silence. During this quiet time, we listened to my mother's signature piano piece: "Rustle of Spring." My cousins knew this music very well: They'd heard my mom play it at more than one family occasion. Once the three-minute recording had concluded, I turned down the volume: I now wanted the music to play in the background for the rest of the service. But something happened instead: In the middle of a selection, the music suddenly stopped and then switched to another track, but not in the prescribed sequence. Take note: My iPod wasn't set to "random play." So I didn't know what had malfunctioned. And then, after another musical piece had been playing for a few minutes, the music again stopped before it switched to another out-of-sequence selection. It was as if my mom were choosing what she wanted to hear at her own service—and for how long—which humorously interrupted the service a few times.

As planned, I shared several important features of my mother's life, including her passions and proclivities. I also told a few stories about my mom and me. Following, my cousins shared their favorite stories about my parents. By 12:15 PM, the ceremony had concluded. My mother was resting in peace.

My cousins and I said our good-byes, Robin joined Chris and me for lunch at the nearby Sly Fox Inn. Afterward, Chris and I drove to LaGuardia Airport for our trip back to California. On board, I felt very satisfied about the gravesite service. I had honored my mother's ninety-nine years in an informal and intimate manner—exactly as we had previously discussed in 1990 and 1996. And my composure had remained in tact throughout the service. But most important, I knew my mom had thoroughly enjoyed her private tribute.

The following day, back in California, I took it easy: I allowed a mixture of emotions to move through my body, ranging from joy to sadness. I was conscious enough to know that I would grieve for a while (no matter what uncertainty I still had in distinguishing life and death). There was no point in denying my grief—or attempting to accelerate it. Mourning my mother would proceed in its own way, as I discovered the very next day.

On Monday, July 31, only two days after the gravesite service, I did what I hadn't done in quite a long time: I drove to Baskin Robbins and had a chocolate fudge, ice-cream cone. I ate this delight while I was walking by a number of stores in a strip mall. Just as I finished my cone, I happened to pass an optometrist's office. Spontaneously, I turned around, walked through the front door, and inquired about contact lenses.

THE COURAGEOUS MOSAIC

I'd been wearing eyeglasses ever since I was a few years old. But I often wondered what life would be like if I got rid of that external contraption and used something more discrete for my vision. In the past, whenever anyone asked me why I didn't wear contacts, I'd say: "Enough's already been done to my eyes. I won't do anything else to them!" But this day, I was mysteriously drawn, without forethought, to enter the optometrist's office.

My lucky day! Dr. Montgomery was immediately available to see me. Within thirty minutes, he gave me an eye exam and selected the proper lenses. To get me started, he put the two contact lenses in my eyes. I had to admit it: I could see just as well with these contacts as I could with my eyeglasses: "Maybe this change will be beneficial for me!"

But the big ordeal soon began: I had to learn to put the lenses in my eyes—all by myself. I repeatedly tried, but my eyes resisted, if not rebelled. It took me a long time and much frustration—before I correctly positioned a lens on the iris of each eyeball. But I had little confidence I could learn to perform this task with ease. Regardless, I recalled the principle that "practice makes perfect" and then left Dr. Montgomery's office with my new contact lenses in my eyes and my old eyeglasses in my pocket.

I spent the next few hours feeling especially anxious, as I drove from place to place doing my errands. On my last stop before going home, I went into a grocery store to pick up a few things. As I walked down one aisle, my attention was magically drawn to a product that my mother used to buy: "Old Fashioned Quaker Oats." Ever since I could remember, my mom had made herself oatmeal for breakfast every morning. Just when I saw that familiar round, cardboard box, the mysterious pull that had drawn me into the optometrist's office hit me like a rock: "Oh, my God! I can't believe it. *Of all the times to put new lenses in my eyes, I choose the aftermath of my mother's death!* It seems my eye/mother pattern said 'hello' to me today. But at least I caught it before I suffered more anxiety."

With that profound recognition, I stopped shopping, returned the items in my cart to their proper shelf in the store, went to my car, and drove back to Dr. Montgomery's office. He was there to see me. I proclaimed my discovery: "The past few hours have convinced me that I wasn't born to wear contacts." But he suggested I give my new lenses an honest chance, by wearing them for a week or more. Even though his request was reasonable for most people, I confirmed my decision: "Thank you, but no thank you. I'm done messing with my eyes!" Dr. Montgomery and I agreed on an acceptable return for my contact lenses: I only had to pay for the eye exam. Greatly relieved, I left his office.

As I drove away from that enlightened mall, again wearing my eyeglasses, a huge smile began beaming over my face. I then started laughing as loudly as I have ever laughed before, and I laughed with such joy for a very long time.

My mother and I had shared a precious journey together, from my first cross-eyed gaze (while she was breastfeeding me) to my last attempt to fix my eyes (soon after I buried her). In that span of time, the woman who took care of me became the perfect mother she had always wanted to be. True, my lazy right eye had shaped every printed word and anxious experience through the first sixty years of my life. But I was now prepared to spend the next sixty years seeing both the reality (and the unreality) of our universe with the perfect vision in my third eye. In the end, I had transcended my recreated patterns by having completely resolved my most challenging relationships: They had fueled my awakenings—from beginning to end.

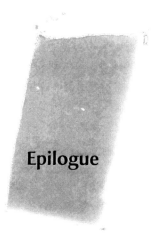

Epilogue

The Courageous Mosaic is a unique blend of stories and theories for accelerating—and deepening—the journey to wholeness. To apply these lessons to your life, I recommend eight action steps:

1. List and then examine the mind/body/spirit modalities that you have previously experienced, are currently undertaking, or will be initiating in the near future, so you can live courageously and thus radiate the higher energies of human consciousness. Investigate how each modality specifically addresses the development of a self-aware and well-defined ego, a flexible and flowing body-mind, and direct and sustained connection with Pure Spirit. *Be sure you're addressing all three aspects: mind, body, and spirit consciousness.* And while you're expanding your consciousness, stay open to having an out-of-body or near-death experience that can help you discover both the reality and the unreality of existence—also known as pure awareness.

2. Explore which of your sacred boundaries have been violated (physical, sexual, emotional, mental, and spiritual) and how one or more of these wounded boundaries have made it difficult for you to develop effective temporal boundaries. The latter, if functioning as intended, will keep your traumas in the past where they belong (past/ present boundaries) and will also enable you to modify your present behavior for future happiness (present/future boundaries).

3. Examine the habitual ways in which you negotiate the truth about what happened in your past—on the distributive dimension (maintaining, conceding, and combining/neutral), on the protective dimension (isolating and combining/negative), and the integrative dimension (synergizing and combining/plus). Remember: *How you approach different versions (and stories) of the truth about your boundary violations affects all the remaining stages for resolving your relationships.* And if you don't heal your boundary violations, you will go through life as a fragmented—insecure—self. If more people could learn the integrative modes for resolving traumatic relationships (as opposed to maintaining a compromised, false, or unhappy version of reality, or staying away from those who might have hurt them)—more souls would awaken and become whole.

4. Examine your energy body, rather than exclusively defining yourself as a biochemical—physical—machine (as the mass media would have you do). By getting in touch with your energy body, you will have more options for knowing—and healing—yourself.

5. Examine your soul's purpose, which includes the particular style—and consciousness—you bring to your love life and work life.

6. List and examine your personal history of physical, mental, and emotional ailments for the signs and signals (chronic miasms), indicating that you haven't been living your soul's purpose. *To honor your soul, and keep yourself healthy and happy for a long time, make sure your ego and soul are taking the same journey.*

7. Explore the systems in society that might be overwhelming your individual efforts at honoring your soul. In the meantime, find opportunities to create consciousness-enhancing systems—or circle organizations—for extended families, educational systems, religious organizations, health-care systems, governments, and workplaces.

8. Periodically review the prior seven action steps to make sure you're courageously living your soul's purpose at all times, as you're bringing greater consciousness to the various systems in our society. In so doing, you'll bring greater joy to our universe.

Think what life would be like if all our systems (from extended families to the United Nations) would encourage consciousness and the realization of pure awareness. From the beginning, all children would be invited to use many mind/body/spirit modalities to know themselves—including their soul's purpose—and how to self-design and self-manage circle organizations. As noted throughout my book, *only by expanding consciousness—in individuals and organizations—will society, systems, and souls be able to resolve war, violence, hatred, poverty, hunger, disease, hopelessness, and the destruction of Mother Earth herself.*

Bibliography

Alcoholics Anonymous. 1939; 2002. *Alcoholics Anonymous: The Story of How Many Thousands of Men and Women Have Recovered from Alcoholism.* Sarasota, FL: Alcoholics Anonymous World Services.

Bakal, D. 1999. *Minding the Body: Clinical Uses of Somatic Awareness.* New York: Guilford.

Ballentine, R. 1999. *Radical Healing: Integrating the World's Great Therapeutic Traditions to Create a New Transformative Medicine.* New York: Three Rivers.

Bartlett, R. 2007. *Matrix Energetics: The Science and Art of Transformation.* New York: Atria.

Bradford, L. P., J. R. Gibb, and K. Benne (Eds.). 1964. *T-Group Theory and Laboratory Method: Innovation in Re-education.* New York: Wiley.

Demartini, J. F. 2002. *The Breakthrough Experience: A Revolutionary New Approach to Personal Transformation.* Carlsbad, CA: Hay House.

DeMille, C. B. 1956. *The Ten Commandments.* Hollywood: Paramount Studios.

247

Epstein, D. M., with N. Altman. 1994. *The Twelve Stages of Healing: A Network Approach to Wholeness.* San Rafael, CA: Amber-Allen.

Gangaji. 2005. *The Diamond in Your Pocket: Discovering Your True Radiance.* Boulder, CO: Sounds True.

Goswami, A. 2004. *The Quantum Doctor: A Physicist's Guide to Health and Healing.* Charlottesville, VA: Hampton Roads.

Grof, S., with H. Z. Bennett. 1994. *The Holotropic Mind: The Three Levels of Human Consciousness and How They Shape Our Lives.* San Francisco: HarperCollins.

Hahnemann, S. 1828; 2007. *The Chronic Diseases: Their Peculiar Nature and Their Homeopathic Cure.* Whitefish, MT: Kessinger.

Harris, B. 2002. *Thresholds of the Mind: Your Personal Roadmap to Success, Happiness, and Contentment.* Beaverton, OR: Centerpointe.

Hart, W. 1987. *Vipassana Meditation as Taught by S. N. Goenka.* San Francisco: HarperCollins.

Hawkins, D. R. 2002. *Power vs. Force: The Hidden Determinants of Human Behavior.* Carlsbad, CA: Hay House.

Hitler, A. 1925; 1998. *Mein Kampf.* Boston: Mariner Books.

Jewison, N. 1971. *Fiddler on the Roof.* Los Angeles: MGM Studios.

Jois, K. P. 2002. *Yoga Mala: The Seminal Treatise and Guide from the Living Master of Ashtanga Yoga.* New York: North Point.

Kilmann, R. H. 1984; 2004. *Beyond the Quick Fix: Managing Five Tracks to Organizational Success.* San Francisco, CA: Jossey-Bass. Washington DC: Beard Books.

Kilmann, R. H. 2011. *Quantum Organizations: A New Paradigm for Achieving Organizational Success and Personal Meaning.* Newport Coast, CA: Kilmann Diagnostics.

Kingston, K. 1997. *Creating Sacred Space with Feng Shui: Learn the Art of Space Clearing and Bring New Energy into Your Life.* New York: Broadway Books.

Kirtana. 1999. "I Am," on the CD, *This Embrace.* Felton, CA: Wild Dove Music.

Lowen, A. 1975. *Bioenergetics: The Revolutionary Therapy that Uses the Language of the Body to Heal the Problems of the Mind.* New York: Penguin.

Robbins, A. 2005. *Unleash the Power Within.* Audio CD. Niles, IL: Nightingale-Conant.

Robertson, J. 1952. *A Two Year Old Goes to Hospital.* Suffolk, England: Concordia Media.

Russell, P. 1998. *Waking Up in Time: Finding Inner Peace in Times of Accelerating Change.* Novato, CA: Origin.

Sagan, S. 1997. *Awakening the Third Eye.* Roseville NSW, Australia: Clairvision.

Sinding, C. A. 1896. "Frühlingsrauschen (Rustle of Spring)," Op. 32, No 3. Leipzig, Germany: C. F. Peters Music Publishers.

Thomas, K. W., and R. H. Kilmann. 1974. *The Thomas-Kilmann Conflict Mode Instrument.* Mountain View, CA: CPP, Inc.

Thurston, M. 1984. *Discovering Your Soul's Purpose: From Techniques Described in the Edgar Cayce Readings and Other Systems of Spiritual Transformation.* Virginia Beach: ARE.

Virtue, D., and J. Lukomski. 2005. *Crystal Therapy: How to Heal and Empower Your Life with Crystal Energy.* Carlsbad, CA: Hay House.

Wilber, K. 2000. *Integral Psychology: Consciousness, Spirit, Psychology, Therapy.* Boston: Shambhala.

Windrider, K., and G. Sears. 2006. *Deeksha: The Fire from Heaven.* Novato: CA: New World Library.

Yao, G. T. F. 1986. *Pulsor, Miracle of Microcrystals: A Treatise on Energy Balancing.* Unknown location: Gyro Industries and Axis International.

About the Author

Ralph H. Kilmann is CEO and Senior Consultant at Kilmann Diagnostics in Newport Coast, California. Formerly, he was the George H. Love Professor of Organization and Management at the Katz School of Business, University of Pittsburgh—which was his professional home for thirty years. He earned his B.S. degree in graphic arts management and his M.S. degree in industrial administration, both from Carnegie Mellon University (1970). He then earned his Ph.D. degree in social systems from the University of California, Los Angeles (1972).

Kilmann is an internationally recognized authority on systems change. He has consulted for numerous corporations throughout the United States and Europe, including AT&T, Kodak, IBM, Ford, General Electric, Lockheed, Olivetti, Philips, TRW, Westinghouse, and Xerox. He has also consulted for numerous health-care, financial, and government organizations, including the U.S. Bureau of the Census and the Office of the President. He is profiled in *Who's Who in America* and *Who's Who in the World*.

Kilmann has published more than one hundred articles and twenty books on such subjects as conflict management and change management. He is also the coauthor of several assessment tools, including the *Thomas-Kilmann Conflict Mode Instrument (TKI)*, the *Kilmann-Saxton Culture-Gap® Survey*, and the *Organizational Courage Assessment*. Kilmann's significant books include *Social Systems Design* (1977), *Beyond the Quick Fix* (1984), *Escaping the Quick Fix Trap* (1989), *Managing Beyond the Quick Fix* (1989), *Gaining Control of the Corporate Culture* (1985), *Corporate Transformation* (1988), *Making Organizations Competitive* (1991), *Workbook for Implementing the Tracks* (1991), *Logistics Manual for Implementing the Tracks* (1992), *Managing Ego Energy* (1994)— all unified in *Quantum Organizations* (2011) and *The Courageous Mosaic* (2013).

Kilmann's hobbies include running, mountain biking, golf, photography, enjoying many types of music (by attending opera, symphony, and rock concerts), and fine dining. He has a passion for home theater—a setting that integrates science, art, music, and intimacy. Yet his long-term hobby, since childhood, is printing.

For more information about the author and his series of recorded online courses on conflict management and change management, visit: www.kilmanndiagnostics.com.

Publications by Kilmann Diagnostics

Self-Report Assessment Tools
Kilmann-Saxton Culture-Gap® Survey
Kilmanns Organizational Belief Survey
Kilmanns Time-Gap Survey
Kilmanns Team-Gap Survey
Organizational Courage Assessment
Kilmann-Covin Organizational Influence Survey
Kilmanns Personality Style Instrument

The Book That Explains the Eight Tracks
Quantum Organizations

Materials for Implementing the Eight Tracks
Work Sheets for Identifying and Closing Culture-Gaps
Work Sheets for Identifying and Closing Team-Gaps
Consultant Schedules for Implementing the Tracks
Logisitics Manual for Implementing the Tracks
Workbooks for Implementing the Tracks

The Book for Expanding Consciousness
The Courageous Mosaic

CPSIA information can be obtained at www.ICGtesting.com
Printed in the USA
LVOW10s0950090913

351537LV00002B/13/P